# EDUCATING AGAINST EXTREMISM

# EDUCATING AGAINST EXTREMISM

*Lynn Davies*

**Trentham Books**

Stoke on Trent, UK and Sterling, USA

Trentham Books Limited
Westview House 22883 Quicksilver Drive
734 London Road Sterling
Oakhill VA 20166-2012
Stoke on Trent USA
Staffordshire
England ST4 5NP

First published 2008

British Library Cataloguing-in-Publication Data
A catalogue record for this book is available from the British Library

ISBN: 978 1 85856 426 5

Designed and typeset by Trentham Print Design Ltd, Chester and
printed in Great Britain by Cromwell Press Ltd, Trowbridge.

# Contents

## Acknowledgements

I want to acknowledge with much gratitude the various colleagues, friends and family who have made this book possible. First, a big thankyou to the team in the Centre for International Education and Research at Birmingham – Clive Harber, Michele Schweisfurth, Chris Williams, Hiromi Yamashita, and former colleague Gordon Kirkpatrick – who read drafts and chapters, and constantly fed me books, journals and newspaper cuttings which they thought relevant. You will get them all back, I promise. But thanks also for the moral support and the laughs: crucial.

An equally big thankyou to my international friends and readers of the drafts who gave me an essential cross-cultural perspective – Muhamad Nazir from Pakistan, Stijn Sieckelinck from the Netherlands, Julia Paulson from Canada and Ådne Valen-Sendstad from Norway. Your erudite and detailed comments and suggestions really helped, as did the necessary corrections so I do not look too foolish. Any inaccuracies of course remain solely my responsibility.

I want to acknowledge Reva Joshee and the Gandhi Foundation of Alberta who kick-started the whole process by inviting me to lecture on extremism at the Gandhi Foundation – an inspirational experience.

Thanks to my publisher, Gillian Klein, who a) agreed to take on what might be a controversial book, b) did not want to change anything major in the manuscript, which was a relief and c) sorted out the expression with such care.

Finally, husband Chris who read it all and said it was Very Good, but didn't like the jokes and the chatty bits. That most are still there is not his fault. But thanks and love to you and to Anna and Russell for everything.

# 1

## The nature of extremism

### Introduction

On Saturday 30 June 2007, a dark green Cherokee jeep loaded with propane canisters was driven into the glass doors of the main terminal of Glasgow airport and set ablaze. The driver was a medical doctor; the other occupant had a doctorate in engineering. Both had written suicide notes indicating they intended to die. The attack appeared rather unsuccessful, and one attacker survived, but this led to heightened security at British airports. The next day, the satirical Scottish newspaper *Daily Mash* ran a spoof article on how the terrorists were going to be prosecuted under Scotland's new tough anti-smoking laws, for 'allowing the vehicle to burn in an enclosed public space'. The reader's forum page included the posting: 'spares/repair: L reg Jeep Cherokee, needs paint, no battery, gas conversion, charcoal interior, tinted windows ... bargain £2,500, will exchange for air miles'.

In this account, there are three points of significance – and curiosity – for this book. First, the terrorists were highly educated, one at least committed by his training to the saving of life. Second, this attack was not predicted or predictable, with government policies on the 'war on terror' seemingly ineffective. Third, humour appears an important, if controversial, response to extremist acts.

Extremism is a huge concern globally, with its links to terrorism and religious fundamentalism. The aim of this book is to explore how education could counter the forms of extremism which present a danger to societies globally. Its main argument is that currently formal education does little to prevent people joining extremist groups, or to enable young people critically to analyse fundamentalism. As will be seen, many suicide bombers have had extensive education in state systems. While literacy is obviously key to enabling people to read and interpret polemic, tracts and messages for themselves, clearly more is needed than basic literacy. Global communications technologies mean that the way young people organise themselves either for peace or for terrorism lies mostly outside the school. But this does not mean that schools are completely powerless. There is an urgent need to look at what formal education can do in the challenge to extremism, and how it should *not* continue to act in a way that may actually support it. The book reviews wider theorising, research and writing with regard to extremism, in order to explore their relation to education; conversely it looks at research on educational contexts to assess the implications for extremism; and finally it suggests ways in which the conclusions from all this can lead to a practical programme for educational institutions. The focus is mainly on schools, but the implications are applicable to non-formal education and universities as well. I propose in this book a very different educational strategy to the conventional tolerant multiculturalism. The task of schooling is to politicise young people without cementing uncritical acceptance of single truths.

Is it being apocalyptic to claim urgency? Human history has been full of extremism leading to persecution, violence and death – whether the Crusades, pogroms, massacres in the name of religion or nationalism and, of course, martyrs. Is there anything new? Clearly there is, because of advanced technology and the speed of communication, and the greater degree of power wielded – and hence the greater unpredictability in terms of how people might use technology. But this technological power also means greater retaliatory strength. The danger from extremism is not just the identified extremists themselves but also the response to them. In his book *Free World*, Timothy Garton Ash writes of the clash of power and vulnerability:

> The 'most powerful man on earth' was told after the 9/11 attacks that any one of those planes he could watch through the windows of the Oval drawing room ... could alter course and hit the White House in about forty seconds. A senior military aide to the vice president told me that the more they learned about possible ways for terrorists to use atomic, biological or chemical weapons, the more alarming it became. However, the people at the top also knew better than anyone what extraordinary, no longer just metaphorically 'space age' military power lay at their disposal. The so-called 'revolution in military affairs' had already taken them another technological generation beyond the satellite-controlled precision bombing of Kosovo. Like the Martians in H.G.Wells's *War of the Worlds*, they possessed the technology to find and destroy almost anything or anyone, anywhere in the world, with the target never knowing what had hit him. Yet it was they, the Martians, who had been hit. They must fight back, and win. But how, and against whom? (2004:118)

As we know, there are political and military 'solutions' to extremism – sometimes more extremism, or extremism disguised as liberation – but in this book I look at educational strategies. These cannot be solutions – education is not that all-powerful – but at least there can be challenges and an attempt at preventative measures. There is a huge growth in writing on terrorism, extremism and fundamentalism. Yet strangely, not much attention has been paid to the role of education or schooling. Education seldom appears in the index of such books. There is equally a growth in writing on education and conflict – including my own (Bush and Saltarelli, 2000; Davies, 2004; Nelles, 2003; Smith and Vaux, 2003; Novelli and Cardozo, 2007). And there is writing on religious education, faith schools and Islamic education which touches on fundamentalism (Apple, 2004; Griffin, 2006; Merry, 2007). But the reason for the present book is that it is time to focus specifically on the extreme end of conflict and radicalism, and to try to bring together the knowledge we now have on extremism with the knowledge we have on how schools can contribute to peace or, conversely, to conflict. The UN Security Council Resolution 1624 (14 Sep 2005)

> calls upon all States to continue international efforts to enhance dialogue and broaden understanding among civilisations, in an effort to prevent the indiscriminate targeting of different religions and cultures, and to take all measures as may be necessary and appropriate and in accordance with their obligations under international law to counter incitement of terrorist acts motivated by extremism and intolerance and to prevent the subversion of educational, cultural, and religious institutions by terrorists and their supporters. (para 3A)

This is the first time that States are *required* to do something within education (as compared to the declarations such as the Dakar Framework (World Education Forum, 2000) which are merely guidelines. The *Convention on the Rights of the Child* similarly does not say 'States must' do various things, but uses the reporting mechanism on what States have achieved in trying to enforce acquiescence – not always effectively. The Security Council however is the highest body, as people can use it to take cases to the International Court of Justice. So their inclusion of education in the countering of incitement to terrorist acts is significant. Their concern with 'subversion' of educational institutions by 'terrorists and their supporters' is nonetheless treated somewhat problematically in this book, as the point is made that schooling may unwittingly support extremism through both the systems of education and everyday practice.

The book considers three questions:

■ How do we prevent people from becoming intolerant and absolutist?

■ How do we prevent people joining extremist or violent movements?

■ How do we enable people to make challenges to extremist or violent movements or to extremist or violent governments?

These questions, predictably, lead into huge areas of identity, religion and justice. They also lead into everything from cartoons to jihadi websites. The book will no doubt offend some people. I sort of hope so. But the nature of offence has also to be subject to scrutiny, and is tackled in Chapter 4.

This introductory chapter considers the necessary definitions of and debates on extremism and fundamentalism and looks at who constitute 'extremists'. The next explores identity and how people become extremists, and also how they might exit from such an identity. Three subsequent chapters look at educational segregation, including faith schools; justice, revenge, retaliation and punishment; and free speech, offence and humour. All these lead into the final chapter on 'critical idealism', which draws together the strands to propose my 'XvX' version of the school which would educate against extremism.

## Definitions: extremism, radicalism, terrorism, fundamentalism

In looking at definitions of terms, themes emerge which are picked up at different points during the book, for example absolutism, anger, perfectionism, politicisation and intolerance. In one of the Doha debates (funded by the Qatar Foundation), Archbishop Desmond Tutu defined extremism as 'when you do not allow for a different point of view; when you hold your own views as being quite exclusive; when you don't allow for the possibility of difference' (Tutu, 2006). Extremism in current usage and understanding therefore is not just doing something to extremes, such as extreme sport. It is the denial of other realities.

> Virtually every movement, from animal rights to feminism, will embrace a spectrum ranging from uncompromising radicalism or 'extremism' to pragmatic accommodationism. For feminist ultras such as Andrea Dworkin, all penetrative sex is deemed to be rape. For some animal liberationists, every abattoir, however humane its procedures, is an extermination camp, while in the rhetoric of pro-lifers such as Pat Robertson, the 43 million foetuses 'murdered' since *Roe v Wade* [an anti-abortion case] are an abomination comparable to the Nazi holocaust. (Ruthven, 2004: 32)

When extremism starts to have a political end – for example to force governments to the table of negotiation or to some changes in their policies – it starts to become coterminous with radicalism. According to the Dutch Intelligence Service, radicalism comprises three aspects:

> The active pursuit of and/or support for fundamental changes in society that may endanger the continued existence of the democratic order (aim), which may involve the use of undemocratic methods (means) that may harm the functioning of the democratic order (effect). (quoted in Sieckelinck, 2007:5)

In educational terms, an indicator of radicalism in students is

> when pupils become intolerant of other people's views; when pupils acquire and apply explicit moral knowledge (in the broad sense, i.e. about good and evil) and orient their actions by a moral hierarchy, rather than by situational components. (Sieckelinck, 2007:10)

This radicalism may not – yet – have political ends, but it is possible to see the forerunners of this. I look explicitly at tolerance and intolerance later, and at the external moral hierarchies which can justify extremist positions.

Extremism is not, however, the same as terrorism. Although one might say every terrorist is an extremist, not all extremists are terrorists. In *The Terrorism Reader,* Whittaker (2007) acknowledges at least 200 different definitions of terrorism, and all the definitions in his book feature terms like violence or force. What is often important is how a definition can be used for policy. The US State department definition of terrorism is 'Premeditated, politically motivated violence perpetuated against non-combatant targets by subnational groups or clandestine agents, usually intended to influence an audience', while the UK government defines it as 'The use or threat, for the purpose of advancing a political, religious or ideological cause, of action which involves serious violence against any person or property' (Whittaker, 2007:4). There is controversy that this definition is too wide, particularly in including 'threat', and that it can lead to the Government restricting or even denying the legitimate rights of a wide range of protest groups.

However, one point of agreement is that terrorism is a pejorative term. It is generally applied to enemies and opponents, or to those with whom one disagrees. Edith King in her book *Teaching in an Era of Terrorism* (2006) includes all sorts of actions as terrorism – bullying, homophobia and female genital mutilation, 'increasingly recognised as a 'terror' for young girls' (p7). Nelles (2003) used the term 'school-yard terrorism' to describe the public bloody massacres by individuals (Colombine, Dunblane and more recently, Finland). Some terrorism is indeed less political, and while it has ends, these are not directed against governments as such. The Army of God, a Christian fundamentalist group in the US that murders doctors who practise abortion, views the American state as Satanic (Gray, 2007:177). The Aum movement in Japan which planted sarin gas in a subway also subscribed to an apocalyptic world view. Terrorists of this kind have more in common with members of cults than with the soldiers and strategists of Hezbollah and the Tamil Tigers.

However, the more conventional definitions relate to political motivation and goals beyond the terror itself, the intent to influence an audience beyond the immediate victims. Terrorism is a chosen strategy, for example to get rid of the occupation in Iraq, or to achieve independence for the Tamils in Sri Lanka, or to gain support for Hamas. It is significant that for the first 30 years of their political struggle, the Palestinians did not use suicide bombing. 'Suicide bombing was calmly and consciously used as a political instrument by the Palestinians and as a *last recourse in trying to resolve past struggles*' (Elworthy and Rifkind, 2006:40, italics in the original).

In the instilling of fear, terrorism is then sometimes seen as distinct from guerrilla warfare and insurgency, for while guerrilla groups are sometimes defined as terrorists by the population they are affecting, terrorists do not function in the open as armed units, do not attempt to seize or hold territory and do not engage with the military in combat.

> Terrorism is designed to create power where there is none or to consolidate power where there is very little. Through the publicity generated by their violence, terrorists seek to obtain the leverage, influence and power they otherwise lack to effect political change on either a local or international scale. (Whittaker, 2007:10)

I would argue that terrorists do attempt to seize territory, but acknowledge this may not be the immediate task of the action undertaken. The key distinction is that terrorists cannot be tackled by conventional means. Scilla Elworthy and Gabrielle Rifkind in their book *Making Terrorism History* explain

> Terrorism is a tactic rather than a definable enemy. There is no finite number of terrorists in the world to be smoked out, imprisoned or killed. Their numbers are controlled instead by the level of anger and hate that drives people to join their ranks. It is that anger and hate which must be addressed. (2006:27)

Addressing anger and hate would indeed seem to have educational implications. Yet Whittaker also points out the difference between terrorism and 'ordinary' criminality:

> The terrorist is fundamentally an *altruist*: he [sic] believes that he is serving a 'good' cause designed to achieve a greater good for a wider constituency – whether real or imagined – which the terrorist and his organisation purport to represent. The criminal, by comparison, serves no cause at all, just his own personal aggrandisement and material satiation. (2007:9)

It is this 'altruism' which makes terrorism so difficult to tackle in education or elsewhere. It is not the same as simple violence prevention measures, anti-bullying or the moral appeals to 'do no harm'. Extremism and terrorism have their own logics and moral codes. Hence there is the need for a critical view of the greater good, which arises throughout this book and which relates to what have been called 'hypergoods'. It is argued that through relationships with others, we become capable of making 'strong evaluations', as we get oriented towards hypergoods,

> on the basis of which we discriminate among other goods, attribute differential worth or importance to them, or determine when and if to follow them ... goods which not only are incomparably more important than others but provide the stand-point from which these must be weighed, judged, decided about. (Taylor, 1989:63)

For many, religious belief constitutes a hypergood, and Taylor claims theism is a fully adequate moral source; in this book, however, human rights is proposed as an alternative base for strong evaluation. Hypergoods instanced by Taylor of liberty, equality and freedom of expression would find an over-arching rationale in the reciprocity of rights and responsibilities; I will argue that human rights are both more direct and less dangerous than theist forms of the 'ultimate good'.

Terrorism is often portrayed as 'mindless'. Yet it can be a rational strategy, with its own logic, its own hypergood. As John Gray (2007) points out, much that is described as terrorism today would earlier have been civil insurgency or un-conventional warfare. Bombing government buildings and assassinating public officials are nothing new, and were the stock in trade of many national liberation struggles. Terrorist techniques are used because they are cheap and highly effective. It could be argued that the actual loss of life is small com-pared to other forms of violence, particularly state violence. One logic is that fewer people die compared to mass state incursions or genocides, or results of state policies such as apartheid, economic exploitation or environmental degradation. Robert Pape in his fascinating book *Dying To Win* (2004) makes the uncomfortable point that suicide terrorism works. Of the thirteen suicide terrorist campaigns 1980 – 2003, seven correlated with significant policy changes by the target state toward the terrorists' major political goals. In Sri Lanka, for example, the government entered into sovereignty negotiations with the terrorists, both in 1993-4 and 2001, 'to create an environment in which people could live without fear' (Chandra Bandaranaike, quoted in Pape, 2004:65). And Reagan actually mentioned the suicide attacks as a reason for withdrawing from Lebanon.

But as mentioned earlier, today's descriptions of terrorists reveal both diverse ends and diverse means, as pointed out by the criminologist Alain Bauer:

> New terrorists have emerged. Today, the real menace is hybrid groups that are opportunistic and capable of rapid transformation – and are not really organisations at all, as the West generally uses the term. They do not have solid, rigid structures. On the contrary, they are fluid, liquid or even volatile. Al-Qaeda is not an organisation like the IRA or the Basque ETA. We must look at and think about terrorism as a continuum. (quoted in Silber and Bhatt, 2007:13)

I similarly examined Al-Qaeda as a 'complex organisation' in my book *Education and Conflict: Complexity and Chaos* (2004). You do not join up and get a membership badge and a constitution. You are a member of a movement, perhaps in the same way as you could be part of a feminist movement; but, like feminism, you cannot identify a physical place, only key leaders, thinkers or open activists.

Finally, fundamentalism must be defined. While often associated with extremism, it is important to establish that they are not the same. The term fundamentalism originated in the specific theological context of early twentieth century Protestant America, and as Ruthven (2004) argues in his book *Fundamentalism: the Search for Meaning*, 'its applicability beyond its original matrix is – to put it mildly – problematic' (pv). It did not begin as a term of abuse or even criticism.

> Put at its broadest, it may be described as a 'religious way of being' that manifests itself in a strategy by which beleaguered believers attempt to preserve their distinctive identity as a people or group in the face of modernity and secularisation. (Ruthven, 2004:8)

Peggy Catron (2008) points out how the early 'fundamentals' aimed to re-affirm the authority of the scripture over the authority of science, and this dialectic between scripture and science has become a defining characteristic of fundamentalist movements. She cites the statistic that 31 per cent of Americans believe that the Bible is the actual word of God and is to be taken literally, word for word. (This would relate therefore to creationism, examined later.) Michele Malamud Kahn (2006) explains how for the USA, groups such as the Southern Baptists, Catholic charismatics, Pentecostals and Mennonites are generally characterised as 'being saved' or 'born again', holding the Bible as the only source of religious authority and supporting proselytising. President Bush is a self-proclaimed born again Christian. Fundamentalists banded together to preserve beliefs such as the inerrancy of the Bible, the authenticity of Jesus' miracles and the virgin birth of Christ.

However, Ruthven (2004) acknowledges that the term fundamentalism now occupies a position at the borders of the semantic field, straying into extremism, sectarianism and ideological purism. He is not sure about the non-religious uses of the word, for while there are similarities between anti-abortionists, animal rights activities, Green Party activists, Islamist agitators and the Six Day Creationists who sit on school boards in Kansas or southern California, they are not all the same. Fundamentalism is 'sharper and more distinctive' than extremism. The original 'Protestant' use of the word anchors it in individual and group selfhoods and identities, the scandal and shock of 'the Other'.

> Although many religious activists (especially the evangelical movements within Christianity and Islam) believe they have a universal mission to transform or convert the world, all religious traditions must face the problematic of their parochial origins, the embarrassing fact that saviours and prophets uttered divine words in particular languages to relatively small groups of people at particular historical junctures: the late John Lennon was correct in stating that the Beatles were more famous in their time than Jesus was in his. (p33)

In the modern age, religious pluralism is inescapable, implying choice and the suspicion that there may be more than one path to salvation. For Ruthven, the surge of fundamentalist movements (or 'movements of religious revitalisation') is a response to globalisation – 'or more specifically, to the anxieties generated by the thought that there are ways of living and believing other than those deemed to have been decreed by one's own group's version of the deity' (p34).

Kahn's particular interest is how such 'conservative' believers take biblical references to same-sex contact as 'truth'. She acknowledges how Christians have used scripture to promote caring for the poor as well as for the abolition of slavery and the death penalty, but at the same time, biblical references have been used to justify sexism, racism and sexual prejudice. In her article on 'Conservative Christian teachers and the implications for lesbian, gay and bisexual youth', Kahn points out how the US Southern Baptists (of which there are 16 million) do not recognise homosexuality as a 'valid alternative lifestyle'. She quotes how the president of The Church of Jesus Christ of Latter Day Saints (approx 12 million members worldwide) contended that 'we want to help these people, to strengthen them, to assist them with their problems and to help them with their difficulties. But we cannot stand idle if they indulge in immoral activity'. The irony apparently escapes him that it is the attitudes of his church which creates the 'problems' and 'difficulties' for homosexuals (or the patronising terminology of 'these people'). The Alabama

State Representative Gerald Allen moved to strip public libraries of books by lesbian or gay authors, promising to 'dig a big hole and dump them in and bury them'.

This homophobia is not just American fundamentalism: President Olusegun Obasanjo of Nigeria supported a law imposing five years of imprisonment on anyone involved in a lesbian or gay organisation or publication or who publicly supported lesbian and gay rights, or even publicly displayed a 'same-sex marriage relationship', while former immigration minister Rita Verdonk of the Netherlands sought to deny asylum to lesbian, gay, bisexual and trans-gender Iranians, threatening to deport them back to a country that imposes the death penalty on homosexual conduct (Human Rights Watch, 2007). I would classify this as an extremist position. Kahn points out how religious beliefs and homophobia are strongly related, quoting studies showing that the stronger the religious conviction, the less tolerant individuals are likely to be towards gays and lesbians. 'While it would be simplistic to blame homo-phobia entirely on religion, there is ample evidence that it has a powerful influence' (Khan, 2006:361).

Of great concern by some feminists is what is seen as the extreme oppression of women by religious fundamentalism. Polly Toynbee (2001:21) for example writes of how

> Primitive Middle Eastern religions (and most others) are much the same – Islam, Christianity and Judaism all define themselves through disgust for women's bodies. There are ritual baths, churching, shaving heads, denying abortion and contra-ception, arranged marriage, purdah, barring unclean women access to the altar, let alone the priesthood, letting men divorce but not women – all this perverted abhor-rence of half the human race lies at the maggotty heart of religion, the defining creed of the holy of holies ... all extreme fundamentalism plunges back into the dark ages by using the oppression of women (sometimes called 'family values') as its talisman.

As she points out, moderate, modernised believers may claim the true Bible/Qu'ran does not demand such things. But the actual situation in Afghanistan for example means that western coalitions have supported the Northern Alliance which can be little better than the Taliban in their oppression of women.

Yet Ruthven (2004) points out the paradoxes in fundamentalism – on the one hand they embrace aspects of modernity if it suits them – radio, television and electronics as well as armaments; on the other hand there is the call to traditionalism, and the lack of acceptance of religious pluralism or equity.

Islamic extremists in Upper Egypt have tried to extract the *jizya* tax from the Christian Coptic minority – a payment that would symbolise their inferior status. The Hindu 'fundamentalists' of the BJP (Bharatiya Janata Party) and RSS (Rashtriya Svayamsevak Sangh or 'national union of volunteers') believe that Indian nationhood must be based on caste, the social categories recognised in classical Hinduism, thus excluding Muslims, Sikhs, Christians, tribal peoples, and even non-resident Indians (NRIs) from their notion of Indian identity. Jewish fundamentalists tend to be narrower in their definitions of what constitutes Jewish identity than secular Zionists. The extremists among them such as Baruch Goldstein, who killed some thirty Arab worshippers at the Tomb of the Patriarchs in Hebron in 1994, and his mentor, Rabbi Meir Kahane, held views about Arabs that were remarkably similar to Adolf Hitler's views about the Jews (Ruthven, 2004:46).

There are also however more subtle fundamentalists, who do damage under the guise of their influential position. The Oxford theologian Richard Swinburne explains 'suffering' as the will of God:

> Although a good God regrets our suffering, his greatest concern is surely that each of us shall show patience, sympathy and generosity and, thereby, form a holy character. Some people badly need to be ill for their own sake, and some people badly need to be ill to provide important choices for others. Only in that way can some people be encouraged to make serious choices about the sort of person they are to be. For other people, illness is not so valuable'. (quoted in Dawkins, 2006:64)

So everything is rosy then. We need not waste our money on medical research because illness is good for our character, or even other people's characters. In his book *The Existence of God*, Swinburne also attempted to justify the Holocaust on the grounds that it gave Jews a wonderful opportunity to be courageous and noble. He said of Hiroshima 'Suppose that one less person had been burnt by the Hiroshima atomic bomb. Then there would have been less opportunity for courage and sympathy...' (2004:264). This is mind-blowing in its twisted logic, but disturbing if anyone agrees with him: the justification for terrorism or inflicting of suffering would be that it gave opportunities to the fortunate who were not annihilated or injured to show sympathy. I would not want to try to explain that to the parents of children killed in land-mine explosions or raped and killed in a genocide.

The problem is that while terrorists are often seen as nutters, Oxford theologians are not, and are in contrast invited onto television and radio to hawk such dangerous ideas around.

So, like terrorism, not all fundamentalists are extremists or terrorists; but this book argues that fundamentalism may predispose its adherents to 'extreme' positions. And extreme positions may be harmful – through either oppression or exclusion, or actual violence or all three. All may share absence of doubt, or the use of justificatory principles, but the differences between them – and their impact – can be summarised as relating to five main dimensions:

- Scale: from individual to state-funded
- Roots: political or religious or combined
- Expansionist: whether continually seeking to draw in new members
- Goals: whether trying to force radical social or political change
- Violence: whether force is seen as desirable or justified.

A fundamentalist group that does not seek to expand itself, nor to take violent action, can be left alone. But when this becomes destructive, or indoctrinatory, or globally revolutionary, then there is a question of how to respond.

## Who are the extremists? Politics and religion

This leads to the question 'who are the extremists'? For our educational concern, what is the scale of the challenge? There is a website (extremismonthe net) which monitors other websites devoted to extremism, and they list 'political fascism, skinhead fascism, Nazi parties, white supremacy, militia groups, Holocaust Denial, race hate, religious cults, anti-homosexuality, anti-semitism, world conspiracy, Islamist militancy, pro-anorexia/bulimia, violent animal rights, sports hooliganism, violent political activism, bomb-making and suicide assistance'. Ironically, many of the Al-Qaeda websites are hosted by US companies.

So is all extremism to be cast as problematic? Gandhi was an extremist perhaps, as was Nelson Mandela or Martin Luther King. We always need such figures, as models of how non-violent action can create social change. Yet this in turn inevitably raises the question of whether violence is sometimes justified. Tibet for example has always followed the Dalai Lama's position on non-violence, but, after 50 years of oppression, would it be time for direct action? Similarly, as I write, the question is being raised in the press of whether massive peaceful demonstrations by Buddhist monks and anti-government protesters will ever bring down the oppressive military junta in Burma. Is Aung San Suu Kyi's insistence on non-violence the right strategy? It is not the place of this book to make judgements, but rather to trace linkages and to argue for a form of education which enables learners to assess the pros and cons for themselves.

In looking at who the extremists are, and why they become so, the key dis-cussion centres round the different mixes of politics and religion. Suicide bombers perhaps represent the extreme form of an already extremist move-ment, but they are not all religious fanatics. In *Dying To Win*, Pape analysed suicide attacks in great detail, looking at 315 attacks over 25 years, and con-cluded (surprisingly?) that 'there is little connection between suicide terror-ism and Islamic fundamentalism or any of the world's religions'. His argu-ment is the territorial one identified earlier, that what they have in common is a specific secular and strategic goal: to compel modern democracies to withdraw military forces from the territory that the terrorists consider to be their homeland. 'Religion is rarely the root cause, although it is often used as a tool by terrorist organisations in recruiting and in other efforts in service of the broader strategic objective' (Pape, 2005:4).

So the link between religion and terrorism is a complex one. We are seeing the politicisation of religion – the rapid growth of political Islam, the political reach of 'born-again' Christianity, Jewish extremism, or the Hindutva move-ment. As Amartyr Sen points out in his book *Identity and Violence: The Illusion of Destiny* (2006), there is the exploitation of religious identity to feed into political polarisation, with the 'Shariah-isation' of Indonesia and Malaysia – despite a history of multiculturalism – and the distinctions be-tween a Muslim country and an Islamic state becoming blurred (for instance, no non-Muslim can be elected President in an Islamic state). State sponsor-ship of extremism then becomes a crucial area. Sen quotes Hussain Haqqani, former Pakistani ambassador to Sri Lanka, who talks of the need to deal with 'the depths of Pakistan's problem with Islamic extremism'. Haqqani argues that the disproportionate influence wielded by fundamentalist groups in Pakistan is the result of state sponsorship of such groups, and he warns that 'an environment dominated by Islamist and militarist ideologies is the ideal breeding ground for radicals and exportable radicalism' (quoted in Sen, 2006: 73).

But many governments, not just Islamic ones, will use extreme measures to achieve their political and economic objectives. We can understand why the US and the UK have been accused of being 'terrorists' in their invasions and their support for Israel. It could be argued that military intervention is justi-fied only if there is genocide or real likelihood of attack – but not just to topple a dictator. Timothy Garton Ash explains:

> There are good reasons why statesmen from the signatories of the Peace of West-
> phalia in 1648 to the authors of the UN Charter in 1945 set such store by respect

for state sovereignty and non-intervention. If I think I'm justified in invading your country, you may equally well feel you're justified in invading mine. Or someone else's. President Putin clearly felt encouraged by America's unilateral action over Iraq to continue his oppression of Chechnya; and China felt it had a freer hand in Tibet. The road back to international anarchy is a short one. (2004:243)

He continues 'I don't yet see a single example of a post-intervention international occupation which has successfully 'built' a self-governing free country'. This reminds me of a nice exercise I found which I sometimes use with students, from a list compiled by the historian William Blum (1999):

---

Here is a list of countries that the US has bombed since the end of the World War II.

| | |
|---|---|
| China 1945-46 | Cambodia 1967-69 |
| Korea 1950-53 | Grenada 1983 |
| China 1950-53 | Libya 1986 |
| Guatemala 1954 | El Salvador 1980s |
| Indonesia 1958 | Nicaragua 1980s |
| Cuba 1959-60 | Panama 1989 |
| Guatemala 1960 | Iraq 1991-1999 |
| Congo 1964 | Sudan 1998 |
| Peru 1965 | Afghanistan 1998 |
| Laos 1964-73 | Yugoslavia 1999 |
| Vietnam 1961-73 | (And now Iraq 2004) |

In how many of these instances did a democratic government, respectful of human rights, occur as a direct result? Choose one of the following:

a) 0

b) zero

c) none

d) not a one

e) zip

f) a whole number between -1 and +1

g) zilch

---

Of course, the instances given above relate to cold war circumstances, and are not directly related to terrorist action as such; but the reasons why interventions mostly do not work often relate to existing fundamentalism. Elworthy and Rifkind argue that:

> Had the Americans been committed not to 'victory' in Falluja but rather to an isolation strategy and the arresting of insurgent groups, then they might well not have inflamed the local community ... it points to one of the most powerful ways in which fundamentalist movements can be unintentionally strengthened by repeated humiliation. In cultures where there have been endless cycles of violence, communities become cumulatively traumatised. It then becomes difficult to enter into the mind of the other, and this in turn makes it hard to build any concern for or interest in the other, or any level of trust – the necessary preconditions for dialogue. This leaves both parties in the position of victim. The culture of perpetual victimhood distorts values, and erodes the vital feedback mechanisms of self-criticism, robbing communities of their most valuable asset, the questioning mind. (2006:18)

Hence the importance of differentiating between modernist and fundamentalist varieties of Islamism, and the overall impact of humiliation (of which more in the next chapter). The International Crisis Group talk of the 'sledge hammer approach' to Islam:

> American and European policy-makers risk provoking one of two equally undesirable outcomes: either encouraging the different strands of Islamic activism to band together in reaction, attenuating differences that might otherwise be fruitfully developed, or causing the non-violent and modernist tendencies to be eclipsed by the jihadis. (ICG, 2005)

While Pape and others would take a political view of terrorism and suicide bombing, there is also the argument that religion is underneath it all – or at least can be harnessed in its cause. Ginsburg and Megahed (2003) concur that there is nothing inherent in any particular religious or cultural tradition that spawns terrorism, but on the other hand there is nothing inherent in any religious or cultural tradition that prevents it being used to motivate violence or terrorism. The anti-abortionists who would kill doctors normally have a religious faith which they say justifies this action because of the sanctity of life – which to others might seem a bizarre contradiction. An interview by Nasra Hassan with a failed suicide bomber found him speaking of the

> power of the spirit that pulls us upward ... we were floating, swimming, in the feeling that we were about to enter eternity. We had no doubts. We made an oath on the Koran, in the presence of Allah – a pledge not to waver. The jihad pledge is called *bayt al-ridwan*, after the garden in Paradise that is reserved for the prophets and martyrs. I know that there are other ways to do jihad. But this one is sweet – the sweetest'. (quoted in Dawkins, 2004:305)

Here one can see a number of attractions: out of the body experiences, yet absolute certainty, a feeling that Allah was there, right next to you, and how being a martyr would put you on a par with a prophet, in a special, exclusionary garden, which run of the mill Muslims presumably do not enter.

But for Dawkins the 'take-home message' is that we should point the finger at religion itself, not religious *extremism,* as though that were some kind of terrible perversion of real, decent religion. He comments:

> Voltaire got it right long ago: 'Those who can make you believe absurdities can make you commit atrocities'. So did Bertrand Russell: 'Many people would sooner die than think. In fact, they do' (p306).

What is pernicious for Dawkins is the concept that faith itself is a virtue:

> Faith is an evil precisely because it requires no justification and brooks no argument. Teaching children that unquestioned faith is a virtue primes them – given certain other ingredients that are not hard to come by – to grow up into potentially lethal weapons for future jihads or crusades. Immunised against fear by the promise of a martyr's paradise, the authentic faith-head deserves a high place in the history of armaments, alongside the longbow, the warhorse, the tank and the cluster bomb. If children were taught to question and think through their beliefs, instead of being taught the superior virtue of faith without question, it is a good bet that there would be no suicide bombers ... Faith can be very dangerous, and deliberately to implant it into the vulnerable mind is a grievous wrong. (p308)

Critics of Dawkins will see him as 'extremist' in his denunciation of religion, as does Karen Armstrong (2006), who argues that hating religion is a pathology, and classifies Dawkins as a 'secular fundamentalist'. I might want to quibble with his argument on the grounds that Sri Lankan suicide bombers and Basque separatists do not have a religious justification or promise, nor did the Baader-Meinhof gangs. But I take his main point that it can be an underlying lack of questioning of beliefs or the rightfulness of causes that can push people into what we see as extremist acts. Hanan Ashrawi, the Palestinian political activist and Member of the Palestinian Legislative council, made a very significant point:

> The Israeli-Palestinian issue is not a religious conflict. It is an issue over land, legitimacy, history and politics. Bringing God into the conflict is a guarantee that it will never be solved. (Ashrawi, 2007)

My supposition would be that the lack of solution would be because of the non-negotiable nature of religion. Other areas could be bargained over, but the absolutism of some types of religious faith and the very fact that there is no evidence and that unquestioning belief is therefore necessary means that this is almost untouchable. There is little exchange currency, and much is seen as indivisible. One side cannot say 'I'll give you the feeding of the five thousand if you'll give me the 72 virgins thing'. In the end, of course, they are not theological arguments but identity arguments (which I look at more in

Chapter 2). Sides do not go to war over actual theological beliefs, over angels and pinheads, but on the *right* to believe and how that belief or culture may condition other material things – such as jobs, homes and prospects. But the injection of something spiritual into the equation ends in stalemate – for example, whose spiritual home Jerusalem is. Even if religion is not the root cause, it has to be identified often for the *maintenance* and *amplification* of conflict, both in its symbolism and in potential justifications for extremism.

## Perfection and Utopia

Both political and religious extremism have in common, however, two traits which are highly significant for education: perfection and absolutism. The first, and one which represents a dilemma, is striving for perfection. Many extremist movements want to return to an idealised traditional world, or to create a new perfect world order.

John Gray's erudite book *Black Mass: Apocalyptic Religion and the Death of Utopia* (2007) examines the drive for a utopian society that is the characteristic of virtually all political movements as well as religions. Soviet communism, Nazism, Mao's China are all based on the vision of the perfect society – as is the Promised Land. He traces the history of 'faith-based violence':

> Utopian projects reproduced religious myth that had inflamed mass movements of religious believers in the Middle Ages, and they kindled a similar violence. The secular terror of modern times is a mutant version of the violence that has accompanied Christianity throughout its history. (p3)

Millenarian beliefs are symptoms of a type of cognitive dissonance in which normal links between perception and reality have broken down. Jesus and his followers believed they lived in an End-Time when the evils of the world were about to pass away. Eschatology (the doctrine of last things and the end of the world) is common – either destruction followed by a new order or simply final disaster. Radical Islam is a millenarian movement. The Mahdist tradition anticipates the arrival of a divinely guided teacher who will reorder the world – a tradition that Bin Laden has exploited when projecting his image as a prophet leader. The teaching of Jesus was that the old world was about to come to an end and a new kingdom be established, with unlimited abundance and the righteous dead raised back to life. 'The new kingdom did not arrive, and Jesus was arrested and executed by the Romans. The history of Christianity is a series of attempts to cope with this founding experience of eschatological disappointment' (Gray, 2007:7).

Again in millenarian terms, Fukuyama's *The End of History* says that we are reaching the end point of mankind's ideological evolution and the universalisation of western liberal democracy as the final form of human government (1992). Such claims, particularly that history is moving towards some 'End,' cannot be refuted or supported by rational argument, but they are dangerous ideas, particularly, as in US, when put together with the assumption of liberal democracy as the only legitimate government. Roberto Ungar (2007) talks of 'democratic perfectionism', with its home in the US: the belief that a free society has an institutional formula or blueprint that, once discovered, needs to be adjusted only in rare moments of national or world crisis. He calls this a 'species of idolatry' (p23).

But Gray would claim that liberal democracy cannot be established in most of the countries of the Middle East, that in much of the region the choice is between secular despotism and Islamist rule. In attempting to impose the American version, one ends up with illiberal democracy, the expression of the popular will and no need to protect personal freedom or the rights of minorities. The interesting question is whether US is actually returning to this anyway, in the use of torture and Guantanamo Bay. Huntingdon's *The Clash of Civilisations* (1996) argued that the age of ideology had ended, to be replaced by cultural and religious conflict. The debate is whether he was prescient in the US invasion of Afghanistan and the various terrorist bombings since 2000; there is a more worrying argument that his analysis acted as a self-fulfilling prophecy, with his ideas influential among neo-conservatives such as US Vice-President Dick Cheney, and with radical Islamists in the Middle East viewing his thesis approvingly (Kepel, 2003).

'The use of inhumane methods to achieve impossible ends is the essence of revolutionary utopianism' (Gray, 2007:18). Means-ends linkages are at the heart of extremism. Marx and Engels were in no doubt that the communism as 'the riddle of history solved' would be reached only after much blood had been shed. Shining Path in Peru carries on this communist ideal, killing tens of thousands of people in pursuit of a world that is better than any that has existed. In that the seeking for perfection can justify all manner of means, the desire for some sort of Utopia is in the end highly dangerous.

Yet we know educationally that we should raise expectations, nourish aspiration and seek through practice to 'perfect' skills. It is necessary therefore to make a simple three way distinction in extremism: extremism which brings pleasure or good; extremism which is wacky but does no harm; and extremism which injures individuals, groups or societies. Hence the person who practises six hours a day to become a concert pianist and seeks near perfection in their work can bring immense pleasure to people. In the second category, the person who indulges in 'extreme sport', paragliding off mountains wearing nothing but a Superman T shirt, does not bring pleasure to thousands, but on the other hand does no harm. It is the third category, the extremism which injures, which is my focus. Like Ruthven, my concern is with those who cannot accept other belief systems or lifestyles and who seek to impose their own.

> Unlike sects such as the Amish, who may be happy to be left alone in horse-drawn, zipper-free isolation, the fundamentalism with which we are primarily concerned has broader ambitions. Seldom content with defending its minority status against the onslaughts of a pluralistic, secular world, it strives to 'fight back' by exercising power, directly or indirectly ... for the activist fundamentalist (as distinct from the passive traditionalist) the quest for salvation cannot be realised by withdrawing into a cultural enclave. (Ruthven, 2004:57)

While we may say that the global obsession with perfection and excellence is a human condition and an excellent thing in itself, it does have undesirable consequences. It is seen increasingly in education across the globe with the obsession with standards and league tables – but I prefer the Swedish National Agency for Education's promotion of '*The Good Enough School*' (Skolverket, 2000). Here the ideology is to make all schools 'good enough' so that parents are content with neighbourhood schools, and artificial choices are not created. Striving for perfection is closely allied to extremist identity, as I examine in the next chapter. Instead, can we not be content with 'goodness of fit'? Indeed, should we not aim for comfort with the inevitable messiness of life? It was interesting how Katherine Whitehorn's first inroads into extolling household sluttishness in her columns in 1963 unleashed so much support from women who otherwise felt guilty of not being the perfect housewife. Readers wrote in to confess their own crimes, such as finding themselves wiping the kitchen table with a kitten. This may seem trivial in this seriously problematic area, but my point will be an educational one: how to combine 'improvement' with acceptance of 'mere' competence, being good enough. I will not digress into my extremist views on Gifted and Talented programmes here.

Utopian ideals are not always revolutionary. And this is not to deny the need for imagination and vision – such as the abolition of apartheid or the slave trade. The problem is the core feature of the utopian dream which is of *ultimate harmony*, leaving behind normal conflicts and clashes of interest. But as Gray and many other conflict experts have pointed out, conflict is normal –

even within us, people want incompatible things: excitement and a quiet life, freedom and security, 'truth and a picture of the world that flatters their sense of self-importance' (p17). As I have written elsewhere, conflict is essential to any sense of progress, as old ideas or regimes are challenged. Democracy is by definition conflictual. It is not a Utopian vision, but one where conflict is ever present and indeed needs to be nurtured. Utopian visions of perfect harmony are dangerously blind.

## Absolutism

The journalist Robert Fisk interviewed Osama bin Laden on more than one occasion in the 1990s.

> He was alarming because he was possessed of that quality which leads men to war: total self-conviction. In the years to come, I would see others manifest this dangerous characteristic – President George W. Bush and Tony Blair come to mind – but never the fatal self-resolve of Osama bin Laden (Fisk, 2005:25)

A twin aspect of extremism, which will be a recurring theme, is an absolutist view of the world – and of oneself. While it is part of the human condition to make distinctions between right and wrong, a manicheaist view regards matter as intrinsically good and intrinsically evil. The world can be divided into enemies and friends, believers and non-believers. In his work on fundamentalism, Ruthven is good on what he calls 'the scandal of difference'. He points out how in a globalised culture where religions are in daily contact with their competitors, denial of pluralism is a recipe for conflict. Yet acceptance of pluralism relativises truth. 'Once it is allowed that there are different paths to truth a person's religious allegiance becomes a matter of choice, and choice is the enemy of absolutism' (2004:48). This is an interesting point: for fundamentalists and those who seek to impose their views on others, there can be no choice. You are offering a whole package, not a menu to select from. The irony is that fundamentalists themselves make strategic selections from scriptures to justify their position. Textual anomalies are either denied, or the burden of proof is shifted from God to humanity. They can then be explained as errors of human understanding, rather than flaws in the text itself.

Tariq Ramadan, in an unpublished speech to the 2007 Education and Extremism conference at Roehampton, acknowledged that there was a particular problem in Islam which lent itself to a binary or absolutist view. Three features explained this: firstly, a politicised and literal reading of the scriptures which led to a dogmatic mindset and the absolute belief in the Celiphate; secondly, a political naivety in this reading, as evidenced by the Taliban's strict and binary interpretations; and thirdly a specific political environment, as in Palestine, Iraq, or the repression in Morocco or in Egypt under Nasser, within which binary interpretations more easily take place.

Similarly, a recent study for the New York police department (Silber and Bhatt, 2007) talk of how the personal search for one's own Muslim identity often dovetails with the desire to find an appropriate Islamic response to the political crises involving Muslims worldwide.

> Complex disputes like the Arab-Israeli conflict and Kashmir are diluted into one large conflict between 'believers' and 'non-believers'. This powerful and simple 'one-size fits all' philosophy resonates with the younger diaspora Muslim populations in the West who are often politically naïve. This powerful narrative provides evidence of an across-the-board plan to undermine and humiliate Islam worldwide. (p17)

Three important educational implications then arise: the need for an emphasis on complexity and on alternative world views; the need for political education, so that young people are not 'politically naïve'; and the need to surface and counter conspiracy theories. Gray (2007) talks of 'demonology' – the Jacobins, the Bolsheviks and the Nazis all believed vast conspiracies were mounted against them, as do radical Islamists today. 'It is never the flaws of human nature that stand in the way of Utopia. It is the workings of evil forces' (p25). But as Nef (2003) points out, this 'friend-foe' doctrine, the 'pedagogy of fear' can infect whole countries (such as US), internalising fear in the name of security and not questioning authority.

For Tariq Ramadan, a binary vision may then be cemented by the way Muslims are viewed in western countries. Terrorists may have been socially and culturally integrated. They may have been intellectually integrated, with language skills and a job. But what is missing is the psychology of integration and belonging, and being trusted. Their vision is still binary – *you* in this society and *us*, Islam on one side and non-Muslims on the other. When there is an official discourse of *you* Muslims, or 'Muslims should do something', this cements the divide. Ramadan's answer is to be serious about equality, so that Muslims are treated not as second class citizens but as groups which can contribute, not just be 'integrated'; it is also to stress commonalities, and to have much dialogue, globally as well as inter-faith.

The other side of the coin in absolutism is the mythical 'logical conclusion' assumption, that everything suspicious will inevitably go to extremes unless we are eternally vigilant. Hong Kong's Chief Executive Donald Tsang had to apologise recently for suggesting that China's Cultural Revolution was 'an extreme form of democracy'. Interestingly, he made this comment to argue that social stability should not be sacrificed for democratic development. 'People can go to the extreme like what we saw during the Cultural Revolution ... [It] was the people taking the power into their own hands. Now that is what you mean by democracy, if you take it to the full swing'. Tsang came under fire for these comments not from the pro-Maoists but from the pro-democracy lawmakers in Hong Kong, who are questioning his full commitment to democracy for Hong Kong (BBC News, 2007). The point in question is how the claim of extremism can be used as a *negative*, the domino effect, if-you-take-it-to-its-logical-conclusion argument. We are right to fear extremism; but we have to be equally careful about threats and putative extensions.

Hence absolutism also appears in reaction to threat. Rizvi argues that

> One of the main problems with the new language of security is that it is often couched in absolutist and binary terms. Far too often, words like 'war'. 'justice', 'victory' and 'security' are used as if they have single, uniform and uncontestable meanings ... This rhetoric serves only to hinder democratic debate about the causes, expressions and outcomes of terrorism and a whole variety of possible remedies that could be considered to meet the new global challenges. (2004: 167)

Alibhai Brown (2007) in similar vein quotes Henry James: 'I hate American simplicity. I glory in the piling up of complications of every sort.' She argues that we have adopted American simplicity in dealing with the piles of complications surrounding terrorism, which have led to an attack on civil liberties and calls to lock up suspects indefinitely. People think in 'unbending certainties' – that bombers do what they do because they hate night clubs, pubs and free life styles. Others are sure it is foreign policy, or the illegal war in Iraq, the occupation of Palestine, the mess in Kashmir and Chechnya, or brainwashing by imams. Alibhai Brown uses a powerful metaphor: 'The disturbing truth, however, is that while all these reasons are bubbling in the cauldrons, as yet we don't know what else is in the brew and what causes the mixture to boil over' (p31).

## Belief into action

As said, not all extremists, however perfectionist or absolutist, want or need to impose these ideas on others. So we need to look at the triggers and drivers of expansionism. An important educational area is the translation of commands in sacred or other texts into action, for much depends on language and whether scriptural exhortations are to be seen as metaphors or as instruction booklet. When at my primary school we all sang 'Onward Christian Soldiers, marching as to war' I don't think we actually took it literally. Nor did it condition my life or make me belligerent – not in the name of Christ anyway. The assumption is that deep down we knew it was an analogy, as much as any 'battle' – against dirt, or indolence, or headlice. But literal interpretation of calls to war can be seen in Christianity as they are in militant Islam. In the Bible, the children of Israel are commanded by God to massacre the Amalekites, an indigenous Canaanite tribe, along with their women, children and flocks. One might assume that this would now be seen in its historical context. Yet for fundamentalist militants such as Rabbi Yisrael Hess, formerly the campus rabbi of Tel Aviv's Bar-Ilan University, the Amalekites of scripture are assimilated to contemporary Palestinian Arabs. An article entitled 'The Commandment of Genocide in the Torah' ends with the chilling words 'The day will yet come when we will all be called to fulfil the commandment of the divinely ordained war to destroy Amelak' (quoted in Ruthven, 2004:91).

Specific *people*, then, do the translation of myth into history, and of belief into future action. Ruthven also tells how Sayyid Qutb, the Islamist ideologue who is the intellectual who shaped the thinking of Osama bin Laden and most of today's political Islamist groups, urged his followers to approach the Qu'ran as a manual for action, as distinct from a source of moral or spiritual guidance. The Qu'ran was not just about acquiring culture or information, to solve scientific or legal problems or remove defects in understanding. Ruthven quotes from Qutb's *Milestones*, where Qutb argues that the first generation of Muslims

> ... turned to the Koran 'to find out what the Almighty Creator had prescribed for him and for the group in which he lived, for his life and for the life of the group'. He approached it in order to act upon it immediately, 'as a soldier on the battlefield reads his daily bulletin so that he knows what is to be done'. For Qutb and his disciples, the 'Sword' verses in the Koran urging Holy War against the enemies of God are to be interpreted currently as operational manuals, rather than as spiritual guidance against the forces of evil. (2004:91)

Apparently, however, 'jihad' is not in fact the same as a 'holy war', and the actual translation is 'effort and resistance', in oneself as well. Yet it has become broadly and loosely used to signify violent action.

This links directly to the role of formal education in interpretation and understanding, and here Sigal Ben-Porath's valuable identification of 'belligerent citizenship' becomes relevant. In her book *Citizenship Under Fire: Democratic Education in Times of Conflict* (2006), she looks at the growth or return of belligerent citizenship when countries are experiencing tension. This reformulates the three components of democratic citizenship, which are normally civic participation; unity and solidarity; and public deliberation. In times of war the form these components take is an emphasis on citizens' contribution to the country rather than on voluntary participation; support for social unity in the form of patriotism rather than diversity; and consequently the discouragement of deliberation, and a silencing of diverse perspectives. The 'belligerence' would imply a highly active role, but not one to defuse tension in the long run, and not one that challenges absolutism.

Globalisation may thus push people into greater insularity, a dichotomy captured by Barber's *Jihad versus McWorld* (1995). September 11 and the attack on US capitalism did make people talk about the global haves and have-nots. And there is awareness that responsibility for international conflict may be very close to home. But in its elision with democracy, free trade is being rebranded as the war on terrorism. In her book *No Logo*, Naomi Klein quotes the owner of MTV (a 24 hour commercial channel in US): 'MTV is associated with the forces of freedom and democracy around the world' (2000:129). As Klein points out, to criticise the US government is to be on the side of the terrorists. We are back to dichotomous friends and foes.

In his latest book *Globalisation, Democracy and Terrorism* (2007), Eric Hobsbawm's views are that terrorism is not the biggest of our problems, and that other long term problems such as climate change cannot be dealt with by our current democratic procedures, by counting votes and measuring consumer preferences. He makes the important distinction that terrorists are symptoms, not significant historical agents. As horrifying as terrorist attacks may be, their real impact on stable, prosperous states is negligible. They do not constitute a threat to our 'way of life', and the megalomaniac counter policy of the US, and the 'irrational fear' created and recreated simply plays into the terrorists' hands. He is cautious about the prospects of recalling this genie, but has a view important for this book: that US assertiveness was contained in past by rival powers, but now it can be restrained only by 'enlightenment and education'.

In sum, the educational task is hugely complex – or devastatingly simple. It is how to give a sense of purpose in life and yet not push people to absolutist 'extremes' and identifications of 'the forces of evil'. The problem is best captured in the winner of the best religious joke for 2006, which is actually about extremism:

Walking across a bridge, I saw a man on the edge, about to jump. I ran over and said: 'Stop. Don't do it.'

'Why not?' he asked.

'Well, there's so much to live for!'

'Like what?'

'Are you religious?'

He said 'Yes'.

I said, 'Me too, Are you Christian or Buddhist?'

'Christian'.

'Me too. Are you Catholic or Protestant?'

'Protestant'.

'Me too. Are you Episcopalian or Baptist?'

'Baptist.'

'Me, too. Are you Baptist Church of God or Baptist Church of the Lord?'

'Baptist Church of God'

'Me, too. Are you original Baptist Church of God or Reformed Baptist Church of God?'

'Reformed Baptist Church of God.'

'Me, too! Are you Reformed Baptist Church of God, Reformation of 1879 or Reformed Baptist Church of God, Reformation of 1915?'

He said, 'Reformation of 1915'.

I said, 'Die, heretic scum' and pushed him off.

# 2
## Identity and radicalisation

Who gets to be an extremist, to form or join extremist groups? Why do some people become extremists and others not, and what are the combinations of influences? What are the radicalisation processes? How do people exit from extremism, if they do? And does education have any role to play either in the entry or the exit? These are the questions for this chapter.

It must be stated from the outset that much extremism and terrorism can only be understood in relation to particular political, economic and historical contexts. In his discussion of the 'pedagogy of violence' and brutality manifested by whole societies as well as individuals, Jorge Nef, for example, sees terrorism as related to five global interconnected manifestations of a political crisis: failed states with economic breakdown and internal conflicts fuelled by a vigorous arms trade; a surge in irredentist forms of ethnic and religious nationalism; the resurgence of neo-fascist right-wing tendencies in developed countries; expanding criminality enhanced by authoritarian or corrupt law enforcement; and the growing irrelevance of democratic politics resulting from neoliberal policies and the erosion of civil society (2003). Identities then have to be understood against specific geo-political developments – for Muslim extremists, this would be the violence and discrimination against Muslims in Palestine (or Bosnia), and the USA's support and huge funding of Muslim seminaries in the 1980s to produce jihadis to fight the USSR in Afghanistan; for Jewish extremists, the persecution in Tsarist Russia and Nazi Germany and the violence they have faced from Palestinian terrorists; or for Hindu extremists, the partition of India on the demand of the Muslim minority.

This book cannot develop all these socio-political analyses and legacies, but focuses on the specific question of why certain individuals and groups *against these same backdrops* become extremists and others not, and whether education is at all significant in radicalisation.

## Identity

First I discuss the contentious issue of 'identity' itself. This is linked to extremism in a number of ways: the identity of the extremist, identity formation, and the protection of collective identities as a justification for extremism. Much of the discourse on educational or multicultural policy plays on the centrality of cultural identity, but this is disingenuous and misleading. In an article on pluralism, identity and freedom of conscience, Kenneth Strike offers an interesting discussion of identity, saying it is far from clear what it means. 'Many of us lack the kind of relationship to some primary group that would allow us to view ourselves as our culture writ small' (2003:82). For some people, their identity is specified by their relationship to some spiritual or moral tradition, but for many others their convictions or values are much more eclectic. Strike finds it difficult, as I would, to use the language of identity to describe his core.

> I can say 'Here are my durable tastes and convictions. This is my core'. But I cannot easily name my core by naming a tradition. I cannot say 'I am a member of this group' in a way that tells you what my core is ... I have many congregations, but no tribe. If having an identity is to have an essence, I do not have an identity. My sense of self is too varied and contextual. The metaphysics of identity does not work for me. I suspect it does not work for many others for similar reasons. This is, I think, a fact of some significance concerning how we think about pluralism. (p83/87)

Pullman (2005), when opposing the religious hatred bill in UK, also worries about the whole focus on identity, particularly when there is a cognitive dissonance that allows people to claim that their 'inner identity' had nothing to do with their actions. 'Yes, I murdered my wife and children, but I'm a good person'. The lawyer of a Texas boy scout leader recently found guilty on a child pornography charge was quoted in the *New York Times* as saying 'I've got to tell you, this is a good man'. So 'being' in the eyes of many people has its own moral qualities which may be good or bad, but which is resistant to any form of change except the miraculous (being born again). Pullman's concern is that 'being' trumps 'doing'.

> It's hard to convey the sheer bafflement and distaste I feel for this attitude towards 'identity'. I feel with some passion that what we truly are is private, and almost infinitely complex, and ambiguous, and both external and internal, and double- or

triple- or multiply natured, and largely mysterious even to ourselves; and further-more that what we are is only part of us, because identity, unlike 'identity' must include what we do. And I think that to find oneself and every aspect of this com-plexity reduced in the public mind to one property that apparently subsumes all the rest ('gay', 'Black', ' Muslim', whatever) is to be the victim of a piece of extraordinary intellectual vulgarity. (Pullman, 2005:4)

Pullman acknowledges that people use 'identity' as a marker, a sort of badge of difference, perhaps for solidarity; but identity claims are not free of con-sequences. They narrow as well as strengthen. In terms of the law, to criticise the religion of someone who makes that religion the primary marker of their identity will be, specifically, to criticise them. It will be criticising what they are, not what they do. Will the law be capable of distinguishing this? Pullman prefers to think of religion as something people *do* – like art – and which should be considered dispassionately in terms of its effects.

Those who are passionate adherents of their faith, who are willing to kill and die for it, are less likely to take a wide and considered view of the subject. And the fact that religion makes people willing to do these extreme things is one of the reasons why we need to examine it. Something in the nature of religious conviction gives be-lievers the chance to experience sharp and intoxicating tastes; those inclined to it can become addicted to the gamey tang of the absolute, the pungency of righteous-ness, the furtive sexiness of intolerance. Religion grants us these malign sensations more strongly and deeply than any other human phenomenon. (p5)

Pullman is like Dawkins in seeing religion as addictive and hence malign. I like the notion of 'the furtive sexiness of intolerance'. These days, those of us who are privileged feel we are not allowed to be intolerant – we are global citizens, well travelled, understanding, networked, multicultural; but we in fact love something that justifies our prejudices and bolsters our sense of superiority.

But it is the 'being-trumps-doing' – that is, who we 'are' is seen to override how we act – which is at the heart of the problem with acceding to 'identity'. I don't care whether people think God created the world in seven days or there are fairies at the bottom of the garden, as long as they do not commit harmful acts as a result of those beliefs and identifications. Philosophers spend much time discussing the differences between beliefs and attitudes, but that is less important; it is what do you do with those beliefs and attitudes that matters. If someone ascribes you an identity and then acts harmfully as a result of that, then you can legitimately claim grievance; but if you choose to assert an identity and claim special treatment on the sole basis of that, there is no justi-fication. The judgement call is on what people have done to you and what you have done to others. And given that any identity, and particularly religious identity, is so multi-faceted and contradictory, if you claim an identity as your sole personification, then you must put up with the criticism of religion.

Yet the question remains of how to give young people a secure sense of self without labelling or hardening this – what is sometimes called an 'essentialist' identity. Essentialism is the notion that a person is 'essentially' a female, or 'essentially' a Christian or Muslim, and that this conditions every part of who they are. Social identity theory suggests that how we think about ourselves tends to vary along a continuum, from the perception of self as unique to the perception of self as very similar or identical to in-group members. In certain situations, we become *exemplars* of them – a process of depersonalisation (Cairns, 1996). Collective identity – and identity politics – is therefore a disturbing force. 'It is through the creation of collective identities that ethnic and national movements, and the land-right claims they make, gain their force ... they mobilise culture, tradition, religion and notions of history and place to evoke a sense of unity' (Cynthia Cockburn, 1998:10).

A strong sense of collective identity may then mean a labelling or even a hatred for 'others'. For Michael Apple (2001), evangelicalism is crucially linked to identity, to 'self' and to 'other'. He describes how, in the USA, the religious Right has a sense of justice which is guided by 'hate' for gays. The majority of conservative evangelicals see themselves as 'nice' people, 'real Americans' who stand for things the rest of us have given up upon, such as 'true' motherhood. There is a Western Baptist site in the US which has the URL 'godhatesfags'. Apple quotes George Marsden, a leading scholar of the evangelist movement, 'A fundamentalist is an evangelical who is angry about something' (p119). Apple describes how the militant anti-Darwinian fundamentalism of the 1940s was kept alive in churches, Bible Institutes and seminaries. They had the problem of seeming too separatist, pessimistic and judgmental, and so moved to an 'engaged orthodoxy' which would reach out to American society and convince them that Jesus Christ was the answer for the world's social, economic and political problems. The new evangelism also gave people 'subject positions', identities, that respond to people's definition of themselves as individuals who have made a personal choice to be reborn. 'How can I interpret my actions as hateful and authoritarian when I am so strongly committed to personal choice and to seeking the 'truth'? (Apple, 2001:162).

Much is made therefore of the need in our multicultural societies to acknowledge the multiplicity of self – being simultaneously white, British, female, mother, wife, music-loving, broccoli-hating and so on. The real problem comes when one identity takes complete precedence. Amartya Sen in *Identity and Violence* claims 'Being a Muslim is not an overarching identity that determines everything in which a person believes' (p65) – although I am not sure whether that is in fact a choice for some Muslims, who would claim a total way of life. But Sen importantly draws attention to the failure to distinguish between Islamic history and the history of Muslim people – that is, not all priorities and activities and values need to be placed within their singular identity of being Muslim.

So there are three questions at this point: the choices that we make about our so-called identities in particular contexts; whether these are part of collective identities; and how we ascribe identities to others. Gandhi, despite being a devout Hindu himself, deliberately decided to give priority to his identification with Indians seeking independence from British rule over his identity as a trained barrister pursuing English legal justice. But the difference was of course that he did not then hate or label all non-Indians. He saw his struggle as a universal one. We know much about ascription of identities from the wars in the Balkans, how Serbs and Croats had to choose, and then would be seen in that light, as with having to be nominated Hutus or Tutsis in Rwanda. They were seen to represent the rest, and the history of conflict – as well as the future. Even five years after the end of the war in Bosnia, a Croat teenager told me 'I'm not sharing a desk with a Serb'.

Extremes of identity claims are often linked to concepts of purity, as seen in attempts to retain 'national purity' in the Balkans, and by Sinhalese in Sri Lanka. In the creation of Pakistan, the literal meaning of Pakistan is 'the land of the pure', thus separate from 'impure' Hindus. The discourse of Islamic purity is found in the Dewan Dakwah movement in Indonesia, 'for which all elements of society must fall into line' (Bakti, 2003:110). Tariq Ramadan's view is that too much of the internal conversation within the Muslim community in Europe at present nurtures a sense of guilt, inadequacy and alienation.

> Young people are told: everything you do is wrong – you don't pray, you drink, you aren't modest, you don't behave. They are told that the only way to be a good Muslim is to live in an Islamic society. Since they can't do that, this magnifies their sense of inadequacy and creates an identity crisis. Such young people are easy prey for someone who comes along and says 'there is a way to purify yourself'. (Interview with Paul Vallely, 2005)

Tom Cockburn (2007) researched the racial identities of young male supporters of the political far right in the North of England. He confirmed that identities are 'multiplicitous' and result from participation in many social worlds simultaneously. Racism and the recent emergence of the far right in England are not products of deep psychological problems, but contain qualities that belong to many in the wider community. The British National Party (BNP) has toned down their vulgar skinhead and racist image to one that campaigns on a ticket of 'patriotism' and the rights of white people. The supporters called themselves 'aboriginal British'. They did not adhere to the stereotype of white, alienated working class young men living on council overspill estates, but were more lower middle class, with some university or college educated. This confirms that prejudice does not come from base ignorance.

Cockburn contends that racism and racist identities are fluid and conditional. The young men could move in and out of far-right ideas quite quickly, and in fact some shifted later to UKIP (UK Independence Party). One survey found that young people between 11 and 21 were seven times more likely to support the BNP than the rest of the population – therefore their support may be a stage of life and part of a biography rather than an essential identity. Interestingly, Cockburn sees racism as 'performances', acts of doing rather than being. This is reminiscent of Goffmann (1956). It also relates to Pullman's argument above, of religion needing to be seen as something one does, not is. In Cockburn's study, racism for these young people was a 'prop' to be used to assist them in getting through the day. There was an overall feeling of insecurity about their economic position, threatened by immigration, or capitalism, as well as cultural insecurity, with a decline of 'white British' values because of the perceived threat of a growing Islam. One young man cited the cases of the Church of England schools being predominantly Asian and the threat this would have to 'our culture'. Although they did not go to church much, the defence of Christianity was part of a general project of 'boundary maintenance'. Identities are formulated in relation to what they are not and what they exclude. Young men had a long list of 'Others'.

> Their resistance is radically conservative in that they seek to bolster or reclaim their economic autonomy, to reassert their political control, and to advocate a system of heterosexual domestic arrangements that firmly subordinates women ... as well as ethnic minorities. Thus the young men hope to restore a notion of manhood that 'they can be proud of'. (T. Cockburn, 2007:551)

Wieviorka (1997) similarly recognises way that an individual's racism can oscillate between 'weak' and 'total' forms, and occupy a range of positions in between. Young men in the Cockburn study were capable of empathy and sympathy towards ethnic minority people. Quotations from two respondents show the mixed orientation:

> I don't have a problem with Muslims and Al-Qaeda. They are just trying to stick up for their own people and their own culture. That's exactly what we are doing: defending our culture.

> I wish we could be more like them. They don't think twice about taking on people who are screwing them.

Interestingly, the young men did have a great deal of respect for Asian people whom they knew in general. The barriers could be overcome when the right circumstances occurred and they were seen as friends rather than competitors. Cockburn argues therefore that anti-racist education should not assume a 'strong' or 'total' form, which would alienate the target audience, but should highlight commonalities and a sense of belonging. In accepting the 'performative' nature of racism, the strategy is to reflect on personal experiences, to debate and learn, to strengthen everyone's sense of identity and to build trust and empathy.

So I think that in the end we need more than the concept of multiple identity, and I prefer Homi Babha's (1994) concept of 'hybridity'. He challenges the constructions and 'exotisisation' of multiculturalism and cultural diversity, which stress recognition of difference, and prefers admissions of long histories of cultural and ethnic mixing. Many writers in Silva's (2002) collection on Sri Lanka draw on this, showing the 'hidden history' of hybridity in culture, art or music, and challenging the notion of single or pure cultures. Hybridity means more than just a collection of multiple identities but rather *new combinations*, and I like the idea of the original as 'repeated as something different – a mutation, a hybrid ... at once a mode of appropriation and of resistance [to the mother culture]' (Babha, 1994:111,120).

In educational terms, the game may be to play up such originality – not push children into camps by getting other children to learn about 'their' Asian food or go on visits to the Sikh temple. The strategy is to enhance the *resistance* to such simple labels and categorisations, and give children status in the uniqueness and the multiplicity of their hybrids. In our study of global citizenship (Davies, Harber and Yamashita, 2005) we found many children claiming a combination of 'identities', usually national/religious ones, and this was also the case in Maylor and Read's (2007) study of curriculum and diversity (see the next chapter). Hybridity is then both a description of reality and also a normative concept, something to promote. The other important message from the discussions above is that extremism, or racism, or religion, is a *performance*, something that one does. Seeing or claiming an 'identity' for it is part of the problem, not the solution.

## Becoming an Islamic fundamentalist in Britain

Later in the chapter, I outline some of the underlying themes leading to extremist behaviour or indeed identity. At this point it might be interesting to look at biographies, at 'real life' accounts from former extremists to test the various theories. Revealing information comes from accounts of young men who have been involved in political Islam and then left. One scours these narratives for patterns or sources linked to education, either in their reasons for joining or their reasons for leaving.

Ed Husain's book *The Islamist* (2007) is a fascinating account of five years as an Islamic fundamentalist in Britain, and provides relevant insights. While his primary school was a haven, with 'colour-blind' teachers who were 'all humanity', Husain's parents' preference for a single sex school landed him in Stepney Green, which was predominantly Asian, compared to his multi-cultural primary school. However, Husain was unhappy, introverted, with-drawn and bullied; there was gang warfare which impacted on the school but which Husain could not be part of. His parents and particularly grandfather were devout and his grandfather well known in Muslim circles; Husain travelled round Britain with him and this made him even more of a misfit at school, where the boys preferred Bollywood films. His family's Islam was not at all militant or politicised however, even though they were interested in politics. Wanting to know more about religion, he read *Islam: Beliefs and Teachings* by Gulam Sarwar, a book that continues to be used in RE class-rooms. One chapter begins:

> Religion and politics are one and the same in Islam. They are intertwined ... Just as Islam teaches us how to pray, fast, pay charity and perform the Haj, it also teaches us how to run a state, form a government, elect councillors and members of parlia-ment, make treaties and conduct business and commerce. (quoted in Husain, p21)

Sarwar commended the efforts of various Islamist organisations that were dedicated to the creation of 'truly Islamic states'. Sarwar was not a scholar of religion but a business management lecturer and the brains behind the separation of Muslim children from school assemblies into what was called 'Muslim Assembly', managed by the Muslim Educational Trust. The per-sonnel belonged to the Jamat-e-Islami front organisations in Britain. Their key message was that Islam was not merely a religion but an ideology that sought political power. This was powerful for Husain at the age of 16, and he became friends with another Muslim 'misfit' to assert a new hybrid – in my terms – identity: 'we were young, Muslim, studious, and London born' (p23). The radical, activist East London mosque became a central part of their lives: 'The people here were interested in *me*. To an isolated schoolboy, that mattered' (p28).

Husain offers an interesting description of how incorporation happens. The Central Executive Committee of the mosque, an all male gathering of long-time activists, organised youth camps, national football tournaments and fund-raising events for the mosque, thereby maintaining a tight grip on the lives of its members. 'The YMO [Young Muslim Organisation] had given me friends, a place in the world'. It had also gained a reputation in Tower Hamlets and beyond as being tougher than the toughest gangsters. Husain's evenings were filled with YMO events and meetings and with reading radical writings such as Mawdudi, and his time at school in organising and leading prayer meetings.

> I was sixteen years old and I had no white friends. My world was entirely Asian, fully Muslim. This was my Britain. (p35)

What adds to the belonging was the feeling of superiority. From Mawdudi's writings, Husain knew himself to be not a mere *Muslim*, like others he knew; he was better. Muslims who did not read the Qu'ran properly were almost as bad as kufirs or non-Muslims. Then, in the more crucial character of Syed Qutb, he learned that Islam is not just a belief but a declaration of the freedom of man from servitude to other men. 'Thus it strives from the beginning to abolish all those systems and governments which are based on the rule of man over man' (quoted on p50). It was in the nature of Islam that it must dominate. The world was divided into two: Islam and *jahiliyyah*, or the ignorant world. Here we see the dualism and simple dichotomies which characterise extremist behaviour as discussed in Chapter 1. The world had been failed by capitalism and communism, and deep down, the Islamists never really objected to the Holocaust. Husain later became even more radicalised by joining Hizb ut-Tahrir, who rejected democracy as *haram*, forbidden in Islam. The political ideology was that people do not rule, Allah does. The task was global domination.

The educational profiles are intriguing. Two central figures within Hizb were a Sheffield university trained town planner who worked for Islington Borough Council and an accountant who worked for J P Morgan in the city. Three members were studying at the London Hospital Medical College. Significantly, the Hizb was legal in Britain but illegal in the Arab world. 'Britain offered the Hizb the freedom to express its ideas freely and recruit uninhibitedly' (p87). Husain is unequivocal about their influence: 'Home grown British suicide bombers are a direct result of Hizb ut-Tahrir disseminating ideas of jihad, martyrdom, confrontation, and anti-Americanism, and nurturing a sense of separation among Britain's Muslims' (p119).

What seem to be the triggers so far, the combination of factors which led to Husain becoming 'an Islamist'? Isolation at school may be one, precipitating the search for comradeship and recognition. Another ex-fundamentalist, Shiraz Maher, who also tells of how he 'escaped Islamism', speaks of how easy it was to join. 'Hizb was a large family in many ways: a group offering social support, comradeship, a sense of purpose and validation. At 21, it was intoxicating to me' (2007). Yet an account from yet another convert to British jihad who then rejected it, Maajid Nawaz, told how he had absolutely no problems making friends and was in the highest sets at school (2007). Nonetheless, Nawaz suffered extreme racist violence, with arrests but no charges, suspecting that the perpetrators had 'friends' within the police. He associated with a 'counter-culture' inspired by American rap music, which he saw as the beginning of his 'politicisation'.

> As time passed I became more aware of identity issues and world conflicts. The Bosnian genocide struck a chord like no other. Here were white European Muslims being identified solely as Muslims and being slaughtered for it. (p8)

He met a member of Hizb ut-Tahrir from his home town who started explaining the ideas. 'My premature politicised mind was ripe to receive an ideology that advocated a black and white solution to the problems I had grown up with.' Thus there is also the appeal of absolutism (see Chapter 1). Although Islam is to welcome people of all creeds, Maher also talks of their worldview 'being being still horribly bipolar. We didn't distinguish on the basis of colour, but on creed. The world was simply divided into believers and non-believers' (2007:19).

Both Nawaz and Husain were in conflict with their parents and their local mosques over their radical associations, so it is not a 'home socialisation' issue. It seems to be the very *special* nature of it all, moving on from an already devout or committed position: 'This was an ideology like no other. Religion had been merged with politics in such a way that we worshipped God through our political activities'. So a sense of self, an essentialist identity was indeed central: 'I had finally discovered who I was. I was a sharp, ideological Muslim whose mission was to create a new world order' (Nawaz, 2007:8). Maher too discovered a new identity, rejecting his British identity and even his ethnic South Asian background. 'I was neither eastern nor western; I was a Muslim, a part of the global ummah, where identity is defined through the fraternity of faith' (2007:19).

So the combination seems to be bad experiences during school years in terms of identity; the appeal of a network and 'family'; the appeal of black and white truths; and the appeal of that network having a special mission and hence oneself having a special place in the world. This would be true for many of us, but, as Rageh Omaar asks of the four July 7 suicide bombers:

> What happened to the young men that made them do this? What failures contributed to turn them and their view of Islam towards such nihilistic violence? Why was it four *Muslims* that blew themselves up? Why have other marginalised communities not produced suicide bombers? (2006:13)

The answer to the last question is of course that they have – in Sri Lanka in particular. But our interest is in what Omaar, in his book *Only Half of Me: British and Muslim: the Conflict within*, says is referred to by security officials as 'Londonistan' – the radical young men from fringe organisations who 'hand out leaflets and sell videos about the conflicts in Bosnia or Chechnya, espousing an ideology of global conflict between Muslims and non-Muslims' (p31). Omaar is interesting on why the bombers selected Edgware Road as one target – the heartland of British Arab Muslim life. The leader was Mohammed Sidique Khan, a 30 year old teaching assistant, father of a young girl and husband of a British Pakistani woman who worked as a teacher.

Omaar says it was because it was a symbol of something that Khan and the movement despised. They attacked Edgware Road precisely because it represented a relationship between Islam and the West, a cultural and ideological abomination in the pure interpretation of Al Qaeda's message. They were challenging the idea that Islam as a religion and Muslims as a community can thrive in the West – in London or Paris or Manchester or Hamburg. They were also attacking the idea that you can have a British identity but still be part of the wider global 'nation of believers'. 'The belief that a western city can ever be part of the modern story of Islam in the world is sacrilegious to the fundamentalist vision' (p37).

Again, we see this combination of the notion of purity and of global identity above nation, above culture. It is a heady mix. It explains why Muslims can be targeted by other Muslims and why Muslims also die in Islamist terrorist attacks. To the extremist, they have sold out, and are on the same level as *kufirs* – just by living and working peacefully in the west.

As a Somali, Omaar is particularly interested in the background of Yassin Hassan Omar, one of the failed bombers of 21 July 2005. All were child immigrants who had arrived in Britain ten years earlier, fleeing wars in the Horn of Africa. Yassin had experienced a relentless cycle of foster families and care homes, and, according to Omaar, would have lost all sense of identity. He was converted by Ibrahim Muktar Said, who became the ringleader of the 21 July bombers. Ibrahim himself had been converted to radical Islam at Feltham Young Offenders Institution, an 'isolated' environment. Omaar is quick to acknowledge that social deprivation or alienation are not somehow to blame for terrorist acts. There are thousands of other refugees, or others who fail to adapt, or who are exposed to intimidating people from a similar background. But he is interesting on the pressures put on refugee groups, quoting Asha, a senior officer in Ealing's anti-racial harassment project:

> When a young Somali boy is bullied at school he may react in the way he has seen people act in a war zone. He may have seen people killed, he may have seen people in refugee camps beating and shoving his mother or sisters in the queues lining up to receive their rations and he reacts as others did there: they fight, they argue, they try to impose their will in order to survive, but most of all, they fight to ensure they won't be humiliated again. (quoted in Omaar, 2006: 202)

He is also interesting on the appeal of Hizb – this time in Dewsbury. A local journalist, Farhana Haq, explained:

> The organisation seeks to help young men come off drugs as part of a social, religious and political process, a kind of Muslim reawakening which, for want of a better phrase, is like becoming a 'reborn' Muslim. Faced with a relative who is addicted to drugs, many conservative Muslims are grateful to these organisations for helping. (p229)

The additional point Omaar makes is that these poor communities turn to such organisations for help, as they feel increasingly unable to do so from the wider world. 'The more marginalised and maligned by the establishment this community is, the more it will turn inwards, reaching for possible extreme forms of salvation' (p230). After criticisms by politicians about women wearing the veil, more British young women started to wear it – 'The veil is now our symbol of solidarity'. The veil is not seen as political by those who do not wear it, but it is seen as deeply political by those who do. Omaar seems to suggest therefore that it is not just imams or radical movements that politicise Islam, but also the establishment. To the identity questions above, we have to add marginalisation and the simultaneous search for purity.

## Causes or triggers to extremist belonging and behaviour

Later in the chapter I look at the exit from extremism by Husain, Nawaz and Maher as well as others. Both entry and exit are gradual processes, but it would be wrong to assume the same steps up as down, nor that the ladders or scaffolding are the same for all. The cases above are intended to give a flavour of the intoxication or addiction. I first explore some of the theories on the causes, triggers or predispositions towards the life of the extremist. These seem to fall within two main but closely linked categories: the experiences one suffers and the psychological predispositions one has.

*Experiences: Trauma and fragility*

Elworthy and Rifkind suggest that there is a direct link between fundamentalism and trauma, with the experience of violence, humiliation and death – as with people who identify with the fundamentalist group, Hamas.

> This is compounded by living in an uncertain, chaotic world in which there is no sense of control and no ability to have any influence. In this situation, fundamentalism offers two things which could give the impression of safety. First is the offer of welfare provision, which cannot be overestimated in terms of providing a material safety net. Second, the presenting of a firm philosophy – albeit extreme in its content – gives the impression of certainty in an uncertain world. (2006:20)

Routine and ritual, such as praying five times a day, also give a sense of familiarity and safety in an insecure world. The Qu'ranic training camps give a sense of community, brotherhood and belonging. But there is also the need for a *moral* certainty, of right and wrong. This psychic need for rigid structures can lead to a calcified view of human behaviour, and a loss of the recognition of its subtle complexities, of people's propensity for both good and bad. Attitudes that stimulate acute political violence become more entrenched.

The need for safety is a recurring theme in the fundamentalist literature. Catron cites Wuthrow's (1998) classification of fundamentalists as 'dwellers' rather than 'seekers'. While seekers are always looking for new spiritual vistas, dwellers find safety in inhabiting a familiar religious space. We saw in looking at Husain's story that he was wanting to move on from the familiar, so this may not apply to all. But Catron reflects on her own childhood as being entirely centred and bounded by the fundamentalist faith community, from which all meaning and purpose arose, and the context in which all life experiences were interpreted (Hood, Hill and Williamson, 2005). Iannacone (1994) suggests that the 'psychological staying power' of fundamentalist religion in a postmodern age lies in its ability to create a unifying philosophical framework that meets personal needs for meaning and provides coherence to an existence that may otherwise seem fragmented. It is not surprising, he concludes, that 'the most successful religions, in terms of growth and maintenance of membership, are those with absolute, unwavering, strict and enforced normative standards for behaviour' (quoted in Hood, Hill and Williamson, p 16).

### Experiences: Fear

The need for safety relates also to fear. Husain spoke of how the radicals 'whipped up Muslim fear'. 'Bosnia today, Britain tomorrow', they declared on their leaflets (p113). Stephan and Stephan (2000) put forward an *Integrated Threat Model* to look at anxiety about outgroups, and proposed that a 'realistic' threat is a threat to political and economic power or physical well being, while a 'symbolic' threat is a threat to the value system, belief system, or worldview of the group. It might seem that for extremists it could be both, which makes the fear much more potent. Catron, in thinking about her fundamentalist students, asks for understanding of the challenges they face: 'Often what appears to be hostility and close-mindedness may really be fear; a fear of new ideas and the potential for personal loss they represent (2008, forthcoming)'.

### Experiences: Humiliation

The trauma experienced by conflict or occupation is often accompanied by humiliation. In an article on 'Intersubjective Dimensions of Terrorism and its transcendance', Diane Perlman explains the impact of humiliation and envy, which together make for 'exceedingly destructive emotions'.

> Being humiliated is like being filled with poison that has to be expelled in order to regain composure. Humiliation carries a narcissistic wound that contains an implicit demand for rectification, often by taking down the humiliator. (quoted in Ramakrishna, 2006:250)

The feelings of individuals humiliated by the outgroup are projected onto this group, so that when there is no way out, terrorism is a way of transforming victimhood into mastery. Terrorists want to *force* the outgroup to taste, however momentarily, their powerlessness, their despair, their dark 'habitus'. Ramakrishna (2006) cites the psychoanalytic view that 'people would rather be bad than weak'. This question of power links to masculinity, discussed below. Significantly, in South Africa under apartheid, the analysis is that the humiliation and brutality experienced by African men at work translated into high levels of violence against the next in line – women. Physical violence becomes a first-line strategy for gaining ascendancy (Abrahams, 2004). A similar

40

point was made about the brutality of youth in the RUF in Sierra Leone. Either excluded from education altogether or denied opportunities to get jobs or access power, the youth suffered the 'wound of invisibility'. Becoming a rebel gave you 'sway over your former master, who used to lord it over you, or the others who might have laughed' (Krech and Maclure, 2003).

In discussing Palestine, Elworthy and Rifkind (2006) also moot a 'powerful correlation' between acts of humiliation and the desire to restore honour and pride by using violence. The treatment of Palestinians, being stripped naked at checkpoints by Israeli soldiers, restricting freedom of movement, seeing their houses demolished, all generate an acute loss of dignity. A dignified death is preferable to living in shame and humiliation. They suggest that a basic way to reduce suicide bombing would therefore be to introduce systematic efforts to restore a sense of respect, or at the very least to remove daily humiliations such as roadblocks, body searches, night raids on houses, and disrespect of women. A positive development in this is, for example, the recently created 'Machsom [Checkpoint] Watch' movement set up by Israeli citizens, which monitors the behaviour of soldiers towards Palestinians attempting to cross.

### Experiences: Alienation and isolation

Alienation can take many forms, chosen or forced. Catron talks of the 'embattlement' of the early fundamentalists, and disenfranchisement from institutions of secular learning such as higher education. 'Alienation became separatism; and separatism became a badge of spirituality readily donned by the warriors of righteousness' (2008, forthcoming). The other form of alienation occurs within a society, when a minority group does not feel fully integrated or accepted. A disturbing account by Eric Silver (2007) of the growth of neo-Nazi activity by Russian immigrants in Israel, cites studies showing that only one third of Russian immigrant teenagers identified themselves as Israeli. The neo-Nazi cells were spray-painting swastikas, vandalising synagogues and attacking visibly religious Jews as well as any vulnerable people. Marina Solodkin, a Russian member of the Israeli parliament and former deputy minister of 'immigrant absorption' was quoted as saying

> 'Neo-Nazi activity is the way a young generation that has not found itself in Israel protests. They've lost their identity. They are not Jews, they are not Israelis. They are Russians who are not accepted, not in schools, not in the families of other children'. (Silver, 2007:4)

The Israeli neo-Nazis draw their inspiration from the thriving radical right in Mother Russia, where there are estimated to be 70,000 white-supremacist skinheads. Antisemitic Russian websites proclaim 'The Jews, through their knavish propaganda, infect the minds of white women and inspire them to look at the Niggers with friendliness and benevolence. We must protect our women. We must liberate their minds from the Zhid [Yid] obsession'. A Russian language bookshop in Jerusalem stocks antisemitic books and Holocaust denial material. Israel has taken pride in fulfilling its Zionist mission and has absorbed more than three million Jews from 100 countries in Africa, Asia, Europe and the Americas over the past 60 years. Yet there is the protest that a country whose *raison d'etre* is to be the state of the Jews has yet to come to terms with multiculturalism.

Because everything centres round the conflict with the Arabs, national minorities in Israel have long been 'cast to the margins' of cultural, public and political life (Silver, 2007:5). Halleli Pinson talks of how Palestinian citizens in Israel often feel excluded not once but twice: once by the Jewish majority in Israel and once by the majority of Palestinians who are not Israelis. She found that in trying to make sense of their unsatisfactory position, some adopted 'supranational' identities such as belonging to the Arab world or the Muslim world (2004). This double marginalisation and replacement with global identity can be seen in Muslim youth in UK too.

Marginalisation also occurs within institutions. J'Lein Liese (2004) quotes 'resiliency research' that demonstrated repeatedly that children who feel ostracised at school are at greater risk of joining gangs or engaging in maladaptive behaviour. Students who feel pain or threat, particularly over something out of their direct control, often come to experience frustration and resentment towards the social groups they blame for their feeling. But perhaps because human beings have a conscience, when young people reach such a level of resentment, they tend to 'build an army' of support for their negative feelings towards other groups among their peers and even prominent adults in their lives. Once they can acquire agreement from others about the characteristics they attribute to their target, any actions stemming from anger, suspicion or rage can be deemed justified. Liese is talking about how the target of American young people's feelings of rage have become Arab and Muslim students, but it could be argued that the psychology also works for Arab and Muslim students themselves, or indeed any group experiencing threat. This response was also found in studies of excluded children in UK, with the experience of loss and threat turning to anger which is then directed at teachers or other students (Leoni, 2005).

*Experiences: Frustration and globalisation*

Terrorism does not necessarily spring from poverty or illiteracy. We know that many terrorists are of middle-class or privileged origins and well educated, and those who support them are likely to be more educated than their fellow citizens. Peter Mansfield argues that Islamic activism was the creation not of the poor but of the frustrated middle class. It gained a following not in the shanty towns of the North African cities but on the campuses of universities and technical colleges. Arab students volunteered to fight in the Afghan jihad in the same spirit as their left-wing European counterparts in the 1930s went off to fight in the Spanish Civil War (2003). The same description of the privileged or frustrated middle class might apply to the Baader-Meinhof group in Germany. The frustration is in not being able to influence government policy or large forces of globalisation. Omaar is clear that the situation in Iraq is crucial for solidifying identities:

> Iraq connects us all. It connects us to the story of the Prophet Mohammed's descendants. It connects us to the story of how Islam broke out of Arabia and became a global religion. It connects us to the story of how Islam was established from a small corner of north-eastern Africa to Asia ... the assault on Iraq has given extremist groups linked to Al Qaeda a chance to explore the anger of ordinary Muslims at what they see as an attack on the cultural and historical things they hold most dear. (p182)

Most of the Islamic terrorists were not long-time practitioners of Islam but became born-again Muslims in Europe. As Roy pointed out in his book *Globalised Islam: the Search for a new Ummah*:

> The Islam they represent does not exist in traditional cultures. It is a version of fundamentalism that could only have developed through contact with the West. It is globalisation that underpins the utopian vision of a worldwide community of believers ... It is the growing de-territorialisation of Islam which leads to the political reformulation of an imaginary ummah. (2004:44)

*Psychology: The need for cognitive closure*

Kumar Ramakrishna (2006) has an excellent analysis of the *Jemaah Islamiyah* (JI) terrorists in South East Asia. He uses the psychology of religious behaviour and some people's need for 'cognitive closure' – the desire for a definite answer to a particular topic, as opposed to confusion and ambiguity. This quest for cognitive closure has been greatly intensified, particularly but not exclusively, in non-western societies by the psychosocial dislocations caused by globalisation. The individualistic, competitive, privatistic and mobile values and attitudes appear to undermine traditional social units such as family, clan and voluntary association. He cites Selengut's analysis that globalisation is destabilising because it promotes the 'desacralisation' of society; encourages religious and moral relativism; places the onus on the individual to determine 'his [sic] values, career, lifestyle and moral system'; and most disconcertingly, undermines traditional ideas about sexuality and the status of women.

The need or preference for 'cognitive closure' does not just relate to globalisation and a fragmented world, and may be part of a 'stuck' developmental phase. Catron cites William Perry's (1999) work on student development, and the conclusion from his research that students move through a number of stages on their way to thoughtful intellectual/moral commitment. The beginning stage is 'Basic dualism'. In this position, students see the world as a dichotomy: 'authority – right – we, as against the alien world of illegitimate – wrong – others' (p66). Perry suggests that dependence on authoritarian structures – an essential feature of fundamentalism – leads to entrenchment in a dualistic view of the world. In this world, morality means unquestioning obedience. To reach 'multiplicity', or the recognition of different possibly valid perspectives, students must be able to extend potential legitimacy to 'otherness'. This is difficult for those who have known only the world of fundamental dualism, witnessing a faith based on obedience to an external code or belief and conduct. The source of the 'innocence' of dualism is its lack of any alternative or vantage point. The difficulty is compounded by the tendency to view anyone who would offer an alternative vantage point as blind to the truth and as a moral threat. This would match Apple's explanation of 'the binary': how evangelicalism depends for its very existence on having a 'constitutive outside':

> Its very meaning and identity requires that there be those who are immoral, lazy, burdens on the state, evil, secular humanists or unsaved. This very binary gives meaning to one's most fundamental sets of interpretive structures. (2004:163)

We can see from this how fear, obedience, threat and dualism come together in arrested behaviour. For Catron, 'the fear of leaving a bounded environment is often greater than the pain of confinement'.

### Psychology: Respect for authority

Obedience links to the question of authority, where Kenneth Strike has an appealing discussion:

> The demand for freedom of conscience is linked to the objectivity and authoritativeness of commands. The voice of conscience may be the voice of God or of reason,

but commands are not commands if they are mere matters of opinion. No one's conscience would be greatly troubled by violating one of the Ten Suggestions. The reasoning that leads to obedience says 'I must do this, because the voice that commands me is true and authoritative'. (2003:80)

As an evolutionary biologist, Dawkins has an interesting theory about socialisation of children. He says that more than any other species, we survive by the accumulated experience of previous generations, and that experience needs to be passed on to children for their protection and well-being. For survival, there will be a selective advantage to child brains that possess the rule of thumb: believe without question whatever your grown-ups tell you. He sees religion therefore as a by-product, a misfiring, of a primitively advantageous trait, such as moths killing themselves on a light because they are wired to steer by the moon. We are wired to accept, however ludicrous, what our parents or elders say – hence the continuation of primitive superstitions such as religion or throwing salt over your shoulder. But the flip side of a trusting obedience is slavish gullibility. The inevitable by-product is vulnerability to infection by 'mind viruses'. For excellent reasons related to Darwinian survival, child brains need to trust parents and the elders whom parents tell them to trust. An automatic consequence is that the truster has no way of distinguishing good advice from bad. 'The child cannot know that 'Don't paddle in the crocodile-infested Limpopo' is good advice but 'You must sacrifice a goat at the time of the full moon, otherwise the rains will fail' is at best a waste of time and goats' (p176). As Dawkins points out, not only do they sound equally trustworthy, but they are delivered with a solemn earnestness that commands respect and obedience.

These ideas then get passed on to the next generation, using the same 'infectious gravitas of manner'. Religious leaders are well aware of getting the child early – the clichéd Jesuit boast 'Give me the child for his first seven years, and I'll give you the man' is an indication of the power of socialisation but also the panic about which of the hundreds of religions or belief sets or miracles a child might absorb as fact, all of which sound weird to those who do not believe them. I like the miracle joke where Jesus at the Last Supper tells the Apostles that he will change the water into wine. 'No', said the others, 'you put your money into the kitty like everybody else'.

Dawkins' analysis is beguiling until you look at the relations with parents of radical Islamists such as Husain. All seem to have had a disjuncture from their parents' views, and conflicted with them. Tom Cockburn (2007) too said that the prejudice of the BNP supporters was not derived from parents – in fact they were in tension with them, and the parents did not want children to draw attention to themselves. Socialisation and constructivist studies now show that young people are not passive recipients of education and knowledge from parents, teachers or the media. Yet where Dawkins' story does make sense is that children may be wired to accept authority, and any authoritarian or strict household will reproduce that obedience. Extremists simply transfer their propensity to obedience to another, stricter, master.

### Psychology: Purpose and love

Another predisposition to unquestioned belief is the desire to find a purpose for everything. I looked at Utopian visions in the first chapter. Dawkins cites psychologists' views that we are naturally predisposed to be creationists, and that natural selection makes no intuitive sense. Deborah Keleman (2004) revealed children as 'intuitive theists', assigning purposes to phenomena, such as in 'clouds are for raining'.

There is also the possibility of a by-product of natural selection of the mechanism of falling in love. Religious faith has something of the same character as falling in love – and both have many of the attributes of being high on an addictive drug. The neuropsychiatrist view is that:

> One of the many faces of religion is intense love focused on one supernatural person, i.e. God, plus reverence for the icons of that person. Human life is driven by our selfish genes and by the processes of reinforcement. Much positive reinforcement derives from religion: warm and comforting feelings of being loved and protected in a dangerous world, loss of fear and death, help from the hills in response to prayer in difficult times, etc. Likewise romantic love for another real person (usually of the other sex) exhibits the same intense concentration on the other and related positive reinforcements. Those feelings can be triggered by icons of the other, such as letters, photographs, and even, as in Victorian times, locks of hair. (Smythies, 2006)

Ruthven (2004) similarly tells of the born again Christians who follow the Southern Baptist theologian E Y Mullins in describing the conversion experience as 'falling in love with Jesus'. Love gives both a purpose and a sense of absolute 'rightness'.

### Psychology: Uniqueness:

Palmer recounts how academics in Peru who were part of Shining Path were advancing their Maoist vision of Marxism by action and by study instead of being satisfied with merely talking about it.

The emerging conviction was that they alone had discovered the keys to Marxist theory and practice by years of diligent study, conscientious application in the field, and the building of close ties between some Ayacucho peasants and the intellectual vanguard which gradually produced a virtually unshakeable faith in their uniqueness, even within the larger Marxist revolutionary community. They saw themselves, if you will, as the equivalent of the reborn Christian, the true carriers of the faith and, therefore, destined to eventual triumph no matter how daunting the odds. (Palmer, 1995:260-1)

There are so many themes here: uniqueness; being the only true saviours or believers; and destiny – that they could not fail because somehow they had been 'chosen'. There is an irony here in a determinedly anti-faith philosophy such as Marxism that people should actually have a religious-like belief in fate, destiny, utopia and the place of followers within this.

*Masculinity*

A final supposition is that a compounding factor would be gender, either as greater masculine propensities for violence, or greater experience of humiliation against their masculine role as protector or as a strong man. The actual picture is complex. First, are women less likely to be involved in extremist movements? Here, the complications of the causes of extremism emerge. Mukta (2000) has a disturbing account of the role of women in the rise of the Hindu right in India, which 'raises salient questions of women's embeddedness within aggressive and violent political movements aimed against the women and men of subordinate castes and the minority religious communities' (p164). We see how structures other than gender – caste and religion – combine to form new political spaces for women. As Sigal Ben-Porath points out, women cannot be considered peaceful by nature, and women soldiers have been charged along with their male peers with 'gratuitous cruelty', showing that the evils associated with masculinity can easily be performed by women in the relevant positions. Women apparently share with men the ability to dehumanise the other and to act forcefully when persuaded that this is the right thing to do.

Robert Pape's demographic profile of modern suicide attackers partially supports the image of them being male, but not entirely. Any link with religion makes it even more complex. Of suicide attackers in Lebanon during the first half of the 1980s, 31 were men and six were women. Pictures of the attackers showed many with stylish haircuts, western clothes and makeup, hardly projecting an image of Islamic fundamentalism. One was a Christian high school teacher. Gender breakdowns do vary across terrorist groups. Of

Pape's survey of 381 suicide attackers, 59 or 15 per cent were female; but some groups use females far more than others. Up to 2003, Al-Qaeda employed no female suicide attackers, Palestinians used six, or 5 per cent, Lebanese used six or 16 per cent, Tamil Tigers used 23 or 20 per cent, the Chechens used fourteen, or 60 per cent and the PKK (independent Kurdish state) used ten, or 71 per cent. The obvious conclusion from this variation is the connection with Islamic fundamentalism (which frowns on female warriors in general). 'This suggests an interesting hypothesis: Islamic fundamentalism may actually reduce the number of suicide terrorists by discouraging certain categories of individuals from undertaking the act' (Pape, 2005:208).

However, this may be changing. On August 20, 2004, the Women's Information Office in the Arab Peninsula released the first issue of a journal called *Al Khansa* which carried articles such as 'Biography of the Mujahidat' (female mujahideen) and 'Raising Children on Jihad's Teachings' (Forest, 2006). While the latter would appear to be using women as the traditional behind-the-scenes socialisers, the former would imply a much more direct role in jihad. The ninth issue of *Sawt Al-Jihad* (Al Qaeda's virtual magazine released on-line in January 2004) contains a special section dedicated to recruiting women for terrorist attacks, in which women are encouraged to assist the warriors by all means. The issue's article, titled 'Um Hamza, an Example for the Woman Holy Warrior' tells the story of the late Um Hamza by her husband, in which her virtues are detailed.

> *Um Hamza and Martyrdom*: Um Hamza was very happy whenever she heard about a martyrdom operation carried out by a woman, whether it was in Palestine or Chechnya. She used to cry because she wanted a martyrdom operation against the Christians in the Arabian Peninsula'. (quoted in Forest, 2006:125)

Another interesting finding by Pape was that women suicide terrorists tend to be significantly more mature than their male counterparts, in their late twenties or older. While there was virtually no evidence of mental illness, some women had experienced trauma (see above). Chechen female suicide attackers are commonly referred to as the 'Black Widows', to make the point that they are seeking revenge for the loss of their family members to Russian military action. Half the Black Panthers of the Tamil Tigers are women, the 'freedom birds', who are supposed to simulate pregnancy carrying high explosive charges under bulging skirts (Whittaker, 2004). Pape's study cast doubts on the prevailing assumption that individuals who carry out attacks are primarily religious fanatics, irresponsible adolescents or sexually frustrated males. Nearly all were well beyond adolescence, most were secular and many – the overwhelming majority in some groups – were women.

Extremist positions *towards* women in terms of oppression or exclusion were mentioned in the last chapter, and here the discussion starts to move towards the construction of 'the other'. Writing on gender violence in Pakistan, for example, Brohi and Ajaib (2006) cast doubt on the usual solution to male harassment of having single sex schools. This works for the immediate future, but

> in the longer term they could have the opposite effect, projecting females as the Other, with whom boys have little contact. This might render girls objects of curiosity and experimentation, almost dehumanising them. The extreme position is where most boys study in *madressahs*, the consequences of which were globally evident in the Taliban's approach to women in Afghanistan. (p88)

Interestingly, Brohi and Ajaib recommend co-education, so that boys and men will view women as more than simply sex objects. Certainly, the single-sex environments of many radical training camps would cement a hard masculinised brotherhood. But masculinity alone would not be enough, even the hard version.

The discussion of gender against all the other predispositions shows how difficult it would be to predict the terrorist, extremist or fundamentalist. It is an obvious point that we all construct our interpretations of the world, and thus our perceptions of fragility, or alienation, or humiliation will be distinct and will be filtered differently through our existing lenses such as gender, as well as through psychological needs such as cognitive closure, or purpose, or uniqueness. We cannot 'catch them young'. This shows the lunacy of former UK Home Secretary John Reid going on September 21 2006 to Leyton, East London, to tell a room full of Muslims how to raise their children so they would not grow up hateful. 'Look for the telltale signs now and talk to them before hatred grows and you risk losing them for ever', he told them. The inevitable heckling that met this amazing display of insult was then interpreted as evidence of how right Reid was, how he would not be browbeaten by bullies (Younge, 2006). This is the same twisted logic as Blair saying that two million people going on the march against the war in Iraq was evidence that we still lived in a free society where people could demonstrate, and therefore this somehow justified defending this right and hence the invasion. Leaving aside the political and social harm done by John Reid, he was simply wrong. There are few 'telltale signs'. None of the suicide terrorists had the pathognomic characteristic of a suicidal personality or past history of suicide attempts. 'Rather, the uncomfortable fact is that suicide terrorists are far more normal than many of us would like to believe' (Pape, 2005:211). But what can be observable is the ways that individuals do become radicalised through exposure to specific 'teachers' and their ideas, to which we turn next.

## Mechanisms for radicalisation

A fascinating 90 page study of the radicalisation process comes from the New York City Police Department (Silber and Bhatt, 2007). The study looks at how 'unremarkable' people are driven to become terrorists, and examines not just US terrorism cases but actual or thwarted cases in Madrid, Amsterdam, London, Australia and Canada. Their conclusions are that the radicalisation process is composed of four distinct phases: pre-radicalisation, self-identification, indoctrination and Jihadisation. As with other studies, the pre-radicalisation phase demonstrates that the majority of individuals involved in the plots began as 'unremarkable' – they had 'ordinary' jobs, lived 'ordinary' lives and had little, if any, criminal history. In the self-identification phase in Islamic radicalism, individuals, influenced by both internal and external factors, begin to explore Salafi Islam. They would gradually gravitate away from their old identity and begin to associate with like-minded individuals and adopt this ideology as their own. The catalyst for this 'religious seeking' is a 'cognitive opening' or crisis, which shakes one's certitude in previously held beliefs and opens an individual to be receptive to new worldviews. Such triggers can be economic (losing a job); social (alienation, discrimination); political (international conflicts involving Muslims); or personal (death or some break up of the close family).

This seems to have close resemblances to a study in the Netherlands (Buijs, Demant and Hamdy, 2006) which identifies several different currents in radicalisation in home-grown warriors, concentrating on three different salafis in the Netherlands – 'apolitical salafis', 'political salafis' and 'jihadi salafis'. The authors argue that openness to radicalism increases as (a) a disadvantaged position and discrimination are seen not as mistakes in a good system but as the expression of an essentially bad system; (b) a disadvantaged situation is seen as an expression of a cultural-religious contrast and of power politics; (c) the idea exists that Islamic identity must be developed in an enclave that is opposed to Western society; and (d) there is no faith in the political institutions and the democratic system.

While the notion in Silber and Blatt's study of the 'cognitive opening' or crisis seems in contrast to the cognitive closure proposed above, the other currents do relate to some of the triggers already mentioned. In this phase, individuals become alienated from their former life, give up cigarettes, drinking, gambling and gangster clothes, and become involved in social activism and community issues. They (the men) may grow a beard and wear traditional clothes. The indoctrination phase occurs when the individual progressively intensifies his or her beliefs, concluding without question that the conditions and circumstances exist where action is required to support and further the cause. The phase is typically facilitated by a 'spiritual sanctioner'. Jihadisation then occurs when members of the cluster accept their individual duty to participate in jihad and self-designate themselves as holy warriors. They begin operational planning, under an 'operational leader'. This component, unlike the others, can be rapid, taking only a few months or even weeks to run its course.

> Much different from the Israeli-Palestinian equation, the transformation of a Western-based individual to a terrorist is not triggered by oppression, suffering, revenge, or desperation. ... Rather it is a phenomenon that occurs because the individual is looking for an identity and a cause and unfortunately, often finds them in the extremist Islam. (p8)

Even more 'unfortunately' perhaps, the study says there is no useful profile to enable the prediction of who will follow this trajectory, which supports my conclusion above. This means that there is no point – and much danger – in teachers or even parents trying to play spot-the-terrorist in Key Stage 2. Class and disadvantage are not predictors. Middle class families and students appeared to provide the most fertile ground for the seeds of radicalisation, with young men from moderately religious families who were upwardly and geographically mobile (p22/3). However sometimes the activities were overt: Saad Khalid, of the Toronto plotters, was a high school student at Meadowvale Secondary School. He formed a 'Religious Awareness Club' and during his lunch time he would preach Islam to other students. He spent a good deal of time with two of the other plotters, Fahad Ahmad and Zakaria Amara. The trio created a chat group called the 'Meadowvale Brothers'. Schoolmates stated that the three began to dress more traditionally and became more withdrawn. There is a problem here – should teachers therefore be hypervigilant or proscribe religious clubs? I return to this in Chapter 5.

Silber and Blatt's study uses the metaphor of the 'extremist incubators' for young, susceptible Muslims – the internet, extremist sermons and study groups, sponsored trips to radical madrassahs and militant training camps abroad. Different venues, from cafes to prisons to halal butcher shops, can be 'hangouts'. The internet is particularly crucial now, in all phases: in the self-identification phase, the internet provides the 'wandering mind' of the conflicted young Muslim or potential convert with direct access to unfiltered radical and extremist ideology. It serves as an anonymous meeting place to share views and experiences. In the indoctrination phase, 'cloaked with a veil of objectivity, the Internet allows the aspiring jihadist to view the world and global conflict through this extremist lens' (p7). It acts as an 'echo chamber', a radicalisation accelerant. The image of the heroic, holy warrior or 'muja-hadeen' has been widely marketed on the Internet as well as in jihadi tapes and videos. This image continues to resonate among young, especially Muslim, men who are most vulnerable to visions of honour, bravery and sacrifice for what is perceived as a noble cause. In male-dominated societies, they will be looking for a male identity. The other catalyst is 'group-think': this acts as a 'force-multiplier' for radical thought while creating a competitive environment amongst the group members for being the most radical. This does seem to relate to the masculinity question raised above.

The study shows that for those groups of homegrown radicalised individuals who do not seek jihad abroad, the dedication and commitment of their leader to jihad is often the main factor in determining whether the group will commit a terrorist act or not. This has implications for how we educate young people about authority. The radicalisation process is accelerating, and the individuals are continuing to get younger. Schools, like mosques or prisons, may be the beginning of the journey. Prisons are especially educational, with their Islamist clubs and groups.

Silber and Blatt's image is of a funnel – entering the process does not mean that one will progress through all four stages and become a terrorist. However, a halt does not mean someone is no longer a threat – individuals who have become radicalised can still act as mentors and agents of influence for the terrorists of tomorrow. It is interesting that Ben-Porath also uses the analogy of the funnel, talking of the shift from democratic citizenship to belligerent citizenship as a 'gradual closing of options, an uneven process of narrowing down perceptions – a slippery slope ... from the wide-open democratic entrance to the funnel, to its authoritarian closed end' (p21). Extremism is not just the end of a continuum or track, therefore, but a severe narrowing of the line.

Bohleber (2003) writes interestingly on shared states of 'aggressive numbing':

> an orientation to the attack ahead, an erasure of all prior scruples, and an extermination of all doubt and any sense of empathy for those who will soon be victims of the attack. This is the submersion into a parallel world where there is no 'point of return' ... What is always killed in such acts is one's own weakness, doubts, and conscience, which are projected upon the other. (Bohleber, 2003)

This would underscore the importance of the written statement or video before an attack – one cannot then back out. The 'shared state' also underlines the sense of duty to brotherhood or peers.

Part of the funnelling is this parallel move from isolation to group think. Elworthy and Rifkind explain that brainwashing is not some sort of magic but a secular, scientific method that acts on the human brain in order to change belief systems. Central to the process is the need to isolate the individual from their own group. In the case of the suicide bombers, this may have happened in the training camps. It also becomes important when brainwashing to narrow the field of view so that everything becomes interpreted through one ideological lens. The brainwashed person needs to be exposed to repetition as the more familiar the idea, the more comfortable he or she becomes. All this is reinforced by the intensity of the group process, his or her identification and sense of belonging to a particular group. This very process is used by cult organisations to draw in members. There is a valuable website of the *Cult Awareness and Information Centre* (www.culthelp.info/) which details the mechanisms, and provides an alarming video called How to Start a Cult, which shows just how easy it is.

In Whittaker's collection *The Terrorism Reader*, there is a discussion of 'moral disengagement' – Bohleber's 'aggressive numbing'. This quotes the social psychology view of 'cognitive reconstrual' (or reconstruction), which transforms normally socialised individuals into dedicated and skilled combatants. There is an odd paradox here. Terrorists see themselves as 'engaging' in a campaign or crusade or in a lone task; observers see them deliberately 'disengaging' from conventional humane, civilised values. Whittaker quotes Albert Bandura, who looks at how radical shifts in destructive behaviour through moral justification are most strikingly revealed in military conduct.

> People who have been socialised to deplore killing as morally condemnable can be transformed rapidly into skilled combatants, who may feel little compunction and even a sense of pride in taking human life. (Whittaker, 2007:267)

If this is easy in military training, it should be no puzzle in terrorism training, which has an equally if not stronger moral message. Conversion is not achieved through altering personality structures, aggressive drives or moral standards, but by cognitively restructuring the moral value of killing, so that the killing can be done free from self-censuring restraints. The task of making violence morally defensible is facilitated when non-violent options are judged to have been ineffective, as we saw in Palestine, and utilitarian justifications portray the suffering caused by violent counter attacks as greatly outweighed by the human suffering inflicted by the foe.

There is a revealing account in Whittaker of Nelson Mandela's 'conversion' from non-violence to a more active mode of civil disobedience. The ANC had looked at Gandhian principles of *satyagraha*, a non-violence that seeks to conquer through conversion, and the ANC originally used industrial action or entering proscribed areas etc. But Mandela, through much self-education and reading, explored other areas and campaigns and armed struggles, in Cuba, China and Israel. In considering four possibilities – sabotage, guerrilla warfare, terrorism and open revolution, the MK (Spear of the Nation) decided to start with the form of violence that inflicted least harm on individuals: sabotage. With a small and fledgling army, open revolution was impossible. And as Mandela recognised 'Terrorism inevitably reflected poorly on those who used it, undermining any public support it might otherwise garner' (quoted in Whittaker, p244). In the end they used more violent methods, with an ANC pamphlet identifying justified targets – the 'racist army', police, death squads, agents and 'stooges in our midst'.

Always there is the ends-means question, the 'just war'. In the West, Mandela is seen as a hero, bin Laden is generally not – except by other extremists. I do not want to spend time going into these moral dilemma questions, although this is a useful pedagogical tool in examining conflict. The point of raising it is to explore the processes by which people shift in their moral focus, and what conditions such shifts.

## Leaving extremism

Finally in this chapter, I turn to how one 'loses' an extremist identity, for this would have implications for education. If one learns to be a terrorist, one can unlearn it. What are the processes of exit? For Husain, it was the promise to study 'properly', and the choice of A-level subjects of history, government and politics and sociology, together with a transfer to a college which had a diverse population. Not since primary school had Husain had acquaintance with non-Muslim British students. There was also his sociology teacher, a committed socialist, who came to find him when he was missing classes.

> He took me aside and uttered only one sentence, then walked away. To this day, I have not forgotten his words: 'If you want to change the world, then you must get an education first'. Most of my teachers disagreed with my politics, yet on a personal level we still got on rather well. I owe that teacher a debt of gratitude for those words and his help later, when the defiant ethos we had created came tumbling down. (p143)

It was also meeting a girl, Faye, whose face did what his used to do a lot: smile. 'As an Islamist, I had lost my ability to smile' (p148). (I look at the role of humour in Chapter 5). She wanted him out. The final push was when a member of Hizb murdered in cold blood a fellow student, a Nigerian Christian, who had been offensive to Muslims. The investigators 'never really understood the seriousness of Hizb's form of violence' (p153), but Husain was beginning to.

Husain's withdrawal from Hizb was gradual, like his entry into it. Violence was now on his own doorstep, not remote in Bosnia or the Middle East. He started having doubts about whether God really wanted government in the name of religion, and why there was failure to establish an Islamic state if God was on your side. He started to learn Arabic to find out more. It wasn't easy, and at first he still saw non-Muslim academics and their interpretations of history as part of a global conspiracy against Islam and Muslims. But a major influence was Professor Denis Judd, a British historian who 'more than any other tutor nurtured my mind with academic rigour, critical thinking and fresh interpretation. He was a warm, approachable and respectful teacher' (p157). Another influence was E.H.Carr's book *What is History?* Carr argued against hero worship, the backbone of Islamism. 'I believed that such men as Mawdudi, Qutb, Nabhani and others swam against the tide, stood separate form the milieu in which they found themselves, and thus sought to guide us to a better, purer age'. Carr hoped to

> discourage the view which places great men outside history and see them as imposing themselves on history in virtue of their greatness, as jack-in-the-boxes who emerge miraculously from the unknown to interrupt the real continuity of history. (Husain, 2007:160)

Husain started to find his heroes were cardboard men, who, rather than being unsullied by Western thought and bearers of pure Islamic intellectualism, had ideas that were derivative, fully formed by Western political discourse but presented in the language of Muslim religious idioms. Hegel and Rousseau had done it all before. He switched to Sufiism, and discovered the way of moderation. Travels to Damascus and then Saudi Arabia also opened his mind. In its treatment of black immigrants, the racism of Saudi Arabia shocked him. It dawned on him that Britain, his home, had given refuge to thousands of black Africans from Somalia and Sudan; they prayed, they had their own mosques, they were free and they were given government housing. How could it be that Saudi Arabia condemned African Muslims to misery and squalor?

> All of my talk of *ummah* seemed so juvenile now. It was only in the comfort of Britain that Islamists could come out with such radical, utopian slogans as one government, one ever-expanding country, for one Muslim nation. The racist reality of the Arab psyche would *never* accept black and white people as equal. (p241)

The London bombings were the final straw. The G8 summit on poverty in Africa was derailed by the events, and forced to think about Arab grievances yet again. The fact that hundreds of children die in Africa every day would be of no relevance to a committed Islamist. 'Who in the Arab world cares that some 6,000 people die each day from AIDs? Let them die, they're not Muslims, would be the unspoken line of argument' (p256). His Saudi students also horrified him:

> Two weeks after the terrorist attacks in London, Zafir, a young Saudi student, raised his hand and said 'Teacher, how can I go to London?'
>
> > 'Much depends on your reason for going to Britain. Do you want to study or just be a tourist?'
> >
> > 'Teacher, I want to go London next month. I want bomb, big bomb in London, again. I want make jihad!'
> >
> > 'What?' I exclaimed. Another student raised both hands and shouted, 'Me too! Me too!'
>
> Other students applauded those who had just articulated what many of them were thinking. I was incandescent. I walked out of the classroom to a chorus of jeering and catcalls. (p260)

Back in UK, Husain finds the radicalism of Hizb unabated, with speakers in prayer halls in Universities preaching all out war, and calling on God to destroy the *kuffar*. Demonstrations against the Danish cartoons were organised, demanding that the USA be bombed as well as Denmark, with preachers cunningly linking the cartoon outrage to Palestine, Iraq or Darfur. Husain is hopeful for a new generation of moderate Muslims, but is by no means sure.

Like Husain, it was mainly education and reading that was to open the eyes of other ex-jihadists. Arrested in Egypt for membership of Hizb ut-Tahrir, Nawaz started to study as much as he could about the ideology he professed to be working for. He became, however, more and more surprised. 'The sheer breadth of scholastic disagreement that I found, on issues I had believed were so definitive in Islam, surprised me'. It dawned on him that what he had been propagating was far from 'true Islam'. This implies to the reader that he is still searching for 'truth', but he does admit he became more and more tolerant the more he learned about Islam. 'Now I am trying to counter the black and white mindset that I once so vehemently encouraged' (2007:8). For Maher, it was his time at university researching the development of Islamic political thought in colonial India that changed him. His research caused him to find marked points of rupture in both the historical and theological narrative of what the Hizb was having him believe. He was able to survey a wide range of Muslim opinion across the Indian sub-continent – in particular the idea so lucidly explained by Abul Kalam Azad, the first central education minister of independent India, that a secular state was validated through Islam.

The stories of the actual difficulties of leaving Hizb and political Islam also have parallels. Maher has met Husain, and they have shared their same feelings of isolation and desperation before they plucked up the courage to leave. Hizb had been an established network offering social support and validation; when Maher left, the network turned bitterly cold and confrontational. 'The inward love was replaced by the external hate'. It would not just be about the loss of networks, but also of self. D. Stephenson Bond (1993) writes with a telling analogy:

> It is an odd thing to fall out of a myth. It is like standing on the shore and looking back in astonishment at the myth from which you've so recently emerged, a beached whale lying in the summer sun. Only yesterday, you were in the belly of the whale, with no idea just how contained you really were, just how much larger the vast sea could really be. Seeing your life now from outside the myth, everything upon which you had formerly stood is revalued, in an instant. And great sadness, like waves washing along the sand, washes over the realisation that such a living body, such a thing of beauty, should lie in silent rigour, exposed to time and long decay until the tide should seek the moon and beat away the bones to untold depths. ( p27)

## Educational strategies for exit

I want finally to contrast two modes of work with fundamentalist or radicalised people to enable them to 'fall out of the myth'. Using yet another metaphor, Catron explains how she talks to fundamentalist students, and how her previous experience was almost crucial in the dialogue:

> I know that to even open one's mind to a new perspective, when coming from a fundamentalist viewpoint, feels like dancing on the rim of the abyss; and it helps to know that your guide is not hostile to your plight and has danced on the rim of the abyss as well – and survived. (2008, forthcoming)

Perry (1999) had suggested that a dualistic mindset is not displaced but modified out of existence, and that for these necessary modifications to be made, there must be modelling by a respected mentor or authority. Other people just being dismissive does not work. A relationship with a respected authority creates a safe space where students have the courage to step out of the safety of dualism. We saw this with Husain in his relationship with the sociology tutor. Worryingly, though, while some students will start to move out of the comfort zone, one response to threat is retreat. The student fortifies himself or herself with 'anger and hatred of otherness' (p198). The role of the teacher is crucial here: for if he or she is perceived as hostile to the student's beliefs, this may be the very impetus that pushes the student into retreat.

Hence, to foster growth, Catron identifies five attitudes, summarised here:

- The raising of students' life experiences, as new knowledge will be related to prior knowledge for deep learning to occur; and discussion of religion should occur in the classroom

- A willingness to reveal our own struggles with faith and intellectual development – our own tentativeness, provisionalism and vulnerability may be the most inviting for fundamentalist students long fettered by dogmatism

- An acceptance of students' views, wherever they are on the development scale, rather than hostility to them, and thus being classified as 'the other', the enemy

- Patience, while a fundamentalist believer apprehends the extent of their loss and learns how to affirm their own responsibilities. There may be regression; and antagonistic expressions of intolerance for new ideas may actually be fearful attempts to fend off growing doubts

- A willingness to engage in dialogue with fundamentalist students, to pose questions and to listen.

These are salutary, and as a naturally confrontational teacher, who (metaphorically) prefers to get students by the throat and bash them against a wall, shouting, 'how can you believe this stuff?', I have seriously learned a lot by thinking about this 'tentativeness'.

In a completely different context, a fascinating account of 're-education' of extremists in Saudi Arabia appeared on the internet on January 18 2006. The Saudi regime had instigated two large-scale projects, one for outreach to Saudi security prisoners and the other a campaign for on-line dialogue with extremists. The counselling programme for prisoners intended to encourage them to renounce their extremist beliefs through one-to-one dialogue and group religion classes. More than 400 prisoners had been released, based on the assessment of the counsellors that they had renounced their views, admitted their errors and wanted to repent. A cynic might think they were doing all this renouncing as a Get Out of Jail Free card, but the article stresses that the prisoners seem to have been persuaded by the re-education process that their interpretation of jihad was incorrect, as well as of the *hadith* that says 'Expel the polytheists from the Arabian peninsula'. (I'm not sure how else you interpret that sentence, but maybe in Arabic it's more ambiguous). But the prisoners admitted being previously brainwashed into thinking that jihad meant the unconstrained and unconditional killing of any infidel, and of anyone who collaborated with an infidel – and that it was an individual 'commandment', like prayer, or fasting. Teachers in schools and universities had apparently been part of this 'brainwashing'. However, the prisoners could be turned round: 'Actually, there was no difficulty with these people, since they were searching for the truth – unlike those who adopted the view of *takfir* with regard to state and society, and who planned to carry out terror operations within Saudi Arabia' (p2). This programme had been done secretly, out of the media eye, but there was now pressure for the counsellors to appear openly on the media to discuss the 'deviant thought' and the 'righteous path' to which the prisoners had been returned.

The on-line dialogue with extremists, called the *Al-Sakinah* (tranquillity), uses some 40 *ulema* and 'propagators of Islam' with Internet skills to enter extremist websites and forums and converse with the participants. The educators counted 130 Al-Qaeda and associated websites, and studied their focal ideas and the principles that guided them in on-line recruitment and mobilisation. Using psychological techniques, conversations had been conducted with 972 individuals, most of them Saudis aged 18-30, over a total of 53,760 hours. 'We saw positive signs during the conversations ... We did not demand that the people with whom we spoke renounce their views by 100 per cent – this would have been a false hope'. The most effective strategy was to draw people into 'side discussions' from the main public dialogues, and exchange views with them at that point.

Six women worked with the team, conducting dialogues either with women who held extremist ideologies, or with the wives and sisters of men who did so. One former high-ranking female member of one of the Al-Qaeda women's organisations, who went by the name of Umm Osama, related how she had come to renounce her views following conversations with a representative of the *Al-Sakinah* campaign. It is worth quoting her account in detail, as there are many educational implications:

In the beginning, I did not know it was an organised campaign. In the forums there were various speakers. There were those who spoke rudely to us or to the commanders, and who made curse-filled accusations. Their tone was harsh and angry. We were not afraid of these people, no matter what they said or how numerous they were in the forums – on the contrary, they made people identify with the Al-Qaeda organisation and its members [even more].

We began to fear those who spoke pleasantly and with well-based religious knowledge. We felt that people were identifying with them, and that we were beginning to lose supporters. Our commanders – whom we did not know personally but with whom we maintain contact via the Internet – wrote a warning and a recruitment letter [calling] to intensify our efforts on the Internet.

We began to talk with [the *Al-Sakinah* representatives] and it was their ideas that were of the highest priority for us. These [people] raised in me, and in many other women I know, serious doubts and questions regarding the beliefs that we held so deeply. There are many examples of this, such as the issue of *takfir* against the Saudi regime, which was indisputable and which we had agreed not to discuss with them. After many discussions we found – or at least I found – that the religious rules that had been dictated to us [by our commanders] were mistaken, and that the Saudi regime was not infidel [at all].

These are interesting techniques – speaking pleasantly, raising questions, demonstrating knowledge, enabling people to identify with you. This is not far from Catron. However – and this is key – the article admits that the representative focuses only on the issue of terrorism *against Saudi Arabia*, and refuses to discuss issues of terrorism outside the country. The representative convinces the participant that Saudi Arabia supports Muslims everywhere, and is 'in the crosshairs of its enemies'. Again, a real cynic might suspect that this government backed campaign is primarily concerned about internal terrorism, that is, jihad in what they call the 'combat regions'; it is not clear whether the 'true path' also proscribes jihad outside Saudi Arabia. But the main issue is the raising of doubt, and presentations of alternative views, which one assumes can only be beneficial.

If we summarise the ways in which extremists become less so – and all the stories above show not a renunciation of religion but a more moderate version – a number of ways emerge. They are not the opposite to the triggers – that is, it is not about somehow *removing* humiliation, threat, fear and even idealism. Instead it is about opening up, presenting *alternatives* to understandings and actions. There is the role of study, not just more study of sacred texts, but of politics, sociology and especially history. This enables the notion that there can be different versions of events, be they different interpretations and translations of scriptures, or different historical views of the Muslim world. There is the influence of a personal meeting, a mentor, a 'respected authority' who, crucially, is not dogmatic, but is warm and sympathetic, and just asks questions. There is the experience of seeing extreme harm or violence or racism perpetrated by other extremists in the name of the cause, which shock and cause doubt about effect and motivation. And there is meeting a girl who smiled.

# 3

## Segregation, faith schools and the myth of equal value

The last two chapters have explored how at least part of extremism is binary thinking, constructions of us and them, and the associated good and evil. In terms of education, the obvious first question is how far schools, universities, and other educational establishments can avoid such dualism and harmful divides. The seemingly incontestable logic is that young people should learn together at crucial stages in their development and in their 'identity formation', so that any absolutes they may experience in the home or community are not cemented. At the same time, there are arguments that minorities have the right to their own schools and that anger at non-recognition can fuel hostility, or a withdrawal from the state system – which has the same isolating effect. This chapter first examines the arguments around physical segregation versus coeducation of children from different groupings in society, particularly religious groupings.

The second question in extremism is how 'difference' is dealt with, whether within a school or across schools. If indeed immoderate or binary views of the Other are linked to the propensity to extremism, then how is diversity and otherness tackled, and what has been the effect of various interpretations of multiculturalism and pluralism? Does the 'contact hypothesis', of bringing people together in different ways, help to ameliorate prejudice? The chapter looks finally at some issues and myths around tolerance, respect and equal valuation.

### Segregation

The debate about segregated schooling takes different shapes in different societies. In an already divided society with clear lines of demarcation of the conflict – Northern Ireland, Sri Lanka, apartheid South Africa – the discussion is about how schools have been part of that divide and whether they contribute to or ameliorate conflict. In a society with multiple points of potential tension – UK, USA – the discussion is either more specific, for example about religious schools versus the rest, or about social cohesion in general. In a society that is divided but peaceful – Switzerland, Belgium, Canada – there is less opposition and indeed a support for pluralism or parallelism. In these countries the divide is predominantly linguistic, and there can be an argument that the upholding of language rights and cultural rights can help defuse any possible tension. It is interesting that Switzerland is held up as a model in Sri Lanka, as having so many parallels (three communities, three languages, similar balances of populations), as successfully managing a federal system and as being a model for peace and non-intervention.

In northern England in 2001, a series of riots quickly took on a racial character, particularly between Asian and white youth, and enquiry teams were established to examine causes and circumstances. The different reports from Burnley, Bradford and Oldham all identified a high level of residential segregation in many of the towns which had created a high level of *de facto* segregation in schools. Segregation between communities seemed to have constrained contact and understanding between them but this, allied with the effects of social and economic disadvantage, had fuelled resentment that some communities were receiving more help than others. The reports identified a key role for schools in 'promoting positive citizenship values, recognising both rights and responsibilities, and suggested that schools ought to explore ways of achieving more balanced intakes' (Gallagher, 2004: 103). Much responsibility is therefore placed on schools. In Wayne Nelles' (2003) collection on education and security, the contributions from Northern Ireland and Sierra Leone show a complex and contradictory relationship between education, cohesion and conflict, with formal education contributing to the deterioration of 'human security' and promoting group difference, while then being asked to reconstruct society after the conflict.

It is therefore the reasons for, and histories of, segregation that are key to the discussion. Single sex girls' schools have not to my knowledge been contributory in themselves to female extremists wanting world domination for women. In Canada, the separate school system for French and English is based on the notion of equal and dual status, solidified in legislation. It is argued that this 'multiculturalism' is actually part of the Canadian identity, and partly in opposition to the melting pot assimilationist conception put forward in the United States. Central to the analysis seems to be that, with the exception of the First Nations people, there are no clear native peoples who claim to be the original peoples of the country. 'To disavow multiculturalism is, in part, to deny one's own particular history as a former immigrant and citizen of Canada' (Gereluk and Race, 2007:123). This is a significant point, or an ideal at least, that all were immigrants once, relatively recently, and have contributed equally to Canadian development. Such a conception is in contrast to the myths of nationalism, national identity and territorial ownership which have caused and maintained conflict in the Balkans (Davies, 2004). It is also in contrast to conceptions of 'original' British values and people, discussed below.

Sri Lanka provides a different example and history of segregation. During 2007, I was part of a team working with the Sri Lankan Ministry of Education to draft a *National Policy on Education for Peace and Social Cohesion* (NIPEU, 2007) – possibly the first comprehensive national policy on peace education in the world, cutting across all sectors. While the ethnic and religious mix of Sri Lanka is actually very complex, the major divide or schism is the majority Sinhalese and the minority Tamils. The 'extremist' element of the Tamils, the Tamil Tigers, have been demanding and continue to demand autonomy and a separate territory. There is no space to go into the history or politics of this, but the relevant point for this book is the segregated school and university system which is acknowledged not to help the situation. While in Colombo and in other urban areas of the South and West, Sinhalese and Tamils may live side by side – although attending separate schools – in other parts, children will never meet a person from the other group. Languages and scripts are different, and while many Tamils will learn Sinhalese, the opposite is less true. Inevitably there is mistrust and suspicion. Tamil schools in the North and East can be recruiting grounds for the Tigers, and headteachers have to be resistant to the messages. Active heads there try to enable their students to meet Sinhalese students through arranging various peace events and exchanges, and try to break down stereotypes, but not all heads will do so. As in Northern Ireland, it is in the end the politics that will decide any end to the conflict, and the education system on its own will not forge a federal system or concessions or a victory by the military over the Tigers. But there is consensus from all groups that segregated and isolationist schooling, as a reproductive force, needs to be broken down (Colenso, 2005).

## Debates on faith schools

Of particular concern in terms of extremism and segregation is the debate on faith schools. In the UK, about one-third of state schools are faith (sometimes called denominational) schools, 600 secondary and 6,400 primary. The vast majority are Christian, with a scattering of Jewish, Muslim and Sikh schools. Parker-Jenkins *et al* (2005) in their book *In Good Faith* take a careful look at the arguments for and against faith-based schools in the UK political context where the government is supporting the extension of single faith based schools funded by the state. The authors try hard to take a balanced approach and review a whole range of studies and views. It is complicated in the UK as our so-called secular schooling, implicitly or explicitly, has an Anglo-Christian ethos. While the arguments that (some) faith schools can accede to minority wishes and therefore promote social justice, and that they do offer high quality education and integrate minority communities, in the concern about extremism and tension, the arguments against them as a totality seem to outweigh all these – although this is not Parker-Jenkins *et al*'s conclusion.

The arguments for segregated schools are fivefold. They appease or recognise cultural or linguistic minorities; they meet demands and ideologies of parental choice; linked to this, they may provide a specific moral value system which is seen as superior to secular or diffuse state systems; they provide a sense of secure identity and safety in a troubled society; and they can be seen to provide a model of integration through deliberate 'accommodation' of others. An exemplar of the latter might be King David school in Birmingham, a 40 year old state-funded Jewish primary school. Judaism is the only religion taught; there is a synagogue on site; the children learn modern Hebrew and celebrate Israeli independence day. Yet half of the students are Muslim, and Muslim parents are queuing up to get their children into this school, even moving house. They like the ethos of the school, and the kosher food, which is somewhat similar to Halal. The school is also respectful to Islam, with a prayer room for the children and provision of Muslim teachers during Ramadan. All year round the children can wear a *kufi* (hat) – although many in fact choose to wear the Jewish *kipah*. A report by Margolis (2007) states that one Muslim mother did not object at all to her children learning Hebrew: 'I think it's great. The more knowledge, the more understanding ... They learn all they need about Islam at mosque school.' Another said 'We're very very pleased with the school. It's so friendly. All the kids mix and go to one another's parties and are in and out of each other's houses. They teach a bit about Israel, but we don't have any problem with that. There are such similarities between our people and our societies'. The good SATs results certainly help, but it is not a particularly privileged intake, with half the pupils having English as an additional language. The head is reported as claiming very few racist incidents – perhaps one a term – compared to multicultural inner city schools where he had taught. So from this we could surmise that whether a faith school does harm or good depends on their makeup and how they tackle religious messages – that is, how 'extreme' they are in themselves. Is King David Judaism-lite?

## Twelve arguments against faith schools

Given that, as discussed in Chapter 1, extremism does not necessarily have a religious base and can be political, a question could be raised about why so much time is spent in this book looking at faith schools and religious identities. The answer is that, unlike political ideologies, this is in many societies an accepted way of dividing children – governments do not sponsor or even encourage a range of 'political' schools in one country for parents to choose from (Marxist, capitalist, democratic, anarchist etc) and would be rightly concerned about the link to extremism. But it has become historically acceptable to permit and even fund schools which exist to promote and protect different religious ideologies. We do need to scrutinise these. In doing so I am aware of their huge range – for example that some faith schools are almost indistinguishable from non-faith schools in their pupil composition, teaching staff and multi-faith ethos. My concern is that less all-encompassing schools can shelter under this apparent ecumenicalism.

Analysing faith schools reveals complications of class, ethnicity and gender, that is, varied combinations of difference. The whole debate about Muslim schools in UK is confounded by the elision of religion and ethnicity/culture, so that it is not just about providing a religious school but about a separation into distinct 'communities', in a way that providing a Jewish school would not do. The arguments specifically against faith schools come from a great range of stakeholders, not just atheists and humanists but also religious leaders of different denominations, philosophers and economists. It has to be stressed that in amassing the arguments, it is not to say that all faith schools are bad – and by implication all secular schools are good – but that in the concern about extremism, the potential for harm seems overall greater in religiously ideological schools, and the potential for social cohesion compromised. I look at twelve aspects of this possibility.

### Isolation
The first relates to exclusion or isolationism. If students rarely or never meet those from other groups, and rely on interpretations of such groups from teachers or the media, then stereotypes are easily transmitted and reinforced. If this is combined with any sense of grievance or injustice or hate, there is

little to counter it. Statements made in the Ouseley report (2001) into race relations in Bradford, UK, suggest that fragmentation of schools on cultural, racial and religious lines has played a key role in heightening racial tensions: ethnic loyalties, cemented at segregated primary schools, remain fixed throughout the years of secondary schooling. These 'community cohesion' reports have been criticised as failing to distinguish between state schools that are secular in their ethos but happen to have high numbers of Muslim pupils, as against voluntary-aided schools that are formally committed to Muslim values (Stone, 2004). But the reports show what can happen when institutions start to cement ethno-religious identities, whatever the school's origins. The argument that racism can occur in secular or multi-faith schools is a diversion from this evidence.

The London Development Centre (2002) raise concerns about whether single-faith schools can contribute to the overcoming of racism, and asks what will happen to those minority ethnic children and families who do not hold religious beliefs, or do not construct their identity around their religion. They argue that the extension of single faith-based schools 'will cause deeper divisions in the Black communities, and a greater stranglehold of the most conservative, anti-women and communal individuals over our children's education and over communities as a whole' (p4). This is an important point. There is the assumption that all ethnic minorities have a religion and want this preserved, but this is not so.

Similarly, different surveys have shown that the majority of Muslims in UK would prefer to send their children to a mixed-faith state school (Policy Exchange, 2007); and 94 per cent of Muslims disagree that Muslims should keep themselves separate from non-Muslims (GfK NOP, 2006). Yet there is often the assumption that groups *want* segregation. Omaar (2007) remarks of government policy: 'At times it has seemed impossible to change the minds of the establishment, to explain to politicians that, if you condemn a group of people for separating themselves from the mainstream, they will only retreat further from that society' (p236). This is a vital insight. Forced feelings of isolation can be compounded by educational isolation.

A significant argument against faith schools comes from a rabbi. Jonathan Romain (2005) thinks they result in religious ghettos or an 'educational apartheid' which destabilises the social health of the country. 'I want my children to sit next to a Sikh in class, play football in the break with a Methodist, do homework with a Hindu and walk to the bus stop with a Muslim before returning to their Jewish home'. I return to the problem of this essentialist categorisation of children later; but Romain makes the valuable point that it is not just the children who are cut off, but the parents too. They cannot meet and form friendships at the school gate, sports days etc. He mentions the Ousely report after the riots in Bradford and Burnley, which blamed the segregation in schools for heightening the divisions between communities.

> We also saw the terrible scenes of Catholic children having to run the gauntlet of screaming Protestants to reach Holy Cross school in Belfast ... Had these Protestant parents mixed with Catholic children 30 years ago, they might have grown up knowing that Catholics are not demons but ordinary kids who eat crisps and enjoy skateboarding.

Romain argues for 'cross-religious' schools, neither allied to one particular faith nor given to regarding religion as a waste of time. Instead, they should treat faith seriously, while accommodating atheism.

> Schools must build bridges, not erect barriers. However good some faith schools are individually, collectively they are a recipe for social disaster. Leaders of all faiths should put aside religious self-interest and make national cohesion a higher priority. (Romain, 2005:9)

The question of self-interest is one to be returned to.

### Parents choosing separation

But it is not just some religious leaders who want separate schools. The Commission for Racial Equality (CRE, 2007) says 'trust' schools and parental choice are leading to some parents choosing schools of their own culture. In an international review of Islamic schools in North America and Europe, Merry and Driessen (2007) describe parents' motivations to protect their children from secular influences in the state schools and society and to cultivate a strong religious identity. For many parents this translates as more discipline. The authors found schools often to be a site for contestation and dispute, for example in striving to provide academic rigour so that students will have the skills and qualifications to succeed in secondary and tertiary education as well as the labour market. Yet Islamic schools also aim to cultivate robust religious identities that will enable pupils to challenge the very trappings of material success many of them will inevitably enjoy. This is consistent with the stated aim of most Islamic schools to promote dual citizenship, one to the global Muslim community (*ummāh*) and one to the wider society from which pupils are drawn.

> Thus in theory, *da'wa* or witnessing to one's faith is consonant with teaching civic virtues such as tolerance towards others. Of course, tolerance is quite different from

*respect* for those with whom one does not agree, and naturally, respect for those who espouse a different reading of Islam, or who are non-Muslim, will be more evident among those with whom there has been positive interaction. Yet for the moment, it remains unclear just how much interaction pupils in Islamic schools have with 'otherness'. This is so for at least three reasons: (1) Some Muslim parents who select Islamic schools are often reluctant to allow their children to form close friend-ships with non-Muslims or even with Muslims from different cultural, racial or theological backgrounds; (2) analogously, 'protection' from different points of view, or, if one prefers, cultural coherence, is partly the *raison d'être* of Islamic schools; indeed, Islamic schools exist at least partly in order to *counter* the prevailing attitudes and cultural norms in liberal democratic societies; (3) finally, the enrolment of non-Muslims in Islamic schools remains very low; indeed, the overwhelming majority of Islamic schools contain no non-Muslim pupils. All of this suggests far less contact with difference for a majority of pupils in Islamic schools, especially in the early years when paternalistic control over what children do is more stringent, and limited contact portends worrying trends for inclusive and democratic educa-tion. (Merry and Driessen, 2007:23)

It is both protectionism and simultaneously wanting achievement within the competitive society which characterises demand. The London School of Islamics, an 'Educational Trust', often writes of radical Islam in their news-letters, but blames

... the western society which is creating extreme Muslims all around the world ... Imams are not solution to the problem for extremism. Extremism is nothing to do with imams. Extremism is not created from abroad, it is coming from within. (London School of Islamics, 2007a)

Their argument is that extremism is created by societal and institutional racism, and the exclusion of Muslims. But this leads not to a demand for inte-grated schools but for separate schools. 'Muslim community would like to see more and more state funded Muslim schools, where Muslim boys and girls could be educated separately by Muslim teachers'. The contention is that 'native teachers' are in no way role models for Muslim children. Much of the argument seems to be around poor teaching of English as well as lack of attention to other languages such as Arabic and Urdu.

The fact is that majority of Muslim children leave schools with low grades because monolingual teachers are not capable to teach Standard English to bilingual Muslim children. A Muslim is a citizen of this tiny global village. He/she does not want to be-come notoriously monolingual Brit. (London School of Islamics, 2007b)

Here we see some admission of integration being a two-way process, and the critiques of Islamophobia and of the British education system are understandable; but the endpoint is to blame these for alienation and radicalism and to make demands for separatist schooling.

The whole question of parental choice becomes highly contested. The Minority Rights Group (MRG) argued that the right to separate schools for minorities is compatible with international standards on human rights, but that an important distinction would have to be drawn between those situations where separate schools are imposed (which MRG defines as segregation), and those situations where separate schools are adopted as a matter of choice (1994). Obviously in South Africa segregation was imposed, and 'institutional pluralism' was not benign. But is it more benign in a situation such as Northern Ireland where schools are indeed segregated by choice? Tony Gallagher (2004) examines the three main alternatives offered to account for the impact of segregated schools there. The 'cultural hypothesis' suggested that segregated schools enhanced community divisions by introducing pupils to differing, and potentially opposing, cultural environments, for example in curriculum – a view echoed in Cannon's (2003) analysis of the different conveying of historical events in the Northern Ireland curriculum. The 'social hypothesis' suggested that regardless of what was taught, segregated schooling initiated pupils into conflict by emphasising and validating group differences and hostilities, encouraging mutual ignorance and mutual suspicion. The third view was that the issue of schools was largely irrelevant, and the conflict was about material inequalities and injustice in Northern Ireland. In the absence of consensus about causes, three broad intervention strategies were curricular, such as Education for Mutual Understanding; contact programmes between Protestant and Catholic children; and the development of integrated schools. The majority of schools are still segregated however, and 'transformed' schools, all originally Protestant, are not always easy to develop from their originally segregated ethos – with concerns particularly from Protestant parents that their schools are being 'taken over'. Cannon (2003) pointed out how schools, particularly separate schools, continue to be the 'flashpoint' between conflicting communities, illustrated by the Holy Cross school disturbances in North Belfast.

### Compounding other forms of segregation

Religious adherence in practice is not spread uniformly across all social classes in a society, and faith schools can cement socio-economic differences. The Young Foundation's study *The New East End* warns that in Tower Hamlets white parents have taken over four church secondary schools, making them virtually all white, so neighbouring secular schools have become 90 per cent

Bangladeshi (Dench *et al*, 2006). The Institute for Research in Integrated Strategies finds that the number of children taking free school meals at Church of England and Catholic schools is lower than the average in an area. This means nearby schools take more, magnifying the difference (reported in Toynbee, 2006). Selection is the secret ethos of church schools, as has been demonstrated by the number of parents who lie about their religious commitment, or start attending church, in order to get their children into a faith school.

The political discourse of choice in the UK has reinforced social fragmentation, and no amount of social engineering in the form of requiring faith schools to accept specified proportions from other faiths will compensate for this. The Leicester Islamic Academy is now state funded, but as Toynbee pointed out, the duty to accept 25 per cent non-Muslims will not trouble it much. 'The Principal said on The Moral Maze [BBC Radio 4] that all girls must wear the school uniform, both the hijab and the head-to-toe jilbaba. Not much choice there'. (2006:7)

### *Lack of opportunity for dialogue*

I quote here another rabbi, Chief Rabbi Jonathan Sacks:

> 'One belief more than any other ... is responsible for the slaughter of individuals on the altars of great historical ideals. It is the belief that those who do not share my faith – or my race or my ideology – do not share my humanity'. (2003:82)

Sacks argues that the best way to live with moral difference and yet sustain an overarching community is 'conversation – not mere debate but the disciplined act of communicating (making my views intelligible to someone who does not share them) and listening (entering into the inner world of someone whose views are opposed to my own)'. Even more strongly he argues that 'the greatest single antidote to violence is conversation, speaking our fears, listening to the fears of others, and in that sharing of vulnerabilities discovering a genesis of hope' (p83).

The argument here is not just that faith schools may separate but that students are deprived of an important learning tool: talk, deliberation and dialogue with those with whom they might disagree. In the encounters that brought together Israeli and Palestinian students, the sharing of fear was an important part of breaking down stereotypes (Davies, 2004).

*Promoting superiority*

It is not just difference which is problematic but possible superiority linked to the message or designation of that school. Parents may send their child to a Catholic school or to a single-sex girls' school because they think the exam results are better, not because they think Catholicism or women are better. That is understandable, and of itself does not breed extremism. It is when the school is badged as exclusive or superior *because* of a religious or ethnic message or identity that the difficulties arise. Children going to that school see themselves as superior to those attending other schools with other messages – always the problem of elite schools – and differences become entrenched. This is the old reproduction hypothesis, normally relating to social class, which I need not go into here. My argument is that when this elitism is combined with a religious or ethnic message which can be matched against particular identifiable groups or communities in a society, it becomes dangerous for social cohesion. Walter Feinberg writes:

> One of the features of many religious schools is that they provide students with the disposition to favour those who share their devotional orientation over those who do not. The fundamentalist message that atheists and members of other religious faiths will not go to heaven; the Muslim view that Mohamed was the last and the greatest prophet with a more complete version of God's message than the others, including Moses and Jesus; the Jewish belief that Jews are God's chosen people; all are, in one way or another, exclusionary beliefs. The exclusionary effect may be even more penetrating when delivered to young children who have not yet had much contact with members of other faiths, and who do not yet comprehend the metaphorical functions of language. (2003:402)

Feinberg argues therefore for critical reflection on the doctrinal errors made by past leaders of the faith, for example Southern Baptist schools in the US might have units on their Church's erroneous defence of slavery and their belated retraction, Catholics on their behaviour during the Inquisition. 'In all religious schools the distinction between the disposition to favour believers like oneself could be mitigated by appeals to humility and the ever present possibility that anyone, religious leaders included, can be wrong about God's will' (p403). I am unsure how much this actually happens in faith schools.

*Locking in cultural identity*

It is significant that Salman Rushdie has opposed the expansion of Muslim-only schools. He thinks that putting children in a single faith environment so early in their lives 'locks in' their cultural identity, and that this is detrimental (reported in Nazeer, 2005). Amartya Sen similarly proposes that a 'confounded view' of a multi-ethnic society led to the encouragement of Muslim schools – 'young children are powerfully placed in the domain of singular affiliations well before they have the ability to reason about different systems of identification that may compete for their attention' (2006:13). For him, faith schools encourage a 'fragmentary' approach to the demands of living in a desegregated Britain.

> Many of these new institutions are coming up precisely at a time when religious prioritisation has been a major source of violence in the world (adding to the history of such violence in Britain itself, including Catholic-Protestant divisions in Northern Ireland – not unconnected themselves with segmented schooling). Prime Minister Blair is certainly right to note that 'there is a very strong sense of ethos and values in these schools'. But education is not just about getting children, even very young ones, immersed in an old, inherited ethos. It is also about helping children to develop the ability to reason about new decisions any grown-up person will have to take. The important goal is not formulaic 'parity' in relation to old Brits with their faith schools but what would best enhance the capability of the children to live 'examined lives' as they grow up in an integrated community. (Sen, 2006:160)

There is then a problem with such multiculturalism of Rabbi Jonathan Romain reported above, and that is the early labelling of children as having a confirmed religious identity. Dawkins describes in *The Independent* a 'charming picture' of a nativity play with the glowing caption of the Three Wise Men played by Shadbreet (a Sikh), Musharaff (a Muslim) and Adele (a Christian), all aged four. He asks, how could any decent person think it right to label four year old children with the cosmic and theological opinions of their parents? He asks us to imagine an identical photograph, with the captions changed to Shadbreet (a Keynesian), Musharaff (a Monetarist) and Adele (a Marxist), all aged four. There would be letters of protest. But such is the privileging of religion in our society that there were no protests about the forced or assumed religious identities. He asks us then to imagine the outcry if the caption had read Shadbreet (an Atheist), Musharaff (an Agnostic) and Adele (a Secular Humanist), all aged four. The parents would probably be investigated to see if they were fit to bring up children (2006).

*Compromising autonomy*

A key question therefore is whether faith schools provide sufficient autonomy in thinking and aspiration. Feinberg defines autonomy as

> the developing capacity of the child to choose a life in accordance with her own critically developed conception of the good. Autonomy requires the ability to reflect upon one's own socialisation process, and to eventually take greater control over that process. (2003:400)

Autonomy is not an all or nothing affair: we critically choose parts of our lives while we leave many others unexamined and unchallenged. The development of autonomy may require different things at different stages of childhood, with the need for a stable self being an important part of early childhood. But Feinberg argues that any state support for faith schools must be predicated on the school advancing individual and social autonomy, producing reflective autonomous citizens.

> One of these conditions is that at age appropriate times children are allowed to gain intellectual and emotional distance over the form of life with which they are most familiar, and to understand that there are many reasonable forms of life. (Feinberg, 2003:402)

A public school 'must aim to reproduce a public', where one learns the skills and attitudes for living together in a democracy, a democracy in which a plurality of different conceptions of the good will be allowed to flourish. However, one important purpose of many religious schools is to raise children into adults who will have the outlook, points of view, beliefs and affiliations of one group of congregants rather than another.

There is however a grey area. Feinberg argues 'Schools that advance a preferred way of life must be distinguished from those that teach intolerance for any way of life other than their own. The former must be allowed; the latter should not be' (p395). Yet if you advance something as 'preferable', this automatically implies a judgement on others. Much would depend I suppose on the sweeping nature of any lack of toleration. One could say healthy food is preferable, but that the odd bag of chips is not a threat to Western civilisation or the world's arteries. It is only when war is to be waged on chip eaters that problems arise. I like Callan's distinction:

> After all, it is one thing to be taught to identify with a particular religion categorically as the locus of meaning and fulfilment for human beings always and everywhere; it is another to learn to see it as the most attractive item on a menu of spiritual possibilities, to be chosen only so long as it maintains its edge over the competition. (1997:57)

I was interested in the paper on *Citizenship Education: A Catholic Perspective* (Battle and Grace, 2006). Gerald Grace tells me I was partly responsible for it, as I had commented in a review of his book on Catholic schools that it would have been useful to show Catholic schools actively involved in citizenship education. The paper does indeed have a number of useful points about the need for new openness and critical thinking, and notes the offerings and 'deeper inspiration' of the Church's social teaching – community participation, social responsibility, good neighbourliness and the need for a basic social morality to deal with crime and drug taking and relationship breakup. But (with apologies to Gerald Grace) I still have two problems with this. Firstly, all these values are not distinct to the Catholic church; and secondly, when things do start to become distinct, the narrowing down and the calculated conflation of issues become apparent. The final section is headed 'How to build a safer world after September 11?' and draws on the work of the US Conference of Catholic Bishops. It begins:

> How to protect the weakest in our midst, innocent unborn children? How to keep the nation from turning to violence to solve difficult problems, by abortion, the death penalty and euthanasia? How to address the tragic fact that more than 30,000 children die every day as a result of hunger, international debt and lack of development? How to defend marriage and support families better? How to combat continuing prejudice, hostility to immigrants and refugees? These are just a few contemporary questions. (p29)

I would add, 'How to explain that children are dying and poverty sustained because of the Catholic position on contraception?' 'How to combat Catholic prejudice against gays?' The questions in the quotation above lead into the paper's final theme of 'solidarity' – yet this ignores the very tensions caused by the assumption of value commonality, and that citizenship education and a 'safer world' can be fostered by very specific Catholic views on, and prioritising of abortion, euthanasia and the sanctity of marriage – rather than the autonomy and self-criticality proposed by Feinberg.

### The problem of critical thinking

This links to the question of possibilities for critical thinking. In jihadist training camps abroad, the Qu'ran is taught as a set of eternal truths, with little reference to its historical context, and the concept of a fairer Islamic society in the form of a caliphate becomes a political aspiration that justifies the use of violence to challenge the dominance of Western values. This is an extreme form of 'single truth' education, but the question is about whether or when sole truths are at the heart of faith based education in western countries.

> Yet while many try to carve out a place for critical thinking and reinterpretation (*ijtihād*) without charges of heresy or innovation (*bid'a*), it is difficult to foster critical thinking when a large number of teachers recruited to teach in Islamic schools adhere to a more authoritarian, teacher-centered pedagogy or when chauvinistic practices that pass for 'tradition' undermine democratic ideals like mutual recognition and the freedom to dissent. (Merry and Driessen, 2007:25)

Brown (2003) examined the complex nature of funding between voluntary controlled and voluntary aided and community schools in UK, and continued:

> Why should pupils who attend voluntary controlled and community schools acquire a knowledge and understanding of a range of faiths with particular emphasis on Christianity, yet pupils in the increasing number of voluntary aided schools learn of nothing but their own religion or denomination or sect at the wish of the governing body? (p110)

The head of the Islamia Primary School, one of the first Muslim schools to be granted voluntary aided status, and with 23 nationalities represented, officially open to all faiths in terms of admissions policy, explained that pupils could practise any religion they liked. They prayed five times a day, learned the Qu'ran with translation, explanation and discussion; but 'One thing we never do is celebrate Christmas' (quoted in Parker-Jenkins *et al*, 2005:132).

Parker-Jenkins *et al* cite the research studies on independent faith-based schools, which demonstrate that their curriculum offerings may be very narrow, due to financial restraints and ideological choice in the selection of curricula. The question then is not just of isolation from others but from mainstream thinking. Fundamentalist schools often drill their students on the most effective creationists' response to scientific evolution, with the purpose of inoculating students from evidence supporting evolution (Feinberg, 2003). The latest in creationist schools is 'creation algebra', according to a recent report in *The Times*. The syllabus from a Baptist school in Texas reads: 'Students will examine the nature of God as they progress in their understanding of mathematics. Students will understand the absolute consistency of mathematical principles and know that God was the inventor of that consistency'. *The Times* comment continues 'Should they have the misfortune to proceed to calculus, they will also discover that God has a foul sense of humour' (*The Times*, 1.10.2007, p16).

Where next? We could have 'creation physics'. During General Zia's Islamisation of Pakistan a proposal was put forward to Islamise science books. Rather than writing in the textbooks that hydrogen and oxygen make water, it was suggested that hydrogen and oxygen *by the will of God* make water. Luckily, before these suggestions could be incorporated into the textbooks, General Zia went to meet his creator (M. Nazir, personal correspondence). The followers of the Church of Scientology on the other hand believe the radioactive souls of aliens, or thetans, have attached themselves to humans and are at the root of our problems. Yet the movement is growing and is exempt from VAT because of its claimed 'educational' purposes. As the chair of the charity FAIR (which cares for families affected by cults) points out 'There is no support under law, since mental kidnapping is not recognised as an offence in the UK' (Gourlay, 2007). The concept of 'mental kidnapping' is a salutary one, and not of course confined to Scientology.

### Imagining community

Much multicultural thinking relies on the concept of community – ethnic and faith communities in particular. As long ago as 1983, Anderson was talking of 'imagined communities' which would bolster the nation state or other political identities. Eric Hobsbawm, who is interested in the globalisation of football and how football's marketability is rooted in nationalism, once wrote 'The imagined community of millions seems more real in the form of eleven named people' (quoted in Hoyle, 2007). Yet within plural societies, these imagined, almost symbolic or metaphorical unities are still constraining thinking and leading to dangerous labelling. 'Community' has a nice feel, with the image of the meeting hall, the village shop, the neighbours, the self-help. Those leaving mental institutions were referred to as being 'released into the community', as if there were some immediate support system which would roll into action, providing the counselling and the bag of sugar. This is mythological, but also has the problem of boundaries and where one 'community' begins and another ends. And as Sen points out, the 'well-integrated' community where residents do great things for each other, can be the very same that throws bricks through the windows of immigrants. When does solidarity become nepotism? More importantly for our study, community, like an essentialist identity, connotes an essentialist grouping of people who somehow have common and distinct values, lifestyles and claims. The notion of religious 'communities' implies that for their members, membership of this community is the most important identity. This is dangerous and divisive.

Ironically, Haque unwittingly points up the paradox of attempts to 'educate' the public about religion:

> Non profit organisations can assist in conducting interviews, research and other activities to help the Muslim community and can play a key role in educating the public about the stereotypes that exist about Muslims and Islam and develop new ways to eradicate them. (p15)

Here is the discourse of community as if this were some sort of homogenous entity. It ignores major divisions between Suni and Shi'ite, with at least 22 sub-divisions as well as national differences. In the same sentence Haque talks of 'the Muslim community' and then complains of stereotypes. It also appears patronising: do 'the Muslim community' want or need to be 'helped'? It reminds me of the old lady in an impoverished location who said 'One thing I have come to dread is being *worked amongst*'. If you replace Muslim with 'gay' in this sentence it would seem almost demeaning. And in days of multiple identities, is 'Muslim' to be the sole reality definer for this research?

Sen's analysis in *Identity as Violence* is valuable here. He worries that the UK is not just an 'imagined community' but now 'an imagined national federation of religious ethnicities' (2006:165). He talks of the 'uncanny similarity' between the problems Britain faces today and those faced by British India, and which Gandhi thought were getting direct encouragement from the Raj. Gandhi was critical in particular of the official view that India was a collection of religious communities. He would have been extremely pained by the sectarian violence against Muslims that was organised by sectarian Hindu leaders in his own state of Gujerat in 2002. But he would have been encouraged by the condemnation of such barbarities by the Indian people and the defeat of political parties involved.

> Much has been written about the fact that India, with more Muslim people than almost every Muslim majority country in the world (nearly as many as Pakistan) has produced extremely few homegrown terrorists acting in the name of Islam, and almost none linked with Al-Qaeda. The growing economy is clearly an influence, but some credit must go to the nature of Indian democratic politics and to the wide acceptance in India of the idea, championed by Gandhi, that there are many identities other than religious ethnicity that are also relevant for a person's self-understanding and for the relations between citizens of diverse backgrounds within the country. (Sen, 2006:168)

It might also be credited to the fact that India has a secular national education system. Gandhi had asked 'Imagine the whole nation vivisected and torn to pieces; how could it be made into a nation?' Sen continues:

> The disastrous consequences of defining people by their religious ethnicity and giving predetermined priority to the community-based perspective over all other identities, which Gandhi thought was receiving support from India's British rulers, may well have come, alas, to haunt the country of the rulers themselves. (2006:169)

Staying with the Indian parallel, it is significant that while Gandhi was religious in a very ecumenical way, the atheist Nehru spoke out strongly against religion:

> The spectacle of what is called religion, or at any rate organised religion, in India and elsewhere, has filled me with horror and I have frequently condemned it and

wished to make a clean sweep of if. Almost always it seemed to stand for blind belief and reaction, dogma and bigotry, superstition, exploitation and the preservation of vested interests'. (quoted in Dawkins p45)

The disaster of the partition of India along religious lines only serves to underscore Nehru's 'horror'. It is crucial that the UK learns from international comparisons and histories before it is too late.

Trevor Phillips, then the chair of Britain's Commission for Racial Equality, gave a famous speech in 2005 entitled *'After 7/7: sleepwalking to segregation'*. He argued that Britain has

focused far too much on the 'multi' and not enough on the common culture ... We have allowed tolerance of diversity to harden into the effective isolation of communities, in which some people think special separate values ought to apply'. (Phillips, 2005:4)

His views and critiques of multiculturalism as being outdated have been controversial in Britain. Yet he is making a significant point around the isolation of communities and their being granted 'special separate values'. This relates to the whole question of whether cultural 'rights' should ever supercede human rights in general, or the convention on the rights of the child. Distinctions within 'tolerance' and 'respect' are explored in the final chapter.

Being assigned to a community – Muslim, Christian, Somali – implies the absence of choice.

When the prospects of good relations among different human beings are seen (as they increasingly are) primarily in terms of 'amity among civilisations' or 'dialogue between religious groups' or 'friendly relations between different communities' (ignoring the great many different ways in which people relate to each other), a serious miniaturisation of human beings precedes the devised programmes for peace. (Sen, 2006:xiii)

Sen's concept of 'miniaturisation' is a useful one, as are his doubts on 'representatives' of a community. The existence of faith schools implies that religious identities are the most important issue in allocating children to education – yet this actually miniaturises them, in the same way that assigning a permanent academic identity can reduce options.

*Gender inequality*
The UK government has not published any gender-specific statistics on faith schools, which has angered gender equality campaigners. The government response is that undertaking research on this would be a 'massively dispro-

portionate' use of taxpayers' money (Hanman, 2006). Questions remain un-answered therefore about whether girls and boys in faith schools are taught a different curriculum, as was found to be the case in a now-closed indepen-dent Muslim school in Scotland. The argument from Clara Connolly from the movement *Women Against Fundamentalisms* is that

> The main problem with faith schools is that their primary purpose is to socialise women into their major roles of wives and mothers. All the most conservative faiths – Islamic, Catholic, Jewish, evangelical – agree that women have a place in the family and that women should be educated towards that aim. (quoted in Hanman, 2006:5)

I am sure that many faith schools will dispute this as a 'primary purpose' and be able to cite high achievement and aspiration for girls. But Connolly cites the Joseph Rowntree Foundation report *Faith as Social Capital* (2006) which says that power inequalities within religious communities can have negative effects, particularly the subordination of women. It states that many faith communities fail to listen to women or young people; and that women usually do most of the work in the community, yet become increasingly less visible in the higher levels of decision-making. Teachers in Catholic schools have to explain to girls why women cannot represent their faith as men do. Hanman interviewed pupils and teachers at the English Martyrs Catholic school in Leicester in 2006. The headteacher said they 'had to stand out against things' and not just go along with every fashion, so that the children had 'a good sense of values'. The school invites Life, the anti-abortion charity, to talk about sex education. The girls are taught abstinence, but not about how to use a condom. 'Chemicals' such as the pill are discouraged as this is said to lead to early sex and breast cancer. One 15 year old student said:

> We are taught about abortion – that it is wrong – and we are taught that we shouldn't use contraception, but we are not really taught about real-life situations. Listening to my friends who go to other schools, I don't know what they know.

The issue here starts to relate to rights – the right to information and to alter-native viewpoints.

### The use of state funding

Another question is whether the state should fund religious schools. Tariq Ali states firmly that there should be a 'moratorium' on state sponsorship of religion. He is concerned over the National Secular Society figures that reveal Labour permitting 40 more non-religious state secondaries to be taken over by the Church of England, with another 54 about to go. The then Education

Secretary, Ruth Kelly, 'a paid up member of Opus Dei, stressed that the 'bombs' would not stop her encouraging the formation of more single-faith schools' (2005:85).

Walter Feinberg (2003) has an interesting discussion on religious education in liberal democracies. His argument is that citizens in liberal democracies are not illiberal if they choose to deny public support to religious schools. A serious objection is that 'it would be tyrannical to take tax funds from one believer in order to advance the beliefs of another' (p387). A democratic consensus could decide to support religious schools, but this support should always be conditional – on the promotion of autonomy and critical thinking mentioned above. Illiberal religious schools should not be supported by state funds. This requires accountability and not just minimalist compliance to state law or state curriculum. With fundamentalist schools, there is always the argument that students will see through fundamentalism and in fact reject it, rebelling in true adolescent fashion against authoritarianism, but that should not be an argument for setting up or supporting authoritarian schools.

A central question arises: if there is a democratic consensus that faith schools are to be supported – and it is not clear there is – then which ones? Former British Prime Minister Tony Blair invoked 'diversity' when challenged in the House of Commons to justify government subsidy of a school in the north of England that taught literal biblical creationism. He said it would be unfortunate if concerns about that issue were to interfere with our getting 'as diverse a school system as we can' (quoted in Dawkins, p331). Yet we have seen how in state funded religious schools which are voluntary aided, the governing body has the power to decide the religious education syllabus. They have the power 'to decide that the content of the subject will reflect only the religious foundation of the school or that other religions or denominations will only receive a cursory amount of time and resources' (Brown, 2003: 109). As Brown points out, the government 'listening' to groups wanting state funding could include Montessorri, Steiner, Zoroastrian and Wicca groups. Roy Hattersley was good on this: 'will the Department of Education endorse the creation of Christian Science, Scientology or a Mormon school? If not, it will have to take the intolerable step of nominating state-approved religions' (quoted in Parker-Jenkins, p195).

A case study is pertinent. Malik (2007) reports that female members of Hizb ut-Tahrir have established two primary schools, in Haringey and Slough. The curriculum contains elements of Hizb ideology regarding the caliphate: according to the Islamic Shaksiya Foundation curriculum document, children aged 7-8 are taught 'our rules and laws come from Allah'; and are asked to contrast Islam with 'other belief systems where human beings make rules'. At age 9-10, children should be taught 'There must be one khalifah (ruler of the caliphate)'. Tahir Alam, education spokesman at the Muslim Council of Britain said he had seen the khalifah being taught as a historical subject but never as an ideological principle. He was concerned about relevance in a UK curriculum that should prepare pupils to be a citizen of this country. The author of the school's history curriculum, Themina Ahmed, has previously written for Hizb ut-Tahrir about her hatred of western society and her wish to see it destroyed: 'The world will, insha-Allah, witness the death of the criminal capitalist nation of America and all other [infidel] states when the army of jihad is unleashed upon them'. One parent said most parents knew that the teachers were from Hizb ut-Tahrir, and although the children were not pressured into joining the group, teachers often invited parents to Hizb events and discussions to try to recruit them. Most worrying of all was that Ofsted was glowing about the Slough school's work, particularly 'the school's provision for the pupils' spiritual, moral, social and cultural development' (Malik, 2007). Hence this school could well apply for state support.

Funding religious schools is therefore a slippery slope, with governments having to face increasing pleas for segregation and with governing bodies deciding religious education. If someone wanted to set up an atheist school, would they or should they be allowed to? While you think about this, here's an atheist joke:

---

### THE ATHEIST

An atheist was taking a walk through the woods, admiring all that the 'accident of evolution' had created. 'What majestic trees! What powerful rivers! What beautiful animals!', he said to himself.

As he was walking alongside the river he heard a rustling in the bushes behind. As he turned to look, he saw a seven-foot grizzly bear charge towards him. He ran as fast as he could up the path. He looked over his shoulder and saw that the bear was closing in on him. He tried to run still faster, so scared that tears came to his eyes. He looked over his shoulder again and the bear was even closer. His heart was pumping frantically as he tried to run even faster, but he tripped and fell on the ground. He rolled over to pick himself up and saw the bear right on top of him raising his paw to kill him.

At that instant he cried out 'Oh my God!' Just then, time stopped. The bear froze, the forest was silent, even the river stopped moving.

---

---

A bright light shone upon the man, and a voice came out of the sky saying,

'You deny my existence all these years, teach others I don't exist and even credit my creation to a cosmic accident and do you now expect me to help you out of this predicament? Am I to count you as a believer?'

The atheist, ever prideful, looked into the light and said 'It would be rather hypocritical to ask to be a Christian after all these years, but could you make the bear a Christian?'

'Very well', said the voice. As the light went out, the river ran, the sounds of the forest continued and the bear put his paw down.

The bear then brought both paws together, bowed his head and said, 'Lord I thank you for this food which I am about to receive'.

---

Actually, and ironically perhaps, my argument would be that opening an atheist school would be undesirable. It would be in the same position as other 'belief systems', of open proselytising. Secular is not the same as atheist. We should not prioritise any belief system, but just let good critical, evidence-based learning do the rest

### Problems of exit

In Chapter 2 we saw the difficulties that Ed Husain and others had when wanting to exit from Hizb ut-Tahrir and from radical Islam. The last of the twelve questions is, do faith schools give the opportunity to leave the faith? Feinberg makes an important point about 'exit'.

> Intensity of commitment should not be confused with indoctrination. One important test is whether students are provided with the skills required to exit a tradition should they later choose to do so. These skills involve both the academic and vocational education needed to take up work in the larger society and the capacity to evaluate different traditional practices. Policy makers need therefore to distinguish between schools that reflect parents' intensity of commitment from schools that use psychological manipulation, selected skill training, or intimidation to inhibit future adults from considering factors that might lead them to exit the tradition. (p395)

Dawkins also talks of how embedded religion is, and how difficult it is to disentangle oneself. He starts in typical Dawkins mode, leading to a significant point about the decision to depart:

> Though the details differ across the world, no known culture lacks some version of the time-consuming, wealth-consuming, hostility-provoking rituals, the anti-factual, counter-productive fantasies of religion. Some educated individuals may have abandoned religion, but all were brought up in a religious culture from which they had to make a conscious decision to depart. The old Northern Ireland joke, 'Yes, but

are you a Protestant atheist or a Catholic atheist?' is spiked with bitter truth. (p166)

These twelve arguments seem powerful; but exit from faith schools in policy terms is equally difficult to individual exit. We cannot abolish non-Christian faith schools in the UK now – there would be an uproar – so one argument is to abolish all state-supported faith schools. I agree with Tariq Ali that there should be a moratorium on more state-funded religious schools, as all sorts of unsuitable ones do creep in on the equity principle, and it is not long be-fore there has to be acceptance of bizarre variants and hate-inspiring institu-tions. However, while the evidence would support secularisation of schools, in UK at least a policy shift is unlikely. Hence the strategy is to make faith schools as non-singular and non-exclusive as possible. Parker-Jenkins *et al* (2005) suggest that the religious dimension of identity can be explored within a concept of citizenship. 'Also very useful for new faith-based schools is the opportunity to study media literacy and to encourage the critical analysis of images of racism, Islamophobia and homophobia, exploring their construc-tion and their often misleading representation' (p144). But will this happen? We saw the narrowing of curriculum that can occur. Parker-Jenkins *et al* are positive that with compulsory citizenship, there is the opportunity for pupils to explore their identity and how this fits in with citizenship. I am less sure: we know from research that schools will still avoid controversial topics, and, un-less Islamophobia and homophobia – as well as atheismophobia – are com-pulsory and looked for by Ofsted, for example, I could see many schools avoiding them. Citizenship education is crucial, I agree; but one should not be over-optimistic about its impact.

## Tackling diversity in the school

While discouragement of faith-based schools would be the first step in the challenge to extremism, on its own it is not enough. Firstly, unlike in France following the Revolution, this is not going to happen or happen quickly, so one has to be realistic. Secondly, as we saw from Husain's story, attendance at a normal state comprehensive is no guarantee of breaking down isolation. Pupils segregate themselves, or are segregated into streams or sets by the school system – but that's another story. I turn now to the discussion of how schools tackle diversity.

'Diversity' is a mantra in many government policies as an understandable re-action to problems of social cohesion. 'Diverse' is a synonym for ethnically or religiously divided. All societies of more than about three people are diverse – but what do we single out to teach about? Through learning about 'others', can we mitigate against stereotyping and extremist views? The obvious point to make is that as soon as one selects a group for scrutiny, one is casting them as 'other' or 'diverse' or 'different'. Multicultural policies that focus on difference have not only failed but have cemented divides, as we have seen. It is useful to have this confirmed in a major recent study by Uvanney Maylor and Barbara Read on *Diversity and Citizenship in the Curriculum* (2007), commissioned by the Department for Education and Skills. They found that pupils often enjoyed learning about different cultures at the global level, but were more critical at the local level, particularly for religion. One gripe was the repetitiveness of covering Hinduism, Islam, Sikhism and Christianity – 'we do it every year more or less the same stuff'; but also about the lack of match with reality. Religions and cultures were taught as a set of ideal types:

> When you see girls walking down the corridor you're not 100% sure, you kind of think all Muslims, Sikhs and Hindus have to abide by the rules, but when you talk to your friends about it, they don't completely follow it ... They [teachers] only say what they should do not what they actually do'. (2007:77)

Pupils got tired of hearing the message 'we're all different' all the time, preferring teachers to 'move on'. Some White British pupils felt marginalised:

> There's either Black History Month or as I said they do Muslims and there's Sikhs, we learn about that, but we don't learn about White people, so we do feel a bit left out as well. (p76)

This quotation possibly sums up the range of the problem – the elision in the pupil's mind between ethnicity and religion, the notion of 'doing Muslims', and the inevitable inward focus on being 'White', as some sort of parallel. No-one would dream of 'doing Whites', not least because it is unclear what one would 'do'; but it is disturbing that schools can happily 'do Muslims'.

In his chapter on 'Muslims in Italy' in van Driel's (2004) collection on Islamophobia, Michele Bertani relates similarly simplistic ideas about 'good practice'. He talks of how 'representatives of the Islamic community are invited to schools to introduce Arab-Islamic history and culture' (which representatives? which bits of culture?) and tells of 'guided tours for students and teachers to the Islamic Community Centre, also the main mosque' (p108). The first is dubious, the second exoticism. To be fair, extracting these from what would be a larger programme of intercultural exchange is unjust, but I merely point up the difficulties of choice in whom to choose or how to expose a belief system to others. I think I will invite religious people to a guided tour of 37, Seclar Drive, to see how a humanist lives. 'Marvel at the ritual consumption of alcohol. See how all are in veneration in harmony in front of old reruns of *Friends*. Look carefully at the preservation of the sacred dustballs under the bed. Note the belief in miracles, that one day this tin opener at the back of the kitchen drawer will suddenly work again'. The problem is that there can be no 'representatives' of non-belief, which is often why atheists are overlooked.

Returning to Maylor and Read's study, they found that the current approaches were 'forced' and did not tackle real issues that meant something. It seems that instead of 'doing' a group as an identity, the way to approach difference and diversity is through a much more politicised approach. This means not ignoring issues of ethnicity or religion, but instead treating them within social or political science, or citizenship, on a 'needs base', with evidence and fact to talk about. It becomes important to talk about difference when there is a social problem of discrimination or underachievement or inequality or lack of representation. It is important to talk about refugees and asylum seekers when this is a local or national issue and would benefit from understandings of migration and how a so-called host country responds. Such discussions may examine culture and belief, but this would be as a means of understanding a greater problem, not just as a stand-alone topic. Isolating groupings for automatic scrutiny is a hidden way of casting them as an actual or potential problem, a subtle form of victim casting.

The diversity curriculum does not include vegetarians, the obese, communists or midgets, either because they are not seen as a problem or because prejudice against them would be worsened by focus. My argument is that singling out groups for inspection and looking at them as bounded entities without looking at their political, social and economic relationships with other – more powerful – groupings is a way to promote extremism and bitterness, rather than counter it. As Connolly (2000) also argues, when all attentions are directed towards overcoming individual psychological stereotyping, the political injustices that can sustain cultural antagonism may be left unchallenged.

There is also the question of whether such scrutiny is done critically, or just as a form of voyeurism in the form of simple 'understanding'. Irshad Manji (2004) in her inimitable style writes:

> Instigating change means not taking the Qu'ran literally, and also not taking multiculturalism literally. Why should forced clitorectomy be indulged? Why should the cops back off when a father (or mother) threatens death to a daughter who chooses to marry outside the religion? Why should a Muslim cabbie who rapes a mentally disabled woman get off under the rubric of cultural sensitivity? To echo the German professor and practising Muslim, Bassam Tibi, why should human rights *belong* to non-Muslims? (p221)

Human rights therefore are central to tackling diversity, not just in equal entitlements but also in equal obligations as citizens, as discussed in the final chapter. As a hypergood, human rights practice overrides 'indulgence' of harmful cultural practices. I look more at cultural 'tolerance' later.

Cockburn's (2007) study of white far right supporters in the North of England, mentioned in the last chapter, found his BNP subjects had all attended schools which had pupils from South Asian backgrounds, and in this sense there was no 'racially segregated schooling'. They had been exposed to anti-racist and diversity awareness. Most were familiar with customs and habits of Asian cultures, knew about the five pillars of Islam. It seems that 'awareness' of other cultures, or proximity, is not enough to foster cultural cohesion, and may undermine it.

> The young people were scornful and angry at the way anti-racist programmes were deployed in their schools. They felt this was delivered in ways that derided them personally and arguably pushed them further from the anti-racist culture of the schools they attended. (p553)

One far right supporter felt the teachers picked on him, that 'they knew my views'. Significant proportions had been bullied by Asian pupils and felt the school took no action. The conclusion is that we should avoid the dualism that places white children as always the oppressors and black children always as victims.

> What is important to stress is that the young men were finding themselves becoming increasingly locked into an educational space where they could negotiate which aspects of education they respected and were going to engage with (i.e. those that will help them do well in qualifications) and those that they would ignore (i.e. diversity training). In this space nobody was interested in listening to them, or realistically engaging in their ideas, or challenging their beliefs in a way that showed respect. (p554)

Instead, they felt 'lectured to', invoked as 'bad characters'. The style of teaching did not seek to encourage a dialogue about identity issues and was seen to prefer to 'lecture the white kids about how great cultures are compared to yours'.

> Researchers have noted that both black and white children have ambiguities about the promotion of 'different' cultures in the curriculum. It leads to embarrassment by black children, while white children resent the apparent privileging of ethnic minority cultures and as a devaluation of their own ... one can think of the obvious need to discuss the appalling legacy and injustice of the British Empire while at the same time acknowledging the positive rewards of British democracy and free speech.

Failure to do this allows the BNP and other far-right organisations to be seen as offering an alternative place of support, friendship and respect. (p555)

Steiner-Khamsi and Spreen (1996) have similarly argued that 'there is not too little but rather too much awareness among youth with regard to cultural diversity, 'race' and ethnic relations' (p27). Cross-race friendships simply see them as 'atypical'. Adult interventions can have some effect on young people, but if handled insensitively can reinforce oppositional identity at the cost of strengthening peer influence.

An interesting study by Daniel Faas (forthcoming, 2008) of white and Turkish students in two inner London secondary schools contrasted the approach of the two schools. At the more working-class school, Millroad, which 'celebrated' diversity and where students' conflict was ethnic or racial, young people found safety in their national(istic) identities. At Darwin, the more middle class school, which worked on integrating students on the basis of common citizenship and where there was only low-level ethnic conflict, young people developed hybrid ethno-national identities.

At Millroad, students sat along ethnic lines in almost all classrooms, with some tables of only African Caribbean students, and other tables with only Turkish Kurdish students. Turkish students had few cross-ethnic friendships and formed an ethnic solidarity group, using this group solidarity in their fight against African Caribbean peers over which group controlled the school territory. Since the Turkish students were disadvantaged both socio-economically and ethnically, this exercise of control within the boundaries of Millroad School was probably their only chance to create a sense of superiority. Faas suggests that using violence and racism thus enabled them to reverse the hierarchy of race. The (minority) white boys at the school also felt uncomfortable; nor did they identify with 'Britishness' – which they called a 'crap' word, that is, without meaning.

Darwin school in contrast drove forward the idea of living in a multiracial, multi-ethnic community, but focused on commonality, with the Deputy Head stressing that '[Darwin] school does not celebrate any faith, we don't celebrate difference, we celebrate similarity'. The school put together Britishness and integration in the sense of portraying Britain or England as a multicultural society to which all could buy in. The concept of ethnicity seemed to play only a subordinate role in relations between youth; most had ethnically mixed friendship groups.

Clearly, the schools were in different socio-economic areas, and direct comparisons are difficult in terms of causation of or challenge to conflict. In Millroad, ethnic conflict outside spilled over into the school. However, the school conflict was not necessarily reduced by the politics of cultural diversity. Intriguingly, the paper argues that a more effective strategy to tackle socio-ethnic marginalisation might be a common identification through social class as a unifying factor. I return to this need for a politicised approach to difference in the final chapter.

## National identity

The discussion above indicates a need to look at whether or how a national identity, or in Britain, Britishness, is a way to unite students and protect against other more extreme or alienated identities. It was interesting that the college Husain attended was unwittingly a hotbed of radicalism. Radical speakers came for Friday prayers at the college. Husain was able to book a lecture theatre to show a film about the killing of Bosnians; and indeed the Bosnian crisis did radicalise many Muslims in Britain. Many students found the literalist approach of Wahhabism attractive, and Husain soon saw several of his fellow students heading to jihad training in Afghanistan in response to Qu'ranic verses urging Muslims to rise up against violence. The interest for our study is the freedom Husain had to promote his views, and how the position of the college was a liberal, tolerant one.

> In the multicultural Britain of the 1980s and 1990s we were free to practise our religion and develop our culture as we wanted. Our teachers left us alone, so long as we didn't engage in public expressions of homophobia or intimidation of non-Muslims. But Britishness and the British values of democracy, tolerance, respect, compromise and pluralism had no meaning for us. Like me, most students at college had no real bond with mainstream Britain. Yes, we attended a British educational institution in London, but there was nothing particularly British about it. It might as well have been in Cairo or Karachi. Cut off from Britain, isolated from the Eastern culture of our parents, Islamism provided us with a purpose and a place in life. More importantly, we felt as though we were the pioneers, at the cutting edge of this new development of confronting the West in its own back yard. (p73-74)

Should one then attempt to replace or supercede a religious or ethnic identity, if this is strong and problematic, by a national one? In the Occupied Palestinian Territory, a national curriculum reflecting national culture, history and identity is analysed as being a positive step to build confidence, even if it does less than it could to encourage peace (Nicolai, 2007). But that is a very different context of nation-building. In their DfES study, Maylor and Read (2007) looked at how diversity was promoted in English schools and whether to incorporate Modern British Cultural and Social History as a potential 'fourth pillar' of the citizenship programme. The idea of the latter is to promote Britishness as a cementing ideal in the multicultural society. The report concluded that this was not a good idea. There was firstly the obvious point of establishing what 'British values' were – and the difference to 'English' values. And secondly, even if one tried, those values would be shared elsewhere, and would not be unique. Ironically, trying to identify Britishness would actually be more divisive.

Nationalistic citizenship curriculum has always presented problems in terms of who is actually included in identifications of 'who we are'. Even if Husain's college had tried, one suspects it would have been counterproductive, that it would only serve to underline differences between Islam and the West, or be seen as an attack on global *ummah*. In the US, the promotion of American 'exceptionalism' and cultural distinctiveness in civic literacy programmes has actually contributed to 'civic illiteracy', according to John Marciano's valuable analysis. Patriotic propaganda and conformity 'leaves citizens and students unable to make reasoned judgements about the terrorist acts of 9/11 and international terrorism in general, preparing them to give unthinking support to US policies' (Marciano, 2000:85). Once more I turn to the use of human rights as a more global ethics and values set which may be able to bring interconnectedness in a far less chauvinistic way.

## Contact hypothesis

Another strategy for countering division is what is called 'the contact hypothesis'. Allport (1954) used the term to refer to the notion that contact between members of conflict groups enhances positive relationships and tackles prejudice. Traditionally it was thought that cognitive processes – *knowing* about people – were the basis for positive intergroup contact, but recent studies have found that emotions are crucial components of racial attitudes, and that affective measurements are better than cognitive ones as predictors of attitudes towards minority groups (Pettigrew and Tropp, 2006). Some of this relates to threat, so that reducing anxiety is more important for reduction of prejudice via contact than is increased knowledge of the outgroup. (The question of fear and threat was raised as a precursor to extremist action in Chapter 2). Empathy and mechanisms for perspective taking are seen to enhance positive relationships – raising interest in the welfare of others, arousing feelings and perceptions of injustice, altering cognitive representations of target group members and inhibiting stereotyping by taking the perspective of a member of another group (Gaertner *et al*, 1996).

Yablon (2007) examined the attitudes of Israeli students towards contact both with Palestinians in Israel and with Israeli religious or secular counterparts, and suggests that the possibility of emotionally based interventions is doubtful for either case. He examined the whole question of the need for time to enable contacts to create change, time which is not always available in situations of extreme tension. Israel has separate school systems for religious and secular students, and has neighbourhoods with either a religious or secular majority. The relationships between the groups are a 'social disaster' in which the two groups are in a process of social separation from each other. Nonetheless, one of the main findings of Yablon's study was that while most of the participants agreed to interact with members of a conflict group based on their religious identity, they did not agree to do so when it came to their *national* identity. Yablon relates this, unsurprisingly, to the intensely negative relationships between Israelis and Palestinians in recent years, which also projects onto the relationships between Israeli Jews and Israeli Arabs, who for the most part identify themselves as Palestinians. He argues that some interactions actually make things worse. 'Thus, contact between Arab and Jewish individuals mostly involves people of unequal status where their contact is usually impersonal, competitive by nature and often opposed by authorities' (p11). Nonetheless around 20 per cent of Israeli students were consistently positive towards meeting Arab counterparts; and this reflects the fact that even during the highest tension between Israeli and Palestinian during the *Intifada*, over 150,000 people in Israel were engaged in coexistence activities.

The issue is therefore whether programmes to ensure contact between groups are likely to reduce extremist views. Much depends on the starting point. Yablon points out 'When two conflict groups are almost totally strange to each other, when even their lifestyles differ, when hate, suspicion and anxiety characterise their relationships, the basis for meaningful and affective contact does not exist' (p12).

In an interesting article, Caitlin Donnelly and Joanne Hughes (2006) compare mixed faith primary schools in Northern Ireland and Israel. The conceptual framework is again Allport's theory of contact: despite variations in the political contexts and the importance accorded to bilingualism in Israel, the schools in both jurisdictions are similarly based on the assumption that contact between divided groups within an educational setting can lead to better inter-group relations. In Northern Ireland and in Israel the traditional policy emphasis has explicitly been upon the preservation of harmony through respecting the rights of each group to have their own school system (as also discussed by Gallagher, 2004). Donnelly and Hughes point out that contact theory never proposed that simple 'body mixing' was enough. Relationships always had to move beyond 'sightseeing' and have the capacity to develop into meaningful friendships. Further conditions included the need for divided groups to see themselves as having equal status within the contact situation (a point also made by Yablon); and that groups should work together towards shared goals.

But there are critiques even here. Donnelly and Hughes explain how American researchers have found that the more contact whites have with blacks the less likely they are to be prejudiced, but in Britain evidence suggests quite the reverse: the more contact whites have with blacks the more prejudiced white people become. So contact alone does not always result in improved relations, and the cultural location is crucial. Rules of engagement may be different too, and Donnelly and Hughes cite the Israeli preference for *doogri* – open and honest patterns of dialogue, a conversational style unadorned by diplomacy and cant. In one of the Israeli schools, two teachers, each fluent in one of the languages, were assigned to co-teach each class. Nothing was translated and the teachers acted as role models for their particular culture, 'often using body language to assist in the teaching process'. The dual-teacher approach is attractive as it requires teachers not only to teach together but also to work closely together in planning the lesson, a process which teachers welcomed as they believed it assisted them in overcoming their own prejudices and fears.

This approach is interesting, as it seems very different from the Sri Lankan model of integrated schools, which either rely on minority children simply working in the language of the majority, or parallel classes existing side by side under one headteacher, or the use of English as a link language. The dual teacher approach was also significant in Feuerverger's (2001) account of the Neve Shalom/Wahat al-Salam school in Israel, where the dual language teachers were described as 'border crossers': able to listen critically to the voices of their students as well as able to critique the language in which histories of conflict was expressed. Another salutary 'dual teacher' approach I was interested in was in a Northern Ireland project, in which two ex-paramilitary soldiers on opposing sides, who had killed for their cause, agreed to talk together to students to encourage reconciliation efforts (*Let's Talk*/80:20, 2001).

But differences between Northern Ireland and Israel were not just about degrees of openness or definitions of 'integrated education'. Donnelly and Hughes point to the different policy environments. The British emphasis on performativity and marketisation, the 'output' orientation, means that the schools focused on the aspects of school activity that they knew the Government would measure.

That there was no clear evaluation scheme for appraising the extent to which the schools met their community relations objectives meant that this aspect of school life was relegated as the schools determined to meet the targets for which they were held accountable ... Hence the standards and results orientation in the Northern Ireland schools, coupled with a strong 'avoidance ethos' left little room for participants to develop empathy with out-group members or to understand the uniqueness and differentiation among outgroup members. (p513-514)

So 'contact' has to be examined within the whole cultural and academic ethos, and can be easily undermined by individualism and competition. The *Guidance on the duty to promote community cohesion* document from the DCSF quotes the Commission on Integration and Cohesion's findings that 'meaningful' contact between people of different groups had been shown to break down stereotypes and prejudice. But to be meaningful required four elements: first for conversations to go beyond surface friendliness; second for people to exchange personal information or talk about each other's differences and identities; third where people share a common goal or share an interest; and fourth where contacts are sustained long-term, with one-off or chance meetings unlikely to make much difference (DCSF, 2007).

Gallagher (2004) similarly looks at all the research on the contact hypothesis, which confirms the importance of 'superordinate goals', that is, goals which most groups want to achieve, but could not achieve independently. For my book, an example of this might be a response to a common threat, such as the shortage of water in the Middle East. Gallagher points out that many of the studies have been in artificial situations, and it is not always evident when some outside event or force will emerge when groups within a society find themselves in a situation of 'competitive interdependence'. As Cockburn concluded in his study of far right groups, the obstacles to engendering social cohesion appear insurmountable. This was because the refusal of young men to mix with Asian people was not confined to supporters of the far right, and attempts to engineer mixed housing spaces resulted in deep resentment and even violence from the settled white population. But in educational terms, 'the conditions of cooperation and shared goals rarely exist in the everyday life of schools, whose prime motivation is 'achievement' through competitive qualifications and school league tables' (Cockburn, 2007:557). This is a very important point, relating to the performativity emphasis in Northern Ireland, mentioned above. Schemes to bring young people together can be hypocritical in the face of larger ways in which schools divide, select and sort.

## Tolerance and the myth of equal value

The mention of hypocrisy relates to the final point discussed in this chapter, which is the treatment of 'tolerance'. Tolerance is often mooted as the opposite or antidote to extremism, as a positive value. Yet it is of course essentially negative – you only tolerate things which you do not like or believe in. Orlenius (2007) rehearses the 'moral philosophy' of tolerance, identifying three aspects: first, it presupposes that the tolerator has a negative attitude towards the phenomenon. If we do not find anything wrong we have nothing to tolerate. Secondly, however, this negative attitude must neither be manifested nor reflected in a disapproved manner. Thirdly, toleration is something deeper than acquiescence or resignation. It concerns a conviction about respect for others and therefore not acting in an inappropriate or unjustified way – it is an issue of power and accountability. Orlenius quotes Burwood and Wyeth: 'The tolerant person is less judgmental towards others. In becoming less judgmental, a person becomes more tolerant. The problem is to avoid slipping into moral indifference with its potential for tolerating the intolerable' (1998:468). This was a point made by Irshad Manji.

In fact, we do not become less judgmental, we simply pretend. This is sometimes acceptable, but it becomes problematic when it relates to major messages that young people receive in school, and to institutional or religious hypocrisy over 'equity'. Philip Barnes (2006) has a thought provoking article 'The Misrepresentation of religion in modern British (religious) education'. In tracing the history of religious education from confessional to the modern notion of 'multifaith', he looks searchingly at the notion that pupils should be taught explicitly that all religions are equal (i.e. epistemically equal as to their truth). John Hull had introduced the word 'religionism' to parallel 'racism', the idea that one's religion in better than others'. It was the denial of the truth of other religious traditions than one's own that was the cause of religious bigotry and intolerance.

Thus after 9/11 a *Declaration by Christian and Muslim Religious Educators in the University of Birmingham* called on fellow Christians and Muslims to 'abandon the competition' which had defined their mutual relations for centuries. Geoff Teece (2005) similarly entreats religious believers to be 'epistemologically humble', by which he means that they should conclude that their own religious convictions are no better warranted than others. This is of course nonsense: the reason why a Christian is a professed Christian is because they see that religion or belief system as better than others. Otherwise they would switch to another brand. The demand for unity is understandable but untenable: it conveniently overlooks this basic fact.

The reasons for religion adherence are indeed complex, but, coercion aside, are in the end no different from any other expression of a market preference. As Barnes points out 'To inculcate in pupils the idea that the religions are complementary and not in competition for each other clearly contradicts both the contemporary self-understanding of most religious adherents and the doctrinal logic of different religions' (p403). Religious identities tend to be exclusive in a way that cultural and ethnic identities are not – you have to 'convert' rather than overlay different identities, as is possible with cultural identities. It is in the end dishonest to portray religions as genuinely acknowledging the 'truth' of each other. It is also contradicted by all other experience – in the home, the media as well as the church or mosque. Barnes points out how systems of belief are often actually contradictory – in notions of the divine, in the religious quest, and the religious end. 'Simply, the different religions all claim to be true' (p404).

In religious education, the response is to gloss over this and focus on what are regarded as communal experiences. As all religions have rites and practices, the focus is on generic themes such as festivals, celebrations, founders, pilgrimage, worship etc. Yet this notion that experience has primacy over concepts and beliefs is again a misrepresentation of reality and the nature of religion. To reconcile different religions would be to change one's own. Barnes looks at the pragmatism of religious education:

> Perhaps the misrepresentation of religion is in fact the lesser of two evils: it may be unethical to misrepresent the self-understanding of religious people in education, but this is eminently preferable to the baleful consequences for society that result from representing religions faithfully and ignoring the bigotry and intolerance they encourage. (p407)

But he then goes on to question this: to present the notion that religions are essentially in harmony is to presuppose that the religions, stripped to their essential features are good. This is questionable, as no religion can purge religious intolerance from its history. Does one then say all religions are good and bad in equal measure? Or that all religions can have a negative effect on society? This would not be popular. Also, the educational strategy of convincing pupils that the religions are in essential agreement with each other actually undermines respect for difference – or respect for those who *resist* the liberal temptation to say all religions are true.

> Equally by devoting its educational energies to the pursuit of this principle it has failed to engage fully with the complex web of inter-relationships between beliefs, attitudes and feelings that combine on occasion to encourage religious intolerance and discrimination. (Barnes, 2006:408)

I would add: to encourage extremism. Barnes therefore argues for a more 'ideologically critical' form of religious education that facilitates dialogue and respect between people with different commitments and from different communities. I would want to go on from this final recommendation to see what this meant in practice. Religious education would simply say that all religions see themselves as true, and then explore the reasons why and the claims made. It would also look at past wrongs done in the name of truth. In this way it would sit alongside education in any other belief or ideological system – Marxism, communism, capitalism or monetarism.

Would this happen? While the pretence at equal value is essentially dishonest and hypocritical, highlighting the hypocrisy worries liberal believers. Pope Benedict XVI, the head of the Catholic Church was strongly criticised by Jewish leaders in July 2007 after he formally removed restrictions on celebrating an old form of the Latin mass which includes prayers calling for the Jews to 'be delivered from their darkness' and converted to Catholicism. God should end 'the blindness of that people so that they may acknowledge the light of your truth, which is Christ'. More liberal Catholics worry about the view of the outside world of a church which sees itself as the sole holder of the truth (Burke, 2007); but do not all churches? Is the Pope not at least being honest about the deeply held convictions of lightness and darkness? It reminds me of the joke about Genesis 1. 'In the beginning the world was without form, and void. And God said, let there be light. And God separated the light from the dark. And did two loads of laundry.' The first task in exploring religious difference is looking at how faiths separate light and dark and on what grounds they think theirs comes out better in the wash than other faiths. Let's at least have an honest and penetrating detergent.

## Conclusion

A recent discussion with a representative from the UK Department for International Development revealed that what they were really looking for from research was what he called 'killer facts'. Forget the nuanced 'on the one hand, on the other hand'; for policy decisions they just wanted it straight between the eyes. So here are the 'killer facts' from this chapter.

■ Schools segregated by faith or ethnicity do not help social cohesion. At best they do little or no harm to integration; at worst they are incubators for unitary views, stereotypes of 'the other' and a dishonest pretence at equity

- But segregation and stereotyping and othering can occur even in mixed schools through well-intentioned diversity or multicultural programmes, with discourses of 'community'

- Contact is important, but not unproblematic. International exchange is valuable, and global links important and possibly preventative, but on their own they are not enough. Finding common ground is undermined by competitive schooling.

The most efficient value-for-money way to protect against extremism is the combination of

- engaging in learning side by side in integrated settings

- having an emphasis on commonality, although not blunt nationalism such as Britishness, nor the pretence that all religions have truth in common

- working together for common goals, whether in school or in contact programmes

- honesty and critical dialogue about belief systems as well as about social and economic inequality as between groups.

# 4

## Justice, revenge and honour

There is an old Chinese saying that 'he who seeks revenge must remember to dig two graves'. The Hamas phrase 'We will not stop killing their children until they stop killing ours' is a chilling one, but by no means exclusive to that movement. One aspect of extremist behaviour and extremist responses is revenge or retribution. It is a primordial, ancient response, and sanctioned in many sacred texts. It links both to regaining status and position and to the projection of injured feelings and abuses – 'now you see how *you* like it'. It is closely linked with some forms of suicide terrorism, in that the 'settlement of debts' is a prerequisite for martyrdom, otherwise the gates of paradise are closed to a bomber. Revenge can be an attempt at an exact parallel – you killed ours so we will kill yours; or it can be a proxy punishment of some sort – killing someone who has raped your relative, or conversely, raping someone from a community that has dishonoured yours. This chapter looks at extremist notions of justice and honour. It also pinpoints how schools use and condone revenge in their punishment regimes, and how this can exacerbate a revengeful disposition. Finally it explores alternatives in the form of restorative justice and how to treat 'wrong'.

### War on terror

The war on terror is at least in part an act of revenge. 9/11 in particular needed to be avenged, and justice sought. Liese (2004) talks of the power of language – that in today's 'war on terror' the dehumanising terms *terrorists* and *evil doers* 'are slurs that have been used to justify retaliatory actions post 9/11'. This was found in President Bush's McCarthyite State of the Union address in 2002.

Parris (2001) pointed out the whole ludicrous and counter-productive nature of the 'war on terror'. You cannot guard all of the modern capitalist world. Borders cannot be sealed. Nor can terrorists be brought down by invasion or troops, or focusing on one 'haven'. The Internet and mobile phone technology make it ever less necessary for conspirators to meet physically in one place in order to conspire.

> The day is coming, perhaps has already come, when terrorists will not need to gather in camps. There will be no HQs to bomb, no cells to track down, no tents to ransack. The concept of 'host' country as geographical location for a terrorist group may already be too weak to bear weight, certainly too weak to justify revenge-bombing of the uninvolved ... We have got a cheek ... to declare ... that the Americans should make no distinction between the perpetrators of a terrorist atrocity and the government which gives it shelter. London and the capitals of Europe offer some of the world's best havens for terrorists and freedom fighters seeking neutral countries from which to hatch their campaigns. (Parris, 2001:9)

Parris argues that we should instead examine what makes a terrorist, and answers that it is 'rage' – against American involvement in the Middle East, propping up favoured states and undermining others. This anger, discussed in Chapter 2, links closely to the psychology of retribution.

Acts of revenge are problematic enough but, worse, they can lead to spirals of reprisal. The dynamics of the Israeli Palestinian conflict take the shape of retaliatory attacks on both sides – with the usual cycles and amplifications. The incursions by Israel into Lebanon in 2006 were a classic example of using one incident to justify a massive attack and loss of life; but many of the criticisms centred round whether the attacks were 'disproportionate' – as if there were ever anything proportionate about killing civilians. Is revenge all right as long as it is 'proportionate' and matched – same eyes, teeth, civilians, children? This chapter seriously questions such discourses.

Chapter 2 examined how humiliation and trauma are a trigger for joining terrorist movements, and Elworthy and Rifkind say that until trauma and powerlessness – such as experienced in Iraq – are addressed, revengeful cycles of violence will continue. They give a diagram of the 'cycle of violence' which goes like this: atrocity – shock – fear – grief – anger – bitterness – revenge – retaliation – atrocity. They say that the cycle needs to be broken at the point before anger hardens into bitterness, revenge and retaliation.

> At moments of provocation, a deep sense of fear is stimulated – especially in the case of the US marines, when all their training in containment has been challenged. The natural response to humiliation is a desire for some kind of revenge or retribu-

tion. But, at pivotal moments in any conflict, the desire to use overwhelming force needs to be measured against the potential to provoke more violence. It takes enormous self-restraint and wisdom to pause and think of non-violent responses to acts of provocation. However, to seek revenge will only unleash a further cycle of violence. Mature democracies need to find ways to be reflective and contain the violence in moments of fear. (2006:17)

These cycles of fear and anger can be applied to the school situation too, as examined later on.

An even greater problem is that terrorism and revenge attacks are changing shape, with nuclear capability a possibility. The risks have been increased by Bush pulling out of arms control agreements and by a change in US nuclear doctrine that allows the pre-emptive use of nuclear weapons against countries believed to have WMD programmes. As Gray points out:

> Above all, after Iraq everyone knows that the only way to be safe against American attack is to possess the WMD capability that Saddam lacked. Obviously an attack on Iran would increase nuclear proliferation and a large swathe of the Middle East would become a zone of armed conflict. The legitimacy of the Iran government and leadership would increase. Agents of mass destruction cannot be threatened with annihilation if their identity is unknown. Military history offers no lessons that tell nations how to cope with a continuing global dispersal of cataclysmic means for destruction. (2007:183)

As I write and ponder these analyses, I have to think about whether education is powerless in the face of such global 'cataclysms', whether it is already too late. While I have no confidence that people have natural goodness, I have to hang on to the idea that sanity or pragmatic self-interest will prevail. Education must attack and question the legitimations or rationalisations for revenge, which justify leaders and those who vote for them – in democratic states at least – blindly engaging in tit-for-tat ventures. It will need to do this within its own processes of treating 'wrong', not just through political education. Therefore we need to look firstly at how revenge is sanctioned, and what drives it.

## Legitimations for revenge

I look at three aspects of how revenge is seen to be justified, and how it becomes deep-seated in our search for 'justice'. These are religious calls for 'blood'; histories and myths of blame; and honour and shame.

## Religion and blood

Buddhism rejects violence – as does Jainism even more – and the Dalai Lama is very well aware of the spirals of revenge:

> If we use violence in order to reduce disagreements and conflict, then we must expect violence every day. Furthermore, it is actually impossible to eliminate disagreements through violence. Violence only brings even more resentment and dissatisfaction. (2001)

Other religions are less cautious, and can be openly bloodthirsty. In talking of the sanctioning of Christian homophobia, Michele Kahn (2006) quotes Leviticus 20:13: 'If a man also lie with mankind, as he lieth with a woman, both of them have committed an abomination: they shall surely be put to death. Their blood shall be upon them'.

Blood and bloodshed then are both symbolic and real. Ruthven (2004) cites the case of Baruch Goldstein, an American educated physician who opened fire in a Muslim prayer hall in Hebron in February 1994, killing at least 29 worshippers, including children. He became a hero for a group of recent settlers, and the Israeli government allowed his funeral cortege to pass through the streets of Jerusalem. A rabbi, Israel Ariel, commended Goldstein in his eulogy as a 'holy martyr' who from now on would act as the settlers' intercessor in heaven.

> Goldstein heard the cry of the land of Israel, which is being stolen from us day after day by the Muslims. He acted to relieve that cry of the Land ... The Jews will inherit the land not by any peace agreement, but only by shedding blood. (quoted in Ruthven, p162)

Mark Steel is wonderful on the lunacy of the laws to protect religious hatred (of which more in the next chapter), pointing out that God could actually be indicted under the law. One of the ten commandments begins 'You shall have no other Gods before me ... for I, the Lord your God am a jealous God, punishing the children for the sins of the fathers to the third and fourth generations'. Steel recounts how he once went to a Pentacostal service which began with a vast and joyous sing-a-long, with the words highlighted on a big screen. 'So 800 people joined in with the opening verse 'Our Lord loves us dearly/He kills all his enemies/la la la la la'. (2004:39)

Allah, too, is seen as vengeful. Manji cites the imam of Al-Aqsa mosque, Sheikh Anu Sneina, who in interview with Bruce Feiler, stressed Islam's presumed perfection. 'In London-honed English, he told Feiler that 'you must follow the last prophet' whom God has sent. Otherwise 'you'll die' under God's blowtorch, just as millions of Jews had been 'grilled alive' with divine sanction by Hitler' (p43).

The worry for Irshad Manji and others is that this view is actually mainstream, unlike the apocalyptic Christians or Jews who are a small minority.

> In trying to answer how I reconcile my Muslim faith with the barbaric lashing of a rape victim, I concluded that I couldn't reconcile them with breezy confidence. I couldn't glibly say, as I've heard so many Muslim feminists do, that the Qu'ran itself guarantees justice. I couldn't cavalierly say that those whacko Nigerian jurists who apply Sharia law have sodomised my transparently egalitarian religion. The Qu'ran is not transparently egalitarian for women. It's not transparently anything except enigmatic. With apologies to Noam Chomsky, it's Muslims who manufacture consent in Allah's name. The decisions we make on the basis of the Qu'ran aren't dictated by God; we make them of our own free will.
>
> Sounds obvious to a mainstream Christian or Jew, but it's not obvious to a Muslim who's been raised to believe – as most of us have – that the Qu'ran lays it all out for us in a 'straight path', and that our sole duty, and right, is to imitate it. This is a big lie. Do you hear me? A big, beard-faced lie. (2004:47)

I am reminded of a newspaper report of a schoolgirl in the UK who had recently converted to Islam. She was delighted that everything was set out for you. The chilling phrase for me was when she said 'You don't have to keep weighing things up'.

Manji also discusses the post 9/11 mantra from Muslims that the Qu'ran makes it absolutely clear when jihad can and cannot be pursued, and how the terrorists unquestionably broke the rules.

> You know the chapter and verse that's cited as 'unequivocal'? It actually bestows wriggle room. Here's how it reads: 'We laid it down for the Israelites that whoever killed a human being, except as punishment for murder or other villainy in the land, shall be regarded as having killed all mankind'. Sadly, the clause starting with 'except' can be deployed by militant Muslims to fuel their jihads. (2004:54)

The critiques of the cultural base to human rights and to human rights education are therefore an issue, and alternatives such as the Universal Islamic Declaration of Human Rights warrant examination. This Declaration (1981) at first glance appears very similar to the Universal Declaration of Human Rights (UDHR) – with articles on the right to life, freedom, equality, justice, education, protection of minorities etc. There would however be major distinctions. The source of human rights is seen to be the Divine Law, and all references to 'the Law' – as in being equal before it – are to Shari'ah Law. There would be a right to a fair trial, but definition of a crime and its punishment shall be awarded according to Shari'ah Law – not national or State law. Articles that would not be found in UDHR are such as 'The Right to Protection of Honour and Reputation (Article VIII), whereby 'every person has the right to protect his honour and reputation against calumnies, groundless charges or deliberate attempts at defamation and blackmail'. This does not specify how such honour would be protected, but one can only assume it would not be in contradistinction to other articles such as the right to life – although the notion that no one shall be exposed to injury or death 'except under the authority of the Law' might offer some different interpretations.

Most Muslim scholars would entirely reject the claim that Islamic injunctions can require or sanction or even tolerate terrorism, although, according to Tariq Ali, many of them would argue that a person would not cease to be a Muslim even if he were to interpret his duties differently, as long as he adhered to the core Islamic beliefs and practices. I suppose we would ask what was 'core' and whether this included non-violence. Tariq Ali cheekily comments 'Meanwhile, 'good' Muslims are being paraded on TV arguing that violence is not advocated in the Qu'ran and therefore the bombers are wrong. The implication here is that, if the Qu'ran permitted them, such actions would be fine...' (2005:86). So the question is, where do we get our rules for behaviour and response to others' behaviour? What is there to avenge, and for how long? These are school questions too.

### Histories and myths of blame

Ed Husain's God was not loving and caring, but a God who was full of vengeance, a legislator, a controller, a punisher. Husain relates how his Saudi students were compelled to study Islamic Culture at university, often memorising such books. The texts had entire pages devoted to explaining to undergraduates that all forms of Islam except Wahhabism were deviation. There were prolonged denunciations of nationalism, communism, the West, the Jews, free mixing of sexes, observing birthdays, even Mother's Day. Readers were warned about the evil effects of plurality and political parties, democracy and a parliamentary system. In like vein, a current website in UK, *Islambase.co.uk*, also warns of the 'tools' which the *kuffar* use 'to promote integration with them', tools of the democratic system, citizenship, the education system, national curriculum, law and order, media and fashion. An author of the Islamic Culture series was Mohamed Qutb, teacher to Osama bin Laden and brother of the founder of Islamism, Syed Qutb. Bin Laden's idiosyncratic jihad includes the violent overthrow of Arab governments, an idea first expressed by Syed Qutb from his prison cell in Cairo.

> The *Islamic Culture* series catalogues Muslim history and the recent decline in Arab imperial glory by doing what most Islamists do: blaming others. Islamists of various

shades (including wahhabis and jidahis) are masters of blaming the Zionists, the Jews, the British, French, and Italian imperialists, the Turks and the Freemasons, but never themselves'. (Husain, 2007:252)

Al-Qaeda documents claim God has sanctioned the punishment on the west, with the right to destroy not just villages and cities but 'the economy of those who have robbed our wealth and to kill civilians of the country which has killed ours' (quoted in *Sunday Times* 17 November, 2002, p2). From this and *Islamic Culture* we see not just religion as such but territory and imperialism as drivers for action, plus blame of others who have denied wealth and power.

Irshad Manji quotes a Palestinian writing in the *Journal of Palestine Studies* who returned to Gaza after years away. He found a society 'blanched of honesty', grasping at every excuse to vent old grievances.

> There were the newly whitewashed walls ... walls, which, only a few days later, after a Palestinian was killed by a stray Israeli bullet, were plastered with obituaries composed by all the known and obscure organisations claiming him as a hero and martyr and threatening terrible vengeance on his killers. Truth and the gleaming white walls were sacrificed, for it is certain that the victim belonged to none of those organisations. The thirst for martyrs is consuming, a dominant passion. (2004:108)

'Old grievances' are the clue here. Not all vengeful campaigns have a religious base. The fanaticism of the Tamil Tigers derives from its skewed interpretations of Marxist-Leninism, and now from intense nationalism. They claim adherence and financial support from a worldwide network of backers, reputedly 70 million in perhaps 40 countries. Whittaker talks of the significance of myth and tradition for the Tigers, a myth that proclaims that only revolutionary struggle can reassert group identity, restore inalienable rights and promote self-determination, regardless of cost. Yet the JVP party (Janatha Vimukthi Peranmuna) is or was also a revolutionary force in Sri Lanka, brutally trying to take over the government in 1989.

> People executed by the JVP were not only identified as government stooges, or as behaving in defiance of JVP authority, they were also presented as offending local moralities ... People killed by the JVP included rapists, seducers, thieves etc. The killing occasionally followed the course of longstanding village disputes and exhibited the passions of local enmities and the desire for revenge. (Kapferer, 1997 p182-3)

Such 'longstanding' disputes are typically part of the cycle, with long historical memories able to be invoked. I often draw on Kate Adie's insights into the Balkans:

It was an object lesson and I heard it over the years from Croats, Serbs, Bosnians and Kosovans. Everything grew out of history – the theft of a cow, the burning of a village, the driving out of hundreds of thousands from what they always thought of as home. The events of yesterday – the previous twenty-four hours, such a vital element in my journalistic tradition – were but a recent drop in the ocean in the mighty historical flow. How could you possibly talk of a few hours when centuries were clamouring to be heard? (Adie, 2002:250)

### Honour and shame

One disturbing aspect of retaliation is what has come to be called 'honour killings'. Among some Pushtuns of Afghanistan, a bride who does not bleed on her wedding night may be killed by her father or brothers (Ruthven, 2004). Brohi and Ajaib (2006) describe how in areas of tribal control in Pakistan, girls have been attacked or kidnapped from school premises or from outside schools to settle scores of tribal enmity. Girls have been kidnapped for revenge or ransom even from urban areas such as Karachi. In Layyah, Pakistani Punjab, a rejected suitor recently threw acid on a girl returning from school, a common punishment in Bangladesh too.

Irshad Manji recounts how she grappled with whether to bid goodbye to Islam, and whether there is something cardinal, something inextricably core, within Islam that makes it more rigid today than its spiritual siblings, Christianity and Judaism.

What disturbed me wasn't just the story of one Nigerian rape victim. Pick a Muslim country, any Muslim country, and the most brutal humiliations will grab you by the vitals. In Pakistan, an average of two women every day die from 'honour killings', often with Allah's name on the lips of the murderers. (2004:39)

Manji links all this to tribalism. Your honour is not yours alone; stepping out of line dishonours your kin and often your kind.

And maybe the desert personality of Islam is why a Muslim woman can be raped to compensate a dishonoured clan, even if that clan's honour was violated not by her but by someone else. Because a woman belongs to her family, raping her is shaming her family, making the woman a fitting pawn in family blood feuds. (p155)

While she knows that people will say: this is culture not religion, she asks the significant question of why it is so difficult to extricate from local customs, tribal customs, if there wasn't something profoundly tribal about Islam in the first place? 'Here the desert tribalism takes the act of closing ranks to a crushing level.'

Tariq Ramadan has got into trouble with fellow Muslims for speaking out against Islamic punishments such as cutting off hands for theft, stoning for adultery and the use of religion to oppress women. While the penalties are Qu'ranic, Ramadan (2006) argues that the conditions under which they were set are 'nearly impossible to re-establish' and 'almost never applicable' – which would fit with Manji's descriptions of tribalism. But he states that Islam is being used to degrade and subjugate women and men in certain Muslim societies; and that this literal and non-contextualised application of Shari'ah law is a betrayal of the teachings of Islam. I would want to know in what 'context' it is OK to stone women, but I must leave that to their own self-criticism.

As we saw Manji herself admitting, it is difficult to disentangle religion and culture, and other examples in the press indicate that honour killings are equally found in parts of Sikh culture in Pakistan. They should not be stereotyped as a Muslim phenomenon. Randa Abdel-Fattah, the writer of the novel *Does My Head Look Big In This?* about being a teenage Muslim girl in Australia deciding to wear the hijab, explained in an interview (Cassidy, 2006) that agents for the novel constantly asked:

> 'Is there an honour killing in it?' Every time you read a book about Muslims it's always either about the Saudi royal family, the Taliban or an honour killing. (p12)

Her book in contrast is about what to her is the average Muslim experience and being a normal teenager – rebellion, eating disorders, spots, smoking and alcohol. Ruthven too points out that

> 'honour killings' for alleged sexual misconduct by women are far from being limited to mountainous, tribal regions: they occur in many other parts of the world, and though Jordan, Egypt, Syria and Iraq furnish numerous examples, honour killings are far from being confined to Muslim countries. The culture of 'honour and shame' in which masculine honour and identity are predicated on female virtue, is also found in Catholic Spain and Sicily and the Orthodox Balkans. (Ruthven, 2004:107)

The interesting question is why this should be, and why it is not declining as a traditional practice. Brohi and Ajaib quote a father on the benefits of schooling: 'What is more important in society? My honour or her knowing where Yunaan (Greece) is?' They continue:

> Where girls and women are the object of collective honour, they are also repositories of culture and identity. Accessing the educational system leaves them susceptible to a range of perceived polluting influences which may threaten this culture and identity. Much resistance to girls' schooling stems from this belief. Religious clerics in Pakistan have taken to denouncing girls' education in their sermons, as

> endangering ideology, culture and identity. This has led to a new trend of rising violence against girls. In Karak recently, a cleric stood outside a school, publicly denouncing all girls entering the school as *fahaash* (vulgar, of loose character). In February 2004, six girls' schools were torched in the Diamer district in the Northern Areas. Another was blown up with a hand grenade ... the local authorities and police have placed the blame on orthodox mullahs. (Brohi and Ajaib, 2006:87)

Such extreme violence against women is thus explained by needing to protect both family and collective honour or culture. The family and family reputation become almost sacred, so that the behaviour – invariably of a woman – that is seen to undermine that reputation must be publicly repudiated. She is not just banished but must be disposed of, so that the family is not contaminated any more. There are strong links to witchcraft as well as blasphemy laws, where the reputation of God is seen to be challenged. But there is also the economic imperative:

> 'Honour' demands sacrificing your individuality to maintain the reputation, status and prospects of your husband, father and brothers. But to question this existence is to indicate that you're not communal property. (Manji, 2004:179)

So honour is closely bound up with male prospects and hence gender relations and female subordination.

In his chapter 'Controlling Women', Ruthven similarly quotes the views of anthropologists such as Anita Weiss: for example in Pakistan, while the men view their womenfolk as more capable than in the past, they also feel threatened by the potential of uncontrolled, educated and economically independent women to compromise their honour and therefore their status among other men. For Lebanon, Ruthven cites Michael Gilsenan's observation that *Sharaf*, the honour of person and family which is particularly identified with control of women's sexuality, is crucial to the public, social identity of men. I like Ruthven's conclusion to the chapter, about fundamentalisms not however being static:

> By formally accepting male authority when moving into public arenas formerly the preserve of males, fundamentalist women hope to soothe men's anxieties while quietly taking over their jobs. (p125)

Honour killings can therefore be tackled on legal and criminal grounds, ensuring they are classified as murder and, like rape, not allowing mitigation of 'provocation'. But what should the educational response be? Increasing the education of women appears in some ways to compound the problem, but no one except the Taliban and some orthodox mullahs would support cutting back female education. The direct approach would be for schools and other places of learning to raise the topic for discussion and treat it within a human rights framework, as argued later; indirectly, strategies would presumably have to include other mechanisms to restore male pride, and ensuring alternatives to status other than female ownership.

Yet the whole notion of shame is not just about male control over women: both boys and girls were seen in Victorian times – and still are? – to 'bring shame on the family' through some reckless behaviour, as in a Hardy novel. Deviant pupils are told they 'bring shame to the school'. The idea is to compound any guilt they might feel by projecting harm on to anyone or any institution surrounding them. One hears so often the litany of the teacher saying to the offending pupil 'You've let yourself down. You've let the school down. You've let your parents down.' I'm surprised they don't continue 'You've let Aston Villa down. You've let England down. You've let the prospect of a Middle East settlement down'. One can understand the logic in such an approach – that by seeing behaviour as reflecting on others whom they are close to, miscreants will be less likely to misbehave in the future. Yet in trying to think about reparation, the focus might more usefully be put on the victim of the offence and how any direct harm to them might be repaired, or avoided in the future. The problem with actions that are designated 'shameful' are that many are actually 'victimless crimes'. The various dress codes which offend does not actually harm anyone; yet there is an attempt at control by calling such dress 'shameful'. Shame is often more about image than it is about hurt. Chapter 6, in examining rights and responsibilities, looks at how children can be enabled – in the same way that they distinguish 'wants' and 'needs' – to distinguish responsibility for one's own actions from responsibility for others' response. This is a message often given to battered women or those subject to the obsession of co-dependants who threaten suicide if you leave them: you are not responsible for another's extremist and violent response.

## Schools and revenge

Robin Richardson (2004) begins his chapter on confronting Islamophobia in education with a narrative of how during the 2003 Iraq war a secondary school student in UK approached one of the staff:

> She was of Pakistani heritage, as was the member of staff. She was being teased, she told the teacher, by other students in the playground and on journey to and from school. 'We killed hundreds of your lot yesterday ... Saddam's your dad, you love him, don't you ... we're getting our revenge for what you Pakis did to us on 11 September...' The teacher asked if she had told her tutor. Yes, she had told her tutor, and her tutor had said: 'Never mind, it's not serious. It'll soon pass. You'll have to expect a bit of teasing at a time like this.' (p19)

Schools have certain tasks in examining revenge. As Gray points out 'It is not always because human beings act irrationally that they fail to achieve peace. Sometimes it is because they do not want peace ... Nothing is more human than the readiness to kill and die in order to secure a meaning in life' (2007:186). While killing and dying is not normally part of the school regime, revenge can be deeply satisfying – as well as being seen as normal. A core problem is that schools condone and use revenge in their punishment regimes – actions unrelated to the offence, such as detentions for rudeness, or in some countries, beating a child for being late or for giving the wrong answer. The message to children is that it is acceptable for the powerful to exact swift retribution. Even though much of the research indicates that teachers actually create more conflict by humiliating students (Leoni, 2005), they then act surprised if students are rude back, and crack down through an escalating series of punishments.

While not all sanctions would be seen as vengeful, violent punishment has a retaliatory feel. Violent reprisal can be sanctioned or even demanded by parents as 'correction', and both parents and teachers will use religious texts to justify such punishments for children. As amply noted in Clive Harber's book *Schooling as Violence* (2004), corporal punishment is rife in many countries and accepted as normal. From studying violence in a range of forms, Harber concludes that there is a direct link between schools as violent places and societies which condone or even celebrate aggression. Which came first? is the obvious reply. Yet violence in schools in the form of corporal punishment persists long after this has been officially outlawed and countries have signed the declaration on the rights of the child (Harber, 2004). In 2007 this still continues: in spite of the Supreme Court banning corporal punishment in 2000, a schoolboy in India died after a beating by his teacher for scribbling over the teacher's signature in his notebook; another from having to run endless laps of the school for being 15 minutes late (O'Connor, 2007).

In our action research in post-conflict Angola, we asked the children about their teachers. One said 'Our teacher is very good. He only hits us if we don't learn' (Davies, 2007). Considering some of the barriers to change, my report identified authoritarian forms of student discipline as one constraint:

> The change process did not seem to have altered the traditional forms of pupil discipline such as corporal punishment. In Tome, a control school, the parents said that they liked the teachers to take control, be given power to discipline children for bad behaviour. They wanted teachers to 'correct' it. Teachers should not be 'shy' to educate bad pupils, they should be free – 'educate' here being synonymous with beating. 'Parents used to get angry when teachers beat their children, but beating

is pedagogically one of the ways to correct bad behaviour. Parents do not investigate why, so they come to the school to complain'. One of the downsides therefore of increased teacher-parent communication is the agreed justification for corporal punishment and the collusion in this as educationally sound.

At Mahumbulo, a parent recounted how the teachers would hold a meeting with the parents to know why the students had not come and the parents did not know they had not come, finding they were collecting wild fruits on the way. Sometimes in these meetings, the parents advised the teacher to beat the students so that they became frightened, so they knew how to behave. The father would also beat them if they did not do their homework.

The Director, when asked whether they ever consulted pupils, said 'we do not consult children. We just consult their parents instead of them'.

I do not need to go into all the research on how violence begets violence and how children who experience violence in the home or at school are more likely to act violently towards others. Similarly, children and teachers in conflict societies will bring that into the school. Mansour (1996) referred to the 'Intifada generation', forced to be aggressive as the Israeli army invaded their daily lives, whether in the school, the home or in children's nightmares. As Mansour said, the pupils of today are simultaneously the young people of the Intifada, the same who just the day before were demonstrating and throwing stones at Israeli soldiers. But in conflict societies, the whole system may be predicated on violence. This does not exclude teacher education: Hitler achieved indoctrination into violence by taking over teacher education institutions, requiring teachers to swear an oath to train students in Nazi ideology and even taking over their professional organisations (Cairns, 1996).

A fascinating account of primary education in Afghanistan examined the curriculum funded by the US from 1984 to 1994, which developed textbooks for use in refugee camps. A 4th grade textbook contained the following question:

'The speed of a Kalashnikov bullet is 800 meters per second. If a Russian is at a distance of 3,200 meters from a mujahid, and that mujahid aims at the Russian's head, calculate how many seconds it will take for the bullet to strike the Russian in the forehead'. (Craig, 2000: 92-93)

When the Taliban took power in the wake of the Soviet withdrawal, the curriculum was implemented across the country – and continued even after the defeat of the Taliban after 2002, as well as continuing to be used in madrassahs in Pakistan (ICG, 2002). The 'hate' curriculum is discussed more in Chapter 6.

Here I reiterate the point that schools and countries that have renounced such curricula and corporal punishment may still be using methods of discipline which are equally counter-productive and based on antiquated ideas of how 'learning to behave' occurs. Epp and Watkinson's (1996) *Systemic Violence* is a classic book which revealed the 'complicity' of schools in Canada in supporting violence, dehumanisation and stratification. There are 'normalising' discourses, like the normalising discourses for revenge above. I often use this quotation:

> When a child forces another to do his or her bidding, we call it extortion; when an adult does the same thing to a child, it is called correction. When a student hits another student it is assault; when a teacher hits a child it is for the child's 'own good'. When a student embarrasses, ridicules or scorns another student it is harassment, bullying or teasing. When a teacher does it, it is sound pedagogical practice. (Epp, 1996:20)

The task is to replace normalising discourses of punitive measures with those that do not lead to cycles of escalation, and, for our concern in this book, do not teach or reinforce the idea that revenge is legitimate, whether by students, by teachers or by governments. Extremist behaviour has to be dealt with in the school, but not by extreme or retaliatory measures. Maud Blair (2000) states that:

> The connection between suspension, expulsion and the criminal justice system has been well demonstrated and needs to be part of the serious reflection that should take place when considering disciplinary measures against students. (p165)

She quotes a dean of an American urban school who compares his job to being a pilot on a hijacked plane. 'My job is to throw the hijacker overboard'. Blair continues:

> This school administrator adopts a language that constructs an image of children as terrorists who put the lives and liberty of other students at risk. Such a description ensures that consensus will be achieved on the sometimes extreme sanctions that are applied in schools. (p161)

The impending risk is what has been called the 'school to prison pipeline' (Fuentes, 2003). Such a direction would not fit the current UK *Every Child Matters* strategy which aims at well-being, safety and making a positive contribution to society.

This leads to a discussion of the alternative of restorative justice and its applicability in the educational context.

## Restorative justice

The opposite or alternative to revenge is restorative justice, sometimes called reparative justice. In legal terms, this is an attempt to refocus crime as a conflict between people, to bring together the people directly involved and to address the impact of an offence on the victim, the offender and the community. Unlike retribution, unlike the eye for an eye ideology, the theory of restorative justice has developed from utilitarianism which seeks the greatest good or greatest happiness for the greatest number. No more suffering should be inflicted; collaboration seeks to repair damage, giving the offender an opportunity to express remorse and make amends. It is often part of truth and reconciliation programmes, for example in South Africa, Rwanda and, more recently, Sierra Leone.

Wrapped up in decisions on the types of transitional justice bodies are questions of justice, impunity, accountability, reconciliation, memory, forgetting, forgiveness and vengeance, not to mention more tangible questions of political will and the support of the international community, as Minow (1998) well discusses. Hayner (2002) identifies five aims of Truth Commissions:

- to discover, clarify and formally acknowledge past abuses

- to respond to specific needs of victims

- to contribute to justice and accountability

- to outline institutional responsibility and recommend reforms

- to promote reconciliation and reduce conflict over the past.

This would have interesting applications to schools: if teachers are the victims of student disruption or violence, do the punishments meted out to students meet the teachers' needs? Do they meet the needs of other children? Does the acknowledgement of past abuses include teachers' treatment of students? Is institutional responsibility outlined as well as, or as opposed to, individual responsibility?

Such commissions or 'transitional justice bodies' are in themselves paying increasing attention to educational issues. Julia Paulson (2006) looks at the Sierra Leone Truth and Reconciliation Committee (SLTRC). Its work included the recommendations in 2004 that human rights education and SLTRC materials be incorporated into all levels of education, as well as outlawing corporal punishment and addressing gender imbalances. Paulson found, however, that this incorporation was patchy. Corporal punishment was discouraged, but evidence pointed to it continuing. With the support of UNICEF, a child-friendly version of the SLTRC had been produced for primary schools, but distribution of the primary and the secondary versions appeared to be erratic, as none of the schools she visited had copies.

> When I asked principals about human rights and peace education in their schools, one explained briefly how the rights and duties of the child are taught before going into a lengthy description of discipline practices in the school, listing the number of lashes doled out with the cane for different offences committed by pupils. (p345)

Even if the principles of truth and reconciliation were known in the school, it would seem that they were not put into practice in punishment regimes. There seemed little holistic understanding of the implications of the rights of the child. I return to this in the final chapter.

The '3Rs' of restorative justice outlined by Titus Alexander in his book on the *Citizenship School* (2001) are: recognition of the *reasons* behind the action and the needs driving the behaviour; the perpetrator takes *responsibility* for their actions and accepts they have done wrong; the perpetrator makes *reparations*, which might include restitution, restoration and reconciliation to settle differences. That's even more Rs, but they are all useful strategies – as long as they are understood and accepted.

The big question however is identification of 'the perpetrator' and of who committed 'the offence' – which links to the cycles of retribution outlined above. In the school equivalent to a war crime, if a child suddenly attacks a teacher with a knife, it might be quite legitimate to say that this child per-petrated an offence and should make some sort of reparation. However, much punishment in school is instigated at a far more mundane level and at some point in what is a whole series of perceived offences by both sides: a student saunters in late, the teacher attempts to regain control by humiliating the student, the student responds angrily, the teacher responds even more angrily and so on. The student's perception is that the teacher started it by their 'extreme' and uncalled for response; the teacher's is that the student was the cause of disruption. In a situation of unequal power, the taking of respon-sibility is not equally allocated. Another school-based problem links to the generalised 'offence' such as a uniform infringement or lateness, whereby a victim to whom one might make reparations cannot be established.

## Tolerance, acknowledging wrongs and forgiveness

Therefore we need to look more closely at the whole question of past wrongs and how these can be dealt with in education. In some countries there is also the need to teach about conflict and past wrongs committed by different social groups – groups who may be represented within the school. Should we just tell children – or teachers – to 'be tolerant' of others whom they perceive to have wronged them? Sigal Ben-Porath's analysis is useful. In her book *Citizenship Under Fire* (2006) she is clear that the notion of cultural 'tolerance' fails to be applicable in the field of international reconciliation, particularly to the effort of overcoming past and present conflicts – say about territory – through education. Ben-Porath comes closer to the notion of 'recognition' rather than tolerance. This means introducing all members of society to the 'unique features of subgroups with whom they share the public space', in that our identity is partly shaped by recognition or its absence, often by mis-recognition of others. I would have problems with the latent stereotyping of 'uniqueness' (as discussed in Chapter 2) and the hardening of identities, but I can see the point. Ben-Porath tells how the multicultural demand for recognition and for the acknowledgement of past wrongs is evident in the bulk of literature pertaining to Native Americans and African Americans, aboriginal cultures and Canadian First Nations. But as she points out, examining the consequences of past wrongs is far from claiming that what is required is an economy of an eye for an eye. Looking at ways to understand the past does not ideally entail calculations of blame and contestation on the role of the victim.

> A racially just American society cannot be expected to first punish all those responsible for or those who profited from slavery, and not only because it is a matter of the past. For Israelis and Palestinians to rebuild the Middle East as a peaceful region, there can be no realistic expectation to calculate all the various ways in which each side victimised, terrorised or oppressed the other. What the requirement for acknowledgement does mean is that all sides need to look at their common history and their respective current conditions from a more complex perspective than is usually available to them. (p98)

Ben-Porath considers education to be the proper institution to undertake the task of acknowledgment, of getting over denial and the focus on 'deficiencies', for it is the first formal institution that all (future) citizens encounter. As well as the influence on individuals, it has a crucial 'declaratory' role in the social and political life of the community. One fundamental way of publicly expressing acknowledgement is the studying of past wrongs in state schools (which in my previous chapter was argued also for religion). In Ben-Porath's view of 'expansive education', acknowledgement is also about allowing former adversaries to hold on to their separate, often conflicting versions of the conflict and of other aspects of their histories. It is not so crucial to get compatible accounts, although these should not be allowed to be self-congratulatory or demeaning. This links to what Ben-Porath calls 'reverse patriotism' – not invalidating patriotic feelings, but not just doing mythic stories of heroism and triumphalist nation building. 'Rather it encourages the students and teachers to understand and identify with their nation (or group) with its complex history, to own it, and thus be willing to amend what needs to be amended (p103). Ben-Porath is aware of the challenges of all this, of consciously reconstructing collective memories, and of the whole problem of forgiveness.

Forgiveness presupposes an identification of the other as guilty; this other must also acknowledge his or her guilt or wrongdoing in order for the forgiveness to reverberate in the public sphere. Michael Ignatieff (1997) asserts that a public acknowledgement of violence, oppression or atrocities accompanied by an appropriate apology can establish the sole basis necessary for the evasion of war. This seems a bit optimistic but, on the other hand, it is rarely tried. Ben-Porath is very good on the difficulties of 'unconditional' pure forgiveness which expects nothing, tracing its religious roots in the work of Jacques Derrida, or Hannah Arendt, and pointing out that this type of forgiveness, albeit noble, bears little relevance beyond the religious and interpersonal context. In the public or political sphere, forgiveness has to be linked to the restoration of justice for it not to happen again. She looks at three models of forgiveness – the unconditional; the strict, which asks for repentance of the wrongdoer; and the 'relaxed' or 'no problem' model. The latter is the one most commonly used in educational settings, particularly with young children. We are to teach children to forgive easily and show a generous acceptance of those who have caused hurt. But as Ben-Porath points out, this is more of a social nicety than a duty, deriving from the norms of politeness, and assuming some sort of equality between the two sides. It would be irrelevant to serious crimes and communal conflict, and is not translatable to different cultures.

> If we teach that one must always work on one's internal ability to grant forgiveness, mainly in the hardest of circumstances when she suffered the worst harms, we place the burden of reconciliation solely or mainly on the victim, in addition to replicating the power relations that made her victim. (p107)

Ben-Porath talks of other models therefore, focusing more on the offender than the victim. In the history curriculum, 'learning to regard ourselves as blameworthy from some other group's perspective can be a sobering educational experience. More often than not, schools focus on 'us' as a morally blameless entity' (p109). It will be interesting to see how schools cope with the Iraq war when it becomes a formal part of the history curriculum.

## Conclusion

In summary, extremist action is often linked to the desire to take revenge and to blame. This can lead to spirals of retribution, and is never good for conflict resolution. The justifications for revenge as a reaction to a perceived wrong come from sacred texts, but also from notions of ancient historical grievances or from the need to protect family or community honour. Education has a key role in challenging revengeful dispositions in two parallel ways:

- Open acknowledgement of, and learning about past wrongs and different perceptions of wrongs that one's own groups, countries or religions have inflicted, but without counting up blame

- Modelling restorative justice through reconciliatory processes such as peer mediation, as well as students mediating between teachers and students; and having mechanisms for reparation of acknowledged wrong that are closely linked to the needs of the wronged – which would also enable scrutiny of who exactly has been wronged and what constitutes an offence in a school.

This question of offence leads nicely into the next chapter.

# 5

## Free speech, offence, humour and satire

The Danish cartoons episode has become a hallmark of the dilemma of free speech. Repression of humour or of freedom of expression is a sign of authoritarianism, yet can people legitimately claim offence from satire or cultural representations? There are a number of educational tasks to be examined in this chapter: when and how to allow freedom of expression, especially extremist expression; when educational practices cause offence; and how to deal with extremist responses to such offence.

From the days of blasphemy laws and swingeing punishments for laughing at one's monarch, we have had periods of greater freedom. Yet we may be returning to the War on Sacrilege. This comprises not just threats to writers such as Salman Rushdie, but actual murder, for example of the Dutch film maker Theo van Gogh. Various opera and theatre productions are being cancelled because of threats by religious extremists or fundamentalists, whether Christian, Sikh or Muslim. One example was the suppression of Gurpreet Kaur Bhatti's play about a rape in a gurdwara. Timothy Garton Ash calls these ideologues '*fanatiques sans frontières*', and worries that the spaces of free expression, even in old-established liberal democracies, are being eroded. What happens eventually is 'self-censorship' because of fear of threat, not the threat itself. 'But self-censorship can also flow from a well-intentioned notion of multicultural harmony, on the lines of 'you respect my taboo and I'll respect yours' – what I've described ... as the tyranny of the group veto' (Garton Ash, 2006:23).

Rageh Omaar has a slightly different position on the free speech and extremism issue. He talks of Ayaan Hersi Ali, the Somali born woman who became a member of the Dutch parliament. From being a devout Muslim, she 're-made' herself to being vehemently anti-Islam. 'Her university experience showed the first signs of 'the zealotry of a new convert, rejecting a set of beliefs which has previously defined their identity, and embracing everything to which those beliefs seem diametrically opposed' (p48). Later she rejected separate schools for migrants and recommended curtailing immigration. With the populist right wing politicians, she mounted virulent attacks on Islam as a faith and as a culture which she argued was incapable of integrating into Western liberal society. She collaborated with Theo van Gogh in the film *Submission*, designed to show Islam as inherently brutal, and violent towards women. In a famous interview, she said of the Prophet Muhammad that 'measured by our standards he is a pervert. A tyrant'. She received death threats, but was awarded various prizes for freedom and democracy, and featured as *Time Magazine's* one of the 100 most influential people on earth. But Omaar argues:

> Freedom of speech is a principle that cannot be compromised or given up. Yet writers and publications who correctly support Ayaan Hersi Ali's defence of this principle seem unable or unwilling to distinguish between defending the principle of free speech and acting as the handmaidens of hate and the dehumanisation of a community ... If people in prominent positions set out to provoke and offend, why are they so surprised when people feel provoked and offended?
>
> The promotion of the views of Ayaan Hersi Ali stands in terrible contrast to the abandonment of the faceless and nameless victims of the violence and hate directed at Muslims. When Nick Griffin, the leader of the British National Party, urges people to decide whether Britain 'should become an Islamic Republic or a democracy' is he so very different from Ayaan Hersi Ali? Yet we condemn one as a fascist and we promote the other as a pioneer of free speech and a representative of the Muslim community in the West. (p59)

For Omaar, the characters of Yassin Hassan Omar (one of the July 21 bombers) and Ayaan Hersi Ali are more similar than one might imagine: one absolutely rejects the West, the other utterly rejects Islam. 'With equal ardour they both reject the only thing there is: hope' (p60).

## Free speech in educational sites

Tackling these differentiations presents a big educational task. The collection by Barry van Driel (2004) on *Confronting Islamophobia* raises the question of the balance between the right to free speech against the freedom to be protected against discrimination. In the Introduction he recounts an occasion when high school students were debating whether the neo-Nazi party NPD (Nationaldemokratische Partei Deutschlands) should be banned in Germany. More than one student expressed the view that what the party said about the

Muslim threat was justified and should be spoken out; the three Muslim students were silenced; the remaining students (and the teacher) were by-standers, not 'coming to the defence' of their Muslim classmates. But what should the role of the school and the teacher be? Not to permit the expression of potentially harmful views? To intervene? To defend those likely to be offended? I present some relevant and salutary case studies.

A fascinating account by Gereluk (2007) looks at various cases of students in American schools being expelled because of expressing their political and social views, either through the clothing they wore or their actions. Interestingly, the US has not focused on banning religious symbolic clothing, as in France or Turkey, but is increasingly attempting to control other forms of dress – and in some cases imposing uniform. Gereluk traces the difference between various 'rulings'. One was in 2003 on a boy who wore a T shirt to school with a picture of George Bush on the front that read 'International Terrorist'. The school insisted he remove it or go home, for fear the shirt would cause 'disruption' amongst students. In 2004, a student similarly wore T shirts with a peace sign, anarchy symbols, an upside down US flag and an anti-war quote from Albert Einstein. When the student tried to defend his right under freedom of expression, the administrator said this right did not apply to students. Both cases were overturned when taken to court.

In 1965, in a landmark ruling about students wearing black armbands to protest against Vietnam, the judges had noted that 'undifferentiated fear or apprehension of disturbance is not enough to overcome the right to freedom of expression'. Later cases however have ruled in favour of the school, for example, when a boy was suspended for drawing a confederate flag in maths class, with the court acknowledging that with overwhelming evidence of growing racial tensions in the district, the curtailment of free speech was a necessary action in keeping law and order. Much seems to hang on the interpretation of the *potential* of an act or expression of clothing to cause disturbance.

Conversely, compulsory uniform has been allowed by the courts on the grounds that the school board's interests in improving student behaviour outweighed the students' right to freedom of expression – and this is in spite of the lack of any evidence on the effectiveness of uniform policies on student behaviour or academic achievement. Small scale empirical studies have suggested that students who wish to engage in delinquent behaviour such as fights, assaults, shoplifting, vandalism or joyriding will do so whether a uniform policy is in place in schools or not. Yet as Gereluk comments, 'What is happening is that the parameters for what is deemed offensive or potentially disruptive has widened at the school board's discretion' (p12).

The Donnelly and Hughes (2006) study of Israel and Northern Ireland found similar difficulties dealing with symbols in what people wore. Some Northern Ireland students were wearing Celtic or Rangers shirts under their school uniforms as cultural and political expression. Teachers and governors agreed they would ignore this behaviour. Yet

> although this response is understandable it could have the potential to fuel sectarian tendencies; pupils remain convinced that cultural symbols are displayed only as an act of defiance, intimidation or prejudice and are never afforded the opportunity of understanding the real cultural significance of such artefacts. (p509)

The implication is that there should at least be discussion rather than disregard.

Orlenius (2007) raised an interesting case regarding a student in a Swedish upper secondary school who was a Nazi sympathiser and member of an established Nazi group. Sven wrote Nazi catchwords on a test, and he involved friends who met not only at his house but also at lunchtime in school. All the staff and the Local Board of Education agreed he should be suspended, as a threat against their values. Orlenius then asked 120 student teachers whether they agreed with this decision, which raised significant issues about tolerance, respect, freedom of speech and rights. 'Tolerance' related to what extent teachers would permit others' right to beliefs and opinions and their right to express their ideas, even if these were contrary to the democratic aims outlined in the guidelines in the national core curriculum. The solid majority of student teachers agreed that Sven was a 'threat against democracy', saying for example 'School should be like a free zone, rid of racist attitudes'. Sven was seen to forfeit his right to be there, as he did not live according to the stated rules; Nazi ideas were not seen to belong in a school where laws and the curriculum emphasised the equal value of all human beings. The implications were that nobody – students or staff – should be exposed to the risk of being offended; the school should be cleaned of anti-democratic attitudes; attitudes like that were racial agitation; Sven contributed to an unsafe environment; and Sven had a negative influence on his classmates.

Orlenius runs through some of the opposing reactions – that the student could be fined or reported to the police for violence and racist attitudes, but not denied attending school; or that efforts should be applied to enable other students to stand up against him, or that those who were offended should be helped. 'Arrange intellectual discussions where hopefully these ideas will be rejected by other students. You can't hush up somebody's opinion; it can only be resisted by good arguments.' Interestingly, there was no indication of violence by Sven, and it is not clear in what way other students were offended. In the real situation at the school, none of the students reported bullying or grave threats. Orlenius made several heretical points:

> According to our definition of tolerance Sven could actually be seen as the tolerant one *if* he does not physically or mentally offend the others. In that case a racist is tolerant if he or she dislikes an attitude but does not act in an inappropriate or un-justified way ... And is it more eligible and sufficient that Sven through his own critical thinking and consideration maintains his ideas than it is that he becomes a good democrat through indoctrination by the school? (pp 9-10)

So there are both philosophical questions of freedom of speech and practical questions of the effects of repression or exclusion of ideas. While sensitivity to context and to the make-up of the student population is appropriate, I would argue that student ideas and ideals should be permitted, and indeed exploited, to provide the basis for debate. Students have to experience real proponents of ideas, not just the moral dilemmas set out in books. Practically, of course, the suspension was unlikely to reform a Sven character. As one student teacher rightly pointed out when arguing for dialogue instead, 'By suspending Sven he will think that the others try to destroy what he is building up. Then his hatred grows even more and also against school, which also can cause destruction at the school' (p10). This was indeed the case in the study mentioned in the previous chapter of the far right boys who felt attacked by the school.

What then of 'zero-tolerance'? In the US this was mainly started in 1994 by the zero tolerance against weapons in school and the Gun-Free School Act, but it has now been applied very much to racism and bullying. But there is a problem about applying the concept and attendant policy to everything faintly nasty or unwelcome, such as swearing, and it may need to be more selectively applied. Certainly no school will ever need to tolerate anything which threatens the physical security of students or staff. Neither will it tolerate behaviours which threaten mental health, such as bullying and the more recent cyberbullying. However, racist *attitudes* are not in themselves harmful. It is when a person with racist views acts to harm others as a direct result of those views that zero tolerance kicks in. Otherwise, in the interests of dialogue and surfacing of the views that are out there in society, a racist view could be tolerated or even taken advantage of.

At higher education level, an interesting discussion is found in Thomas and Bahr's chapter 'Faith and Reason' (2008), which looks at the role and responsibility of HE regarding the changing role of religion in American public life. They point out how religion appears on campuses regardless of whether it is formally on the curriculum, not just students demanding exemptions based on their belief, but

> accusations of indoctrination and discrimination by students against faculty for behaviour that students view as 'liberal' or biased toward a secular views; parents and legislators challenging assignments or academic programming that offend their religious views; student blogs on the out-of-class speech of their professors; religiously-affiliated high schools suing universities to force them to accept credit for courses that use textbooks that place 'God's word above science'; and concerns over the distinction between 'sincerely held religious beliefs' and sham excuses. (2008, forthcoming)

As the authors point out, these are matters of academic freedom, of who can teach, what should be taught, how university property is used and who decides. They ask, what happens when a student refuses to study a particular text, citing her right to the free exercise of her religion? How should a university respond to the faculty member who teaches the Apocalypse as part of a history class? What should a professor do if a student refuses to engage another in class, claiming religious reasons? Thomas and Bahr set out the limits on academic freedom – that lecturers cannot exploit or coerce students, or discriminate; and they have to be competent:

> A geography teacher cannot deny the existence of Israel ... Professors can ask controversial questions or unpopular questions and can employ provocative teaching methods, but they cannot cross a line and indoctrinate. Students are not entitled to not be offended; they are, however, entitled to not be humiliated or harassed. (2008, forthcoming)

The last sentence is the key one. If I take offence at something you say, is that my problem or yours? And do I have the right to take offence at second hand about, say, a criticism of a political or religious leader, a movement? This often overlaps – 'I am offended' and 'this is offensive' are mooted as the same thing. Before looking specifically at offence in schools, a brief examination of the actual legal position may be warranted.

## Legal initiatives and rights regarding free speech

Much legal work derives from the various Articles in conventions such as the Universal Declaration of Human Rights, specifically Article 19 on the right to freedom of opinion and expression, including freedom to hold opinions without interference. The question is always whether this could contradict the right to security and the right not to be subjected to 'degrading treatment', nor to 'attacks on honour and reputation'. Children have the right to express an opinion on matters that affect them (Article 12 of the Convention of the Rights of the Child), although this does not yet appear in every country's national or educational legislation.

The debates occur on when there should be restrictions on communication rights. Baxi's view is that participation rights and duties rely on freedom of expression, and they entail a duty *not* to criminalise speech except in the rarest of situations.

> At the same time, the underlying ethic of participation forbids the crime of silence in the face of massive and flagrant violations of human rights, at home and abroad, on the part of individuals and groups ... The notion that the right to speak also includes the right not to speak is fatal to the logic of participatory rights, except in circumstances where the right to silence is an aspect of human rights, as in the case of the right not to incriminate oneself. (1998:102-3)

Hence the right to free speech must entail an equal duty to hear, listen and respond.

As Dimitrijevic (1998) pointed out, permissible restrictions on rights treaties are not used as a means to protect peace, but primarily to protect the interests of the nation state – on the grounds of prevention of disorder, or preventing disclosure of confidential information.

> Such a collection of grounds appears to offer more protection to the military and patriotic establishment, with its insistence on secrecy, territorial integrity and its glory and reputation, than to interests of peace and peace activists, who can be easily blamed for acting contrary to national interest. (p55)

A further question is freedom of speech versus freedom of religious belief. There has been significant debate about the Resolution of the United Nations Commission on Human Rights called *Combating Defamation of Religions*. This started out as 'defamation of Islam', in the face of growing Islamophobia and association of Islam with terrorism, and was proposed by countries of the Organisation of Islamic Countries (OIC). It was then broadened to defamation of religion generally. The International Humanist and Ethical Union (IHEU) argues the Resolution is 'unnecessary, flawed and morally wrong'. While freedom of religion is an unalienable right of every human being, the significant point is that these freedoms are vested in the *individual*, not the group. It is individuals, believers and non-believers, who have rights, not religions.

Also, it has become a fashion to style every criticism of religion as hate speech, specially in the case of Islam. 'Islamophobia' is being used as a blanket term to cover both criticism of Islam and hatred of Muslims. It is used by Muslim leaders to demonise even those who express legitimate concerns about any aspect of Islamic practice, such as the stoning of women for adultery, by equating such criticism with hatred of Muslims. (IHEU, 2007:3)

What is happening through this resolution are attempts to apply internationally, and in a different form, the blasphemy laws that are in force in many countries which are pushing the resolution. It actually threatens freedom of religion as well as freedom of speech, as the expression of one set of religious beliefs could be interpreted as defamation of another's, as apostasy. Freedom of religion is about the right to practice, and does *not* include the right *not* to have one's religious feelings or beliefs challenged or criticised – which actually would be at the heart of religious reform and social progress. There is no right, nor no freedom not to be offended – which confirms Thomas and Bahr's statement above.

Maxim Grinberg, a international lawyer, also points out how the Resolution did not protect the rights of individuals to choose or change their religions, did not prohibit state-sponsored educational systems that taught prejudice against non-Islamic religions and failed to criticise defamation of religions other than Islam. India called the Resolution 'obscurantist and self-serving' (Grinberg, 2006:5). It is also unnecessary, in that Article 4 of the International Convention on the Elimination of All Forms of Racial Discrimination already requires States to forbid not only the advocacy of hatred, but 'all ideas based on racial superiority or hatred, and the provision of assistance to racist activities'. IHEU make the significant point that 'There are deeper moral issues because a religion that needs the power of a state and the threat of punishment for criticism loses its persuasiveness and its moral character' (2007:5).

It was significant that the European Court of Human Rights overruled Turkish courts that convicted and sentenced a lawyer to jail for publishing a book and article criticising Turkish policy against Kurds. According to Turkey, publications containing the words 'Kurds' and 'Kurdistan' constituted separatist propaganda. The European court recognised that Article 10 of the European Convention on Human Rights on protection of reputation did not apply to political expression or debate on matters of public interest. 'The Court explained that freedom of expression constituted one of the essential foundations of a democratic society. Even expressions that offend, shock, or disturb are protected' (Grinberg, 2006:9). Turkish authorities had failed to have a sufficient regard for the public's interest to be informed of a different perspective on the policies of Turkey towards the Kurdish people. From the perspective of my book, the right to competing information is an important part of challenging absolutist thinking.

The promotion of the tradition of *ijtihad*, or independent reasoning in Islam (discussed more in the next chapter) talks of the necessity of assuring freedom of expression in order to permit the open exchange of ideas (Smock, 2004). The 2003 Arab Human Development report remarks that self-censorship has become a deeply rooted aspect of intellectual and civil society in the region, in large part due to ambiguous laws regarding freedom of speech that a government may invoke to prosecute and silence an individual or organisation perceived as threatening to the state (Zaki, 2005). These factors support Gesink's (2006) assertion that 'there exists a tension between an intellectual culture promoting ijtihad and a bureaucratic demand for acceptance of hierarchical authority' (p344). Yet as Grinberg points out, criticism of religious or social norms is consistent with international law, especially when it is critical of norms that are contrary to civilised norms of behaviour. Interestingly, the law is that criticism of government or public officials is based on value judgements that are not susceptible to being proven false, and hence not capable of being defamatory.

One problem is the ringfencing of religion as having some sort of special protection. In the trial of Abu Hamza for inciting violence, his defence stated – accurately – that many of the offending passages in his sermon consisted of quotes from the Qu'ran. They argued, implicitly, that if it is in a religious book, it cannot be condemned. For religion, there is also the constant claim to parity with anti-racism and anti-sexism, in terms of discrimination. But there is a key difference: the religious choose their faith. We do not choose our skin colour nor our biological sex. But people of faith could in theory leave that faith tomorrow. And if they choose to remain, and choose to follow others' edicts, then people must be free to critique such choices.

## Giving and taking offence

Does this legal framework help then in what constitutes offence? As with sexual harassment, it would be important to be able to show that something has genuinely injured and distressed a person, to the extent that this hinders the capacity to work or study. What also happens however, is that people claim offence o*n behalf of others* – usually God, but sometimes all women or all ethnic minorities or all people with disabilities... If it is held to offend God, this becomes blasphemy.

This last point is the key one which surrounds all the others, the distinction between claiming offence and being personally humiliated. In educational contexts, in challenging what one sees as an unreasonable aspect of a faith, 'the trick is to do so in ways that do not denigrate the student, religion in general, or the religion with which the student is affiliated' (Thomas and Bahr, 2008:7). This is easier said than done, particularly if students claim, as with the Danish cartoons, that they are personally humiliated when their God or the God's writings are mocked or challenged. I recall that this was what we were supposed to do as feminists – when stereotypes of females were used in meetings, when sexist language was used, we were supposed to say 'I feel offended by that remark/usage/assumption' – that is, the personal is political, and vice versa. In fact, such a statement about offence is not personal; it is actually saying 'I represent not just myself but the female race in general, and I am taking offence on behalf of others here'. Such 'offence' is strategically quite useful, and we found that if enough of us were boring in meetings, always drawing attention to sexist usage, bristling with indignation, the culture gradually did change – together of course with codification in the form of written guidelines and policies. So is there a difference? I think there is. As feminists, we were objecting mainly to exclusion or to automatic stereotyping. We were not objecting if challenging questions around gender were raised. On the contrary. It was mainly the invisibility of women altogether. And we could cope with the sexist jokes, because there were plenty of reverse ones. I have a lovely volume, given to me by a male friend, called *The Little Book of Stupid Men*.

> Why did the stupid man get so excited after he finished his jigsaw puzzle in only 6 months? *Because on the box it said 'From 2-4 years'*.

> How do you save a stupid man from drowning? *Take your foot off his head.*

But the comparison between gender interests and religious interests is a seriously useful one, and helps in drawing the fine lines – such as between fact and belief. Gender inequality can be evidenced; belief in a supernatural being cannot. Hence it would be legitimate to claim religious discrimination – as with sex discrimination – if there were evidence that a person did not get a job or acceptance into higher education because of their professed beliefs. It is *not* legitimate to claim offence because someone believes something different from you and expresses that belief. Unless it harms you, it is *not* legitimate to claim offence if someone behaves in a way in which you yourself would not behave. If men want to get into serious male bonding at football matches and sing chants and get paralytically drunk, that's fine. If people want to spend Sundays or Fridays praying and genuflecting and listening to people telling them how they should behave, that's also fine. I cannot claim I do not want to sit next to them because they do these things and I would not do these things. Nor would I reject all men and all believers because of certain things that some men and some believers do, sometimes, on Tuesdays or when it's raining. Extremism is the inability to see and break down one's own and others' complex pieces of belief and behaviour into its different parts, complexities and contradictions. It is the ultimate stereotyping.

A discussion in *The Economist* in 2004 centred on whether to strengthen blasphemy laws to prevent films from offending Islam; or to insist more aggressively on liberal values. One commentator was of the view, 'there is no way you can appease Muslim radicalism ... if you go down that road, you will end up banning the sale of alcohol in the supermarkets ('A Civil war on terrorism', *Economist* Nov 25, 2004). This unknowingly foresaw Sainsburys allowing Muslim checkout staff who refuse to sell alcohol to opt out of handling customers' bottles, as reported in the *Sunday Times* in September 2007. They 'are told to raise their hands when encountering any drink at their till so that a colleague can temporarily take their place or scan items for them' (Foggo and Thompson, 2007). Some senior Islamic scholars have nonetheless condemned this practice, saying that Muslims who refused to sell alcohol were reneging on their agreements with the store, that it was 'over-enthusiasm' and showed a lack of professionalism and maturity. What is equally encouraging is that the *Sunday Times* felt able to publish a cartoon at the side of the article showing a Muslim behind the checkout with the 'Next Customer' sign replaced with 'Next Infidel'.

If we can laugh at such extremism, there is hope for it not to be taken too seriously or to spread. One does think, what next? Refusal to sell pork? Anything not halal? Bacon flavoured crisps? Yet this fracas was followed by the account of some Muslim medical students in the UK who refused to attend lectures or answer exam questions on alcohol-related or sexually transmitted diseases because they claimed it offended their religious belief (Foggo and Taher, 2007). This has extended to refusing to see patients who are affected by diseases caused by alcohol or sexual activity, or refusal to see patients of a particular gender. The GMC has not supported this, nor has the Muslim Council of Britain nor the Muslim Doctors and Dentists Association, but it is a trend to watch.

Dawkins perceives a widespread assumption, which nearly everybody in our society accepts – the non-religious included – that religious faith is especially vulnerable to offence and should be protected by an abnormally thick wall of respect, in a different class from the respect that any human being should pay to any other. He quotes a speech by Douglas Adams:

> Religion ... has certain ideas at the heart of it which we call sacred or holy or whatever. What it means is, 'Here is an idea or a notion that you're not allowed to say anything bad about; you're just not. Why not? – because you're not!'. If somebody votes for a party that you don't agree with, you're free to argue about it as much as you like; everybody will have an argument but nobody feels aggrieved by it. If somebody thinks taxes should go up or down you are free to have an argument about it. But on the other hand if somebody says 'I mustn't move a light switch on a Saturday, you say 'I respect that'. (p20)

Yet how deep is this respect? Mark Steel is particularly scathing about the actual hypocrisy by the government of the incitement to religious hatred proposals:

> The attitude seems to be that you shouldn't upset a Muslim by deriding his religion; if you want to upset one, the correct method is to demolish his city – as long as it's not likely to stir up hatred. After you've fired a cruise missile into his mosque and you're going to shoot the wounded, remember to take off your socks or you'll offend his faith. If New Labour had existed 200 years ago, they'd have decided not to abolish slavery as it was an example of free enterprise, but declared themselves friends of the slaves because they were proposing a law that you weren't allowed to say 'darky' ... Call me a layman, but I'd say if we stopped killing lots of Muslims, then Muslims would be less cross. (2004:39)

The reaction to the twelve cartoons published in a Danish newspaper in February 2006 depicting the prophet Muhammad is a test case in terms of response to offence – and its political use. As Dawkins points out, indignation was carefully and systematically nurtured throughout the Islamic world by a small group of Muslims living in Denmark, led by two imams who had been granted sanctuary there. These exiles went to Egypt with a dossier which was copied and circulated globally, containing falsehoods about alleged mistreatment of Muslims in Denmark and the 'tendentious lie' that the newspaper concerned was a government-run one. The dossier contained the twelve cartoons, which, crucially, the imams had supplemented with three additional images whose origin was mysterious but which certainly had no connection with Denmark. These add-ons were genuinely offensive – or would have been if they had, as the zealous propagandists alleged, depicted Muhammad. One was a photograph of a bearded Frenchman wearing a fake pig's snout, entered for a pig squealing contest at a country fair, and nothing whatever to do with the prophet Muhammad, Islam or Denmark. All this was used to incite hatred.

Danish citizens and, indeed, Westerners generally, were physically threatened. Christian churches in Pakistan, with no Danish or European connections at all, were burned. Nine people were killed when Libyan rioters attacked and burned the Italian consulate in Benghazi. As Germaine Greer wrote, 'what these people really love and do best is pandemonium'. (Dawkins, 2006:23)

The contrast has also been noted between the so-called 'hurt' professed by Muslims and the readiness with which Arab media publish stereotypical anti-Jewish cartoons. At a demonstration in Pakistan against the Danish cartoons, a woman in a black burka was photographed carrying a banner reading 'God Bless Hitler'. But the equally problematic question is that the actions of a minority of such Muslims then act to stereotype the rest, who are not that bothered about the cartoons nor about *The Satanic Verses*. The response which would be infinitely preferable would be satire (discussed more below), as in another *Daily Mash* spoof article:

---

### SATANIC VERSES SENDS SUICIDE BOMBER TO SLEEP

A would-be British suicide bomber failed to blow himself up after he fell asleep on the train while reading Sir Salman Rushdie's *The Satanic Verses*, it has emerged. Mohammed Al Inseini, 32, boarded the 8.04 Cloy to Old Cumnock Express determined to detonate himself on arrival at the Clackmannanshire town in protest at the author's recent knighthood.

Mr Inseini began reading Sir Salman's controversial book in a bid to stoke his religious fervour and give him the courage to perform his terrible act.

But half way through the opening page he nodded off, missed his stop and had to be roused by the guard when the train ended its journey at old Cumnock Halt.

Mr Inseini said: 'When I first woke up I believed myself to be in paradise, yet instead of the 72 virgins I was promised all I could see was a fat sweaty man in a Scotrail uniform'. Mr Al-Inseini said that, on reflection, *The Satanic Verses* was not the most evil book in the world, but instead 'Just a turgid load of old s****'. Frankly, I can't see what the fuss is about'.

Jim McKay, the ScotRail guard who finally confronted the would-be bomber, said he was 'shocked and terrified' by Mr Al Inseini's behaviour.

He said: 'The terrorist lad explained that he only had a one-way ticket to Old Cumnock because he had planned to blow himself up and assassinate the rest of us. When I pointed out that his failure to explode was not really my problem and that I wanted another £3 for his staying on to the next stop, he became quite abusive. It really was quite frightening'. (downloaded 30.8.2007)

---

This account could offend Salman Rushdie, radical Islamists, and Scotrail, all in one go – but it has a serious message in its evenhandedness about human

absurdity. Yet what appears puzzling and counter-productive, even for believers, is the portrayal of the Prophet as so weak as to be 'offended'. One
would think him above all this, rather than being portrayed as reacting like a
child insulted in the playground. It seems to demonstrate fragility rather than
strength. As the headmaster of a Cairo school pointed out 'if we were confident about our faith we wouldn't have to react so hysterically' ('Islam and
free speech: mutual incomprehension, mutual outrage'. *Economist* 11 Feb,
2006).

So in terms of how to raise issues of offence in the classroom, analysis needs
to focus on who exactly might be offended, whether they are actually physically or mentally damaged, and how many of a particular group the offended
professes to be speaking for.

## Offence in school

Not giving offence in schools has become a minefield. In the 'First Appoint-
ments' section of the *Times Educational Supplement* in 2005, Victoria Neumark asked 'Can you tiptoe through the entire school day without causing
offence'? In her article, she gives a list of all the areas where different religions
will have taboos or restrictions, in order to help beginning teachers to be
more 'aware'. These areas are: assemblies and celebrations, television/film,
drama, dance, music, computers, art, evolution, swimming, sex education,
menstruation, physical contact/modesty, food and first aid. I would have
thought this pretty much mopped up the entire school day. As well as not
doing evolution, Jehovah's witnesses don't do birthdays or indeed any un-
biblical celebrations such as Guy Fawkes or harvest festival (I thought harvest
festival was biblical, but what do I know). They don't even do Christmas and
Easter, as these are pagan, nor of course other faiths' festivals such as Diwali.
Christmas and nativity plays are supposedly frowned on by many groups,
accounting for the lunatic 'Winterval' celebrations attempted by Birmingham
City Council one year to replace Christmas. Music, although on the national
curriculum, can be forbidden by some branches of Islam, and so needs 'discussion'.

I am ambivalent about this sensitivity. On the one hand, Neumark's article is
very useful, and not just for beginning teachers, to understand why pupils
and parents may be resistant to some aspects of the content and style of
learning. On the other hand, why should religion be privileged as 'causing
offence' and needing special treatment? I should be able equally to claim
offence if my beliefs or value system in human rights were violated, and my
child was denied dignity, for example, by not being allowed to go to the toilet

in lesson time. The school day can be a mass of violations of children's rights, as some schools are realising (see Chapter 6).

And how does a school balance the right to information and health, for example sex education, and respect for what are often referred to as cultural rights? Should a school accede to *all* religious views, even if perceived as extremist by the more moderate within that religion – for example rejecting any textbooks with figures in them, or seeing females as being 'impure' at the time of menstruation? This seems to deny rights and to reproduce the subjugation of women. Under the heading 'menstruation', Neumark cautions 'if pupils object to sitting next to someone of the opposite sex, do not insist'. What? In case a boy has to be sullied by sitting next to an unclean female? This sort of accession is not just a throwback but a severe blow for gender equity. A school has to make a decision about what sorts of accessions to sensitivity or exclusivity are harmless and which actually cement divides, reproduce gender inequality and deny curriculum access and therefore opportunities to students.

Michele Bertani's chapter on Islam in Italy (2004) recounts a court case brought by two Muslim students to remove the Crucifix from their classrooms. Crucifixes are mandatory in all public facilities in Italy. This plea was upheld, but to public outcry.

> Interestingly, a similar request to remove the Crucifix from classrooms attended by atheists or non-Catholic students had been presented to courts in previous years, but did not excite such intense protest or public debate as the 'crisis of the Crucifix' of October 2003. (2004:103)

The stance of my book is that you can have what you like hanging up – a rabbit's foot or a picture of Che Guevara – but be prepared to talk about it. Significantly, in the case above, not all Muslims supported the action or decision. Bertani quotes two views of Muslims in positions of authority in Europe:

> 'The Crucifix or the discussion about celebrating Christmas in the classroom is not a problem. And I think it will not generate any problem for my little child when she will attend school. Because I will explain to her what the meaning of Christmas is and what the Crucifix represents for our Christian brothers.' (Mohammed Guerfi, *imam* of the Islamic Council in Verona)

> 'What do I think about the demand to remove the Crucifix? This initiative upsets and shocks me because it demonstrates the absence of respect for Italian traditions and faith. Moreover, it is an absurd idea to create a sort of religious space for Muslims who are overly sensitive and easily get offended' (Dalil Boubakeur, President of the

French Muslim Council and Rector of the Mosque of Paris) (Bertani, 2004: 103/ 104).

Thomas and Bahr (2008) tell how a group of educators concerned about the questions of religion on campus met and devised a set of recommendations called the *Wingspread Declaration on Religion and Public Life: Engaging Higher Education* (2006). One central message is that colleges and universities should never be conflict averse – and I would add schools into that too. This involved really tricky debates about principles of 'rational enquiry' not tied to an already fixed worldview. Acceding to demands for prayer rooms, separate counselling and so on outside the class was fine, but would acceding to religious views in class lack intellectual rigour? This raises the question of teaching comparative religion:

> Religious studies professors have for decades asked their students to suspend both belief and disbelief in order to understand and empathise with a variety of religious and anti-religious perspectives. Professors themselves are trained to check their personal beliefs at the classroom door. (2008, forthcoming)

But then what happens in assessment? Can one understand something and demonstrate that comprehension on a test, yet not believe it to be true? Charlene Burns (2006) points out that these methods reduce 'cognitive dissonance, creating a kind of permission to 'learn without changing'' (p7). But the problem is that it is necessary actually to *generate* cognitive dissonance if one wants students to learn. Thomas and Bahr ask, 'is it really possible to 'learn without changing?' We would want students to learn about climate change or about their social and political world so that they would evaluate their own place and responsibility in this; and we would hope that this learning would be transformational. But 'is it right to assume that education in certain disciplines (e.g. environmental science) will be transformational, but education in religion cannot be so because it will be viewed as indoctrination?' (2008, forthcoming).

My view – and I think theirs – is that cognitive dissonance is essential in learning, whether about religion or anything else. Comparing what one thought one knew against new and different information or ideas is the essence of education: that's what it's for. One does not have to be a paid-up constructivist or understand nuances of the zone of proximal development to know that all real learning is about change – about either expanding or shifting one's knowledge base, or questioning previously held assumptions. I do not think a teacher or lecturer should necessarily even 'check in' their religious or political values at the door. They do not do this for other areas of life – healthy eating, punctuality, politeness, the value of education itself – where no one questions whether teachers can and should promote a certain value set. In this sense, schools 'indoctrinate' endlessly, and on a daily basis. The key is honesty and transparency – that a teacher can reveal what they stand for, but *not* say 'and this is what you should stand for too'. This is what preachers do. And while they should engage in the necessary task of setting their personal beliefs against others, a teacher does not necessarily have to find 'balance' in absolutely everything, creating space for all ideas equally, on the 'Let's hear it now for Atilla the Hun' principle.

The worry is that teachers are somehow seen as influential role models. Most teachers I know moan 'would I were that powerful!'. We saw from the research on suicide bombers and extremists that their journey towards absolutist beliefs was a gradual process and occurred not through normal state school RE lessons nor a teacher's admission that she was going to vote for the BNP. The main important indoctrinatory role is that teachers believe in something – anything – and are willing to state their positions and be open to critique.

Students in a formal education system in many countries suffer cognitive dissonance anyway – revising for the exams yet praying to God for success, on a sort of all-cover insurance policy. This has been called 'prismatic society', a fusion of traditional and modern (Harber and Davies, 2000). I treasure a letter from 'Shirani' in the Sri Lanka *Daily News* entitled 'Prayer before Examination':

> 'Oh, Great St Joseph of Cupertino, who has obtained from God the grace to be asked only the questions you know, obtain for me success like yours in my examination for with [sic] I promise to make your name famous and cause you to be invoked. St Joseph of Cupertino pray for us (3 times). It has never been known to fail'. (May 18 2007, p8)

Intriguingly, this appeared under 'Obituaries', so I hope Shirani is still alive and that she got through her exams.

## Media and messages

The UN Security Council Resolution (see Chapter 1) has a paragraph:

> Stressing the importance of the role of the media, civil and religious society, the business community and educational institutions in those efforts to enhance dialogue and broaden understanding, and in promoting tolerance and coexistence, and in fostering an environment which is not conducive to incitement of terrorism. (2005: Resolution 1624)

Chomsky defined a democratic society as

> ... one in which the public has the means to participate in some meaningful way in the management of their own affairs and the means of information are open and free. (1997:5)

These statements imply two things: a fundamental responsibility of the media, and the ability of the readership to deconstruct messages. In conflict societies, however, the hate media has been a counter to democracy and peace. Hate radio played a key role in starting the genocide in Rwanda (Gardner, 2002). Privately owned but government controlled, RTLM (Radio Mille Collines) was created in mid 1993 with shareholders that had strong ties to the ruling regime and its security forces. After securing a listenership through pop music, it then broadcast political propaganda and death warrants, encouraging the killing of Tutsis. It even read over the air the names of people to be killed. The International Criminal Tribunal of Rwanda proceedings were unique in that in addition to finding certain media editors and executives guilty for the content of their broadcasts, the Tribunal found them guilty for the *consequences* of their hate propaganda, as though the media leaders had 'personally wielded machetes' (McKinnon, 2004:325). The Hutu run media described the Tutsi people as 'hypocrites, thieves and killers' and as 'inherently evil'. It accused Tutsi women of intentionally using their sexuality to lure Hutu men into 'liaisons' in order to promote the ethnic dominance of the Tutsis over the Hutus. The Rwanda tribunal described this speech as a 'discriminatory form of aggression that destroy[ed] the dignity of those in the group under attack ... .and treat[ed] them as less than human'. (McKinnon p328)

I think it is possible to see the distinction between (false) claims to defamation of religion mentioned earlier and the actual incitement to genocide. Similarly, the 'blood libel' accusation is prominent in some Arab newspapers, e.g. the false claim that Jews kill people, specifically children, as a form of sacrifice and use their blood in mysterious rituals. In 2002, a government newspaper in Saudi Arabia described the Jews as 'vampires who bake cookies with the blood of Arabs', claiming that 'the Torah, the Jewish holy book, requires Jews to demonstrate their joy by eating pastries mixed with human blood'. Such Saudi-backed antisemitic literature is now increasingly appearing in mosques and bookshops in the UK (Vallely, 2007). In 2000, the Mufti of the Palestinian army stated on the cable news channel of Al-Jazeera, *without being challenged*, 'there can be no peace with Jews because they use and suck the blood of Arabs on the holidays of Passover and Purim' (quoted in Grinberg, 2006). Freedom of expression is indeed questionable here, and the responsibility of the media – or at least a free press – is not necessarily to suppress such views but to challenge them, demand evidence and provide alternative views.

In the Balkans, confrontations between the stabilisation force peacekeeping troops and Serb hardliners for control of television stations in Bosnia's Srpska Republic illustrate how valuable broadcasting can be in a conflict situation. Efforts were made also to destroy the enemy's communication lines. It is ironic that in the interests of liberation and free speech, the Americans bombed the Al-Jazeera and Abu Dhabi TV stations which were presenting a different view of the situation in Iraq than the US propaganda (Nelles, 2003).

Responsibility is about both alternative views and accuracy. Hensher (2005) thought it might justifiably be said that the British newspaper which published a story, on no evidence at all, that asylum seekers were killing and eating wild swans was abusing its authority.

> Similarly, we might deplore, on the grounds of 'responsibility' the lie spread, without any medical evidence, by the Roman Catholic church in Africa, that the use of condoms is useless against the transmission of HIV. Such bodies, perhaps, do have a duty to consider the weight of their voices and exercise their right of free speech responsibly. (p6)

But who decides what is responsible? As he points out, the problem with legal curbs on free speech is that it is decided by 'the authorities': 'Responsibility is in the eye of the government, the church, the Roi Soleil, the Spanish Inquisition and, no doubt, Ivan the Terrible' (2005:6).

Haque (2004) says therefore that 'the media must stop using terms such as Islamic extremism, fundamentalism and terrorism unless they consistently apply them to other groups too' (p13-14). This is a valid point, although I am not sure whether all groups can be so labelled. Sandy Fox, the comic and Buddhist, had a routine: 'The Buddhist demo was a nightmare. There were 10,000 Buddhists shouting 'What do we want?' 'Nothing'! 'When do we want it? ... (silence)'. But it is important that children think about how representative so-called 'spokespeople' are. In his chapter on Muslims in Italy Bertani talks of the few radical Islamic leaders who regularly appear on television. They seem to exploit the lack of knowledge of Islam in the media and their need for an audience. 'Although they represent only a minority of the Muslim population, they are, thanks to the media, seen as representing the entire Muslim community. Recently, one of these leaders invited the Pope to convert to Islam, while another voiced his support for the views of Osama bin Laden on the Western world' (2004:97). The Islamic establishment had itself often criticised such comments, but it was the radical views that were seen as newsworthy. The media certainly bear some responsibility for the rise of Islamophobia, as is well documented in the Stone report *Islamophobia* of 2004.

Media education relates also to analysis of discourse and justification for violence – particularly by politicians. As Gray (2007) points out, in the span of six years, Tony Blair took Britain to war five times. In each case the war was to be a form of 'humanitarian intervention'. This may have had some validity in the Balkans and in Sierra Leone. It was dubious in Afghanistan and duplicitous in Iraq. He justified these military movements in terms of a 'doctrine of international community', that the sovereign state was on the way out – which was nonsense. So called 'rogue states' should be the target of armed force, not just to neutralise threats, but to improve the human condition. Blair said: 'Our values [unspecified] are worth struggling for. They represent humanity's progress throughout the ages and at each point we have had to fight for them and defend them. As a new age beckons, it is time to fight for them again'. In January 2007, he said 'Terrorism destroys progress. Terrorism can't be defeated by military means alone. But it can't be defeated without it' (p100).

So critical media literacy is crucial – both for analysing spin and propaganda and, conversely, for recognising the importance of media in investigative journalism and in freedom of speech and critique. Being part of the public voice is for politicians both a danger and an opportunity. When exploring the justification for extremism we need to look at truth and myth. The power of rumour and distorted information is significant. Lyndsay Bird's account of the role of educative processes on conflict in the Great Lakes region of Africa has important sections on rumour and gossip, and what or who is seen as 'trustworthy' (2006). Similarly, an instructive account of the religious conflict in Ambon, Indonesia shows how this was triggered by wrong information (Poerwawidagdo, 2002). After centuries of peaceful co-existence between Christian and Muslim, a quarrel between two young people quickly spread into a massive conflict resulting in hundreds of deaths and the destruction of property. It was fuelled by rumours about *impending* attacks, which were purposefully spread to provoke fear and defensive violence.

Wrong information can be used intentionally by the political élite or the military, and fear has a strong amplifying effect. Michael Fisher (2007) has assembled a whole annotated bibliography on 'The Culture of Fear and Education' which is disturbing in illustrating the scale of the problem. Vulnerability of groups can mean that fear drives them into pre-emptive strikes. The same fear is what apparently drove the US, aided by UK, into a pre-emptive strike on Iraq. The power of small bits of (mis)information – the 45 minute strike – are enough to cause or justify aggression on a massive scale.

Our question might be how to spread a rumour about peace. Is fear so much more powerful than happiness? Will reporting ethnic violence incite more violence? It is a debatable point whether withholding information for the sake of social and communal peace is morally correct and ethically appropriate.

So who controls history and memory is a key factor in conflict. The use of 'imagined communities' (Anderson, 1983) (discussed in Chapter 3), gives considerable leverage to political leaders bent on using ethnicity as a mobilisation device. Such ethnification of politics is greatly helped by modern communications technology, which

> now enables the most atavistic rhetoric of ethnic leaders to reach a far wider audience, with a great deal more vividness than the old tribal chieftain could ever dream of. Ancient prejudices are transmitted through the most sophisticated media, just as ancient vendettas are carried out with the most modern military weaponry. (Bardhan, 1997:79)

There is clearly a difference between Al-Qaeda and other terrorist movements, in that Al-Qaeda is a global campaign. Most terrorism is national or regional in both its scope and its goals. Even if their funds are derived from across the world, organisations such as ETA in the Basque country of Spain, the IRA in Ulster, the Tamil Tigers in Sri Lanka and the PLO in Gaza remain based in one or two countries. Gray (2003) points out how Al Qaeda is an essentially modern organisation, not only in the use of technology but also in its understanding that 21st century wars are spectacular encounters in which the dissemination of media images is a core strategy. Its use of satellite television to mobilise support in Muslim countries is part of this strategy. It is a truly global multinational. It is organised on the model of an extended family, using ties of trust. It makes considerable use of informal banking systems (*hawala*) that are global in their reach and whose operations are effectively untraceable.

Media coverage is therefore crucial for terrorism – and, like celebrity pop stars, for radicals all news is good news. Husain recounts how in the 1990s their work in university campuses across UK was creating a storm, with local newspapers and national media profiling them, reaching new audiences of millions. It did not matter that much coverage was critical – they knew there was a crucial constituency of Muslims who would look on them as their leaders, their spokesmen against the attacks of the infidels. Their style of debate was confrontational, designed to provoke outrage, to 'destroy concepts'.

Tariq Ali (2005:19) quotes Mark Danner in the *New York Review of Books*:

Power, the argument runs, can shape truth: power in the end, can determine reality, or at least the reality that most people accept – a critical point, for the administration has been singularly effective in its recognition that what is most politically important is not what readers of the *New York Times* believe but what most Americans are willing to believe. The last century's most innovative authority on power and truth, Joseph Goebbels, made the same point but rather more directly. *'There was no point in seeking to convert the intellectuals. For intellectuals would never be converted and would anyway always yield to the stronger, and this will always be 'the man in the street'. Arguments must therefore be crude, clear and forcible, and appeal to emotions and instincts, not the intellect. Truth was unimportant and entirely subordinate to tactics and psychology.'*

Or as Plato said in *The Republic*, 'Those who tell the stories also rule the society'.

Critical analysis of media images, newspapers, TV reporting, and government information campaigns are all essential survival skills, at individual and at national level. Journalists themselves have learned to be disillusioned by information given to them by 'informed officials'. Many reporters in former Yugoslavia have stated that they were at times astonished by claims and information given to them by the United Nations Protective Force, later proved incorrect (Gardner, 2001). Yet political and media literacy in schools is not always seen as a vital part of language learning. In Brcko, I found the teachers who were working on curriculum harmonisation in Bosnia Herzegovina were preferring the safety of literature and comprehension rather than using newspapers as resources, as they felt threatened by anything that appeared 'political'. Teacher training may be key: skills and orientations need to be developed towards teaching controversial issues and analysing discourse. Cheng and Jacob (2003) give a good example of a teaching portfolio from a Taiwanese elementary school teacher who used September 11 to help students reflect on the various roles the media use in disseminating information – the difference between covering a news item and translating a news item, or whether CNN is quoted directly without verification. Analysis of language takes even more important forms when translation of media items is involved.

In his valuable book on media education, Cortes (2000) concludes that 'school education about diversity will *always* be self-limiting in its effectiveness if school educators do not seriously engage the reality – the inevitability – of students learning about 'otherness' through the media' (2000:xvii). He uses a concept of 'media textbooks' – that media products (TV, newspapers, shows etc) ultimately function as public textbooks, and teach. Whether consumers learn is another matter. So whenever embarking on a multicultural programme of 'awareness', we need to find out what students already know. This is like Mark Twain: 'education consists mainly in what we have unlearned'. We need to know what young people *extract* from *The Lion King* to know whether this is racist, sexist, homophobic etc. Cortes classified four types of societal curriculum – the immediate curriculum (home, family, peers, neighbourhood); the institutional curriculum (youth groups, religious institutions, voluntary associations); the serendipitous curriculum (random personal experiences, chance interactions, foreign travel); and the media curriculum. World War Two media was called upon by the Federal government in the US to support mobilisation, and so ridiculed and dehumanised the enemy, particularly the Japanese. *Rosie the Riveter* was a symbol of the government's appeal for women to take their place on the assembly line – although there was afterwards a rapid about face, calling on Rosie to return home, raise her family and leave jobs to their rightful possessors.

Cortes asks teachers to recognise that 'multicultural' learning is taking place, to analyse its patterns, and to provide multiple perspectives. Techniques for multicultural education training might include keeping a media curriculum journal – keeping records of and their reactions to multicultural teaching they encounter; analytical journals of the mass media treatment of a diversity-related topic for a week; working with parents; working directly with the media – PR departments, communicating concern to newspapers etc; and inviting media makers to the school. He warns however about over-simplistic strategies, the endless games of pin-the-tail-on-the-stereotype.

It would be interesting to apply this strategy to recent newspaper accounts of a report on 'hate' material found in a small number of British mosques, material which urged execution of apostates, stoning of adulterers and abhorrence of heretics, as well as identifying 'Women Who Will Go to Hell' (Evans, 2007). Examining the language both of the material and the newspaper accounts reporting it would be revealing.

A report on *BBC Today* on 'de-radicalisation' (7.11.2007) explained how football and other conventional youth activities were being used in a project to bring together young people who might be exposed to Islamist ideology. All they knew of Islam was through jihadi DVDs, and the project used the same material to counter the propaganda. They watched the films together, high-lighting the misunderstandings from the Qu'ran and showing how the DVDs worked on the emotions to get people upset. The aim was to reveal the material's hidden agendas of using the youth as puppets, and to engage with the views espoused, not suppress them.

Other forms of messaging can usefully be given the same treatment, for example in textbooks. There have been numerous accounts of how history textbooks portray 'the enemy', which I need not rehearse here (Davies, 2004). Attempting to sanitise nationalistic materials post conflict leads to dilemmas. Just one example will do: I recall seeing in Bosnia Herzegovina history books on all sides of the conflict with their inflammatory passages blacked out – and of course it makes one desperate to try to read them. Galloway (2006) has a salutary account of the UN underestimating the guile of canton authorities to preserve their versions of history. In one notorious case, claiming to have no black pens, they used highlighter pens to identify the relevant passages in every book in the school, arguing to the UN authorities that this would facilitate the removal of the passages when black pens became available...

## Cyberspace

As well as all forms of print and broadcasting, media education has become particularly important regarding the internet. In the late 1990s, people were already pondering on the implications of internet use, as Symonides explains:

> The use of the Internet for the dissemination of pornography by paedophiles, for the advocacy of racism, xenophobia and violence raises a number of ethical and legal questions concerning the limit of freedom of information and expression ... Should the Internet fall under the law of the press and mass media, or should it be governed by laws regulating private correspondence? Is cyberspace a private or public area? Is state control and censorship justified? (1998:23)

Symonides' view is that there is no need for state censorship and preventive control. Freedom of expression and information should be a guiding principle for the Internet. 'This is the most effective guarantee of cultural and linguistic pluralism and diversity. Therefore the free flow of information should be fully preserved and defended' (1998:23). I agree strongly with this, if only on a practical level. It is almost impossible to police the Internet. The ease with which young people can access not just political blogs but Jihadi sites and even bomb-making sites – whether in or out of the school building – means the duty of the school is to develop skills in analysing what is read, rather than trying to shield their students from inflammatory material. It is also of crucial importance for young people to realise the arguments that are being used by extremists, the use of language, the logic, and the source of the arguments presented. It is not just about receiving messages but about the use of cyber-terrorism itself, employing advanced technology to disrupt financial markets, airports and power stations (Gray, 2003).

The web and cyberspace are dominated by niches, and people head for specific sites. Such sites can be democratic and peace promoting, such as the Middle East Citizens Assembly, or the CyberPeace project involving dialogue between Jewish Israelis, Arab Israelis, Palestinians and Jordanians, using intergroup conversations. They can be useful sources of information, such as TANDIS (the Tolerance and Discrimination Information System), run by the Office of Democratic Institutions and Human Rights of the OSCE. But some sites – such as hate based and conspiracy websites – can also contribute to polarisation and foster bigotry. There is a valuable website called *The Hate Directory* which monitors and lists hundreds of hate sites (www.bcpl.net/~rfrankli/hatedir.pdf). One of the terrorist bombers whose rucksack failed to explode told investigators that the would-be bombers of July 21 had psyched themselves for the attacks by watching films on the war on Iraq, 'Especially those where women and children were being killed and exterminated by British and American soldiers ... [films] of widows, mothers and daughters that cry'.

> The contrast between the price tag the Western media place on their own citizens – the photos of smiling faces, the intimate details recalled by friends and family – and on the tens of thousands of those nameless, uncounted bodies shot, tortured or blown up from 30,000 feet on the command of Bush and Blair, could hardly be starker. It is this that fuels the anger. (Ali, 2005:52)

M15 in the UK are worried about what they term 'self-radicalising kids' – teenagers as young as 15, not members of Al-Qaeda but inspired by images on the internet to carry out their own attacks, driven by emotional rather than ideological inspiration (Evans, 2007). These are extreme examples, but Vallely (2007) also points to the other end of the spectrum: with the internet, videos and tapes, Muslims are now studying texts once reserved for scholars in the higher reaches of clerical training. 'The result is a new highly individualistic theology which often reads holy texts in a literalist way with no understanding of the contexts in which different parts of the Islamic scriptures were framed' (2007:5). The next chapter discusses counter moves in the form of more critical reading of scriptures, but the power of the internet simultaneously to create 'community' and to individualise and alienate is remarkable.

## Humour and satire

Lastly in this chapter I turn to one key role of media in a free society, namely satire. This section ventures onto the thin dividing line between giving offence or insult and engaging in the necessary or harmless derision. There is a wonderful bit in the film the *Life of Brian* when Jesus heals the leper and the leper is furious because his livelihood of begging is gone. 'Bloody do-gooder', he says gloomily. It is significant that the campaign against the proposals for the UK bill against the incitement of religious hatred was spearheaded both by religious leaders and by comedians. Stewart Lee, the co-author of *Jerry Springer the Opera* received a death threat from Christian fundamentalists. His view is 'It's the duty of comedians to attack religious belief because you test the elastic limit of a thing by probing it, and belief systems based on faith rather than facts need to be tested' (*The Independent* on Sunday, 5 December 2004, p3).

Macintyre points out that satire is the mark of a healthy democracy, 'the pricking of pomposity that reminds our leaders that they are not self-anointed'. He quotes George Orwell: 'Every joke is a tiny revolution. Whatever destroys dignity and brings down the mighty from their seats, preferably with a bump, is funny' (2005). Humour can usefully attack pretention:

> And Jesus said unto them 'And whom do you say I am?' And they replied, 'You are the eschatological manifestation of the ground of our being, the ontological founda-tions of the context of our very selfhood revealed'. And Jesus replied 'What??'

Osama bin Laden became a staple of playground humour – tasteless and defiant jokes began to emerge after 9/11, the natural response to the oppres-sion of terror, a tiny revolution against fear. The wonderful female Muslim comedian Shazia Mirza started one of her shows with: 'My name's Shazia Mirza. Or at least, that's what it says on my pilot's licence...'

Black humour, the ability to laugh in the face of adversity, is a powerful tool for resistance. Paul Stokes, the co-editor of the *Daily Mash* which posted the spoof articles quoted in this book, said 'It helps that nobody was killed in the attack [on Glasgow airport], but within hours people were laughing and joking. We're supposed to be terrified by these people [the attackers] but to be honest they're a joke' (quoted in Lister, 2007). Humour here has three func-tions: to raise morale; to not give over-importance to the terrorism whose main purpose is not the deaths themselves but the terror caused; and to make a laughing stock of the terrorists themselves. Some satirical articles drew especial attention to their being doctors, but failed doctors, part of the National Health Service's 'failed terror campaign'. 'The NHS terrorists are good people with good intentions and they are doing their best to incinerate themselves and the public in very difficult circumstances. But it is clear that they need private sector experience. There is too much red tape and form-filling involved in NHS fanaticism. We will outsource that work to a call centre in Pakistan and let terrorist doctors be terrorist doctors' (www.thedailymash. co.uk). In a stroke, the article has a snipe at privatisation ideology as well as at terrorism itself.

But tyrants – and terrorists – try to elevate themselves above humour. Husain talks of how his Islamist group never discussed anything trivial. 'We had to be serious – we were the leaders of the Muslim *ummah*' (p95). Anti-Nazi jokes became punishable by death in Germany, just as they flourished outside it. In North Korea, satire is banned for the simple reason that since the Communist state is officially perfect, there is officially nothing to satirise. 'The first sign that a tyrant's days are numbered comes not with the sound of gunfire but the gentle ripple of disrespectful laughter' (Macintyre, 2005). Before the French Revolution, the monarchy was comprehensively undermined by satire, ribald and unrelenting. Within hours of the unsuccessful attempt to bomb Saddam Hussein during operation Shock and Awe, a joke was already doing the rounds of Baghdad cafes: 'Following the attack, the Iraqi Information Minister has summoned all Saddam's body doubles to a meeting to tell them: 'The good news is that our beloved leader has survived, so you all still have jobs. The bad news is that he has lost an arm'. As Macintyre points out, the snigger is mightier than the sword.

However, while we might all agree that political satire is necessary and important, satirising religious leaders arouses far greater debate. For believers, they are not self-appointed; like Kim Jong Il in North Korea, they are perfect, and to joke about them is to joke about the whole religion or regime. It is puzzling that if they are all-powerful, why can't they take a joke? But nonetheless, part of humour education would be to discuss the whole notion of insult and offence, and when it is necessary and when gratuitous.

In 2005 for example there was a competition in the UK called The Laugh Judgement, whereby more than 4,000 people voted on 700 religious jokes sent in to the satirical Christian website ShipofFools. The aim was to identify the ten funniest and the ten most offensive. The ten most offensive were about Christianity, many involved paedophile priests and one involved Hitler. Most also involved sex. The contest was started in order to highlight potential problems with the Government's new religious hatred legislation, which was, as said, strongly opposed not just by secularists and comics, but also by religious leaders across the denominational spectrum. Would comics be prosecuted under these laws? The editor of ShipOfFools pointed out that 'Ridiculing some religious beliefs, criticising absurd religious practices and offending religious people was a way of life for Old Testament prophets. It's not a freedom so much as a responsibility' (quoted in Gledhill, 2005).

I like the idea of satire as a responsibility. It is the identification of the ridiculous, the sending up of perverted logics by taking them to extremes.

Animal rights extremists for example, use the logic of anthropomorphism – that *you* wouldn't like to be cooped up all day in a chicken farm. The reply is that I also wouldn't like to spend all day bent double pecking up seeds. We should not project a human brain into a chicken brain. The reason why you can never outwit an alligator is that when you have shinned up a tree to escape, they will wait at the bottom endlessly until you fall off through tiredness or come down through hunger. Apparently an alligator has a brain the size of a walnut and never gets bored. Binyavanga Wainaina (2006) has a wonderful satirical piece in *Granta* on 'How to write about Africa':

> Always treat Africa as if it were one country ... Don't get bogged down with precise descriptions. Africa is big: fifty four countries, nine hundred million people who are too busy starving and dying and warring and emigrating to read your book ... Adopt a sad, I-expected-so-much tone. Establish early on that your liberalism is impeccable, and ... how much you love Africa. Africa is to be pitied, worshipped or dominated. Whichever angle you take, be sure to leave the strong impression that without your intervention and your important book, Africa is doomed.

But while humans should be portrayed in stereotypes, animals on the other hand

> ... must be treated as well rounded, complex characters. They speak (or grunt while tossing their manes proudly) and have names, ambitions or desires. They also have family values: see how lions teach their children? Elephants are caring, and are good feminists or dignified patriarchs. Elephants may attack people's property, destroy their crops, and even kill them. Always take the side of the elephant.

Hence analysis of extremist messages would include the over-simplification of humans and the under-simplification of animals.

A powerful form of satire is the analogy. A brilliant article by Richard Dawkins describes the highly additive drug 'Gerin oil' – or Geriniol in its scientific name (an anagram if you hadn't realised). This, he says, acts directly on the nervous system to produce a range of characteristic symptoms, often of an anti-social or self-damaging nature. If administered chronically in childhood, it can permanently modify the brain to produce adult disorders, including dangerous delusions which are hard to treat.

> The four doomed flights of September 11th were all Gerin oil trips: all 19 of the hijackers were high on the drug at the time. Gerin oil fuelled Salem witchhunts, massacres of South Americans by inquistadores, wars of European middle ages, and on a smaller scale, Ireland. Gerin oil addiction can drive previously sane people to run away into closed communities, limited to one sex, and forbidding sexual activity, as well as preventing others, particularly homosexuality. It can be hallucinogenic, hearing voices – but such people can be venerated as leaders. There is bizarre psychedelia such as the cannibalistic fantasy of 'drinking the blood and eating the flesh' of the leader. Oil-heads can be heard talking to thin air or muttering to themselves, apparently in the belief that private wishes so expressed will come true, even at the cost of mild violation of the laws of physics. As with many drugs, refined Gerin oil in low doses is largely harmless, and can even serve as a social lubricant on occasions such as marriages, funerals and ceremonies of state. But experts differ as to whether this is a risk factor, upgrading to more addictive forms. It can lead to mutilation, particularly of the genitals. You might think that such a potentially dangerous drug would top the list of proscribed substances. Yet it is readily available, and does not need a prescription. Pushers are numerous, organised in hierarchical cartels and opening trading on the street and even in purpose-made buildings. Governments grant a tax-exempt status; worse they subsidise schools with the specific intention of getting children hooked. (2005:16)

Dawkins says he was prompted to write the article by a picture of a very happy man in Bali. He was ecstatically greeting the news that he was about to be executed by a firing squad for the brutal murder of large numbers of innocent holiday makers whom he had never met. 'He punched the air, delirious with joy that he was to be 'martyred' to use the jargon of his particular subculture of Gerin oil substance abusers. For, make no mistake about it, this beatific smile, looking forward with unalloyed pleasure to the firing squad, is the smile of a junkie'. Dawkins concludes it is easy to regard such people as evil criminals, but the problem would not arise in the first place if children were protected from becoming hooked on a drug with such a bad prognosis for their adult minds.

A specific debate has emerged about satire and humour *within* Islam. Irshad Manji sometimes gets asked 'why are there no jokes about a priest, a rabbi and a mullah?' She explains that

> Islam has a popular teaching against 'excessive laughter'. No joke. In a booklet entitled *Problems and Solutions* Sheikj Muhammed Salih Al-Munajjid spells out the teaching. While 'the Muslim is not expected to be dour-faced' an abundance of

147

> laughter proves that we Muslims have been manipulated by charm and wit, which softens our character and piety. I recall an uncle lovingly but firmly warning me one New Year's Eve not to laugh too loud as doom would be sure to follow. (p33-34)

However, as with injunctions against images, others will counter the claim that the Muslim world is not used to laughing at religion. Taheri (2006) argues that it is true if you restrict the Muslim world to the Muslim Brotherhood and its siblings in the Salafist movement, Hamas, Islamic Jihad and Al-Qaeda. It is the political organisations that are humourless: 'their attempt at portraying Islam as a sullen culture that lacks a sense of humour is part of the same discourse that claims 'suicide martyrdom' as the highest goal of all believers'. Taheri claims that Islam has always had a sense of humour and that Muhammad himself pardoned a famous Meccan poet who had lampooned him for more than a decade. He gives a number of examples of laughing at religion in the literatures of Islam; and importantly, says that Islamic ethics is based on 'limits and proportions' which means that the answer to an offensive cartoon is a cartoon, not the burning of embassies or the kidnapping of people designated as the enemy. He makes the important point that

> Islam rejects guilt by association. Just as Muslims should not blame all Westerners for the poor taste of a cartoonist who wanted to be offensive, those horrified by the spectacle of 'rent-a-mob' sackings of embassies in the name of Islam should not blame all Muslims for what is an outburst of fascist energy. (p3)

Whether Taheri and others would see Shazia Mirza's particular style of humour as 'proportionate' is not known: she was once attacked on stage by three Asian men after she recounted the time in Mecca when a man touched her inappropriately. 'I felt a hand on my bottom. I ignored it. I thought, 'I'm in Mecca. It must be the hand of God.' But then it happened again. I didn't complain. Clearly, my prayers had been answered'.

Naturally, one should not over-estimate the power of satire and mockery. In spite of his own political and satirical writing, and his original worldview that Central American dictators could not be overthrown until *Not the Nine-o'clock News* had been translated into Spanish, John O'Farrell describes his doubts that 1930s cabaret in Berlin actually did anything much to erode the power of the Nazis. 'Political humour thrived throughout the 1980s, but so did Margaret Thatcher ... we never had UN joke inspectors going into Iraq to check on Saddam's secret sarcasm programme' (2006:28). Yet naturally O'Farrell would not be without satire. Authorities dislike political comedy 'because you can't argue with the sound of laughter – you can't say: 'Actually, that joke doesn't work, because in fact that wasn't our policy at the time...'

> A good joke can detonate an unspoken truth, bring its all-powerful target down to the same level as the rest of us – not to mention the good it does for the morale of those without power. (p26)

And it can be a way in: Amnesty International's cunning use of comedy to fill the Albert Hall in London in the 2006 *The Secret Policeman's Ball* was far more influential than getting some local volunteers to read out distressing case studies. People joined Amnesty after seeing the show, there or in cinemas outside, or on the DVDs. The same is being done through pop music, but a comedy show has a double message:

> It is quite likely that the audience at the Secret Policeman's Ball just came to have a good laugh, and why not? But take a moment to reflect that an event like this could never happen in places like Burma or North Korea. They wouldn't understand a word the comics were saying, for a start. Comedy and music are uplifting and liberating expressions of free speech, so what better way to celebrate the release of prisoners who were locked up just for voicing an opinion? (O'Farrell, 2006:28)

## Conclusion: Implications for schools

The inferences for work in schools appear at two levels: at policy level, deciding the limits of free speech, and at classroom level, analysing how extremism is both expressed and can be challenged. The conclusions lead to five proposals for school strategy:

- Permitting the expression of 'extremist' attitudes, so that they can be discussed as attitudes and logics, and without disparaging the holder – and as long as people are not physically or psychologically harmed

- Understanding and discussing the nature of offence and when it is legitimate to be offended; this will require analysis of rights and of motives, whether using the right to free speech just for the sake of offending or to try to point out injustice or wrong

- Skills in all forms of critical media analysis and discourse analysis including, importantly, analysis of cyberspace and how it is used

- Understanding, reading and producing satire and cartoons as part of political education; this includes questions of power and responsibility, whether one is satirising the powerful who have their own access to media or just poking fun at those who have no means of having their voices heard

- Lots of laughter, and nothing moderate – again, as long as it is not at the expense of the powerless.

149

# 6

## Towards critical idealism: the XvX model

The aim of this chapter is to bring together all the arguments in the book in search of an educational approach which can mitigate extremism. All writers are tempted to propose the ultimate solution, and I enter a dilemma here. Extremism, as we have seen, really has entered a new phase due to the combination of internet communication and nuclear capability. Increased security and military solutions have not always been effective in countering it and can even be counter-productive against amorphous movements with different logics. But unlike some of the fundamentalists in Chapter 1, I am not apocalyptic, and think that education – while not the key to everything – can interrupt extremist processes. It may even be one of the most viable solutions we have in the long term.

So does extremism call for extreme measures in education? I am wary of parodies and over-the-top prescriptions here. Was it the Goons who said 'This calls for extreme measures! Arm the Electric Bagpipes!' I shall not be setting out the electric bagpipe solution, although, on reflection ... but a far less excruciating proposal. This is what I term XvX, a four way model whose components contrast with the more normal model of schooling – and of society (see page 152). I know this sounds like a ten-day detox diet plan – but mopping up the free radicals has a certain resonance here.

The four quadrants or spaces are the organisational base or scaffolding, the values base, the knowledge base and the process base. This book has already tackled significant parts of this model, arguing that the organisational base to the school or system would be integration, a stress on commonalities rather than difference, acknowledging hybrid identities and minimising the various divisive aspects of schooling, such as the obsession with competitive standards and choice. Parts of the process base have also been discussed. These

151

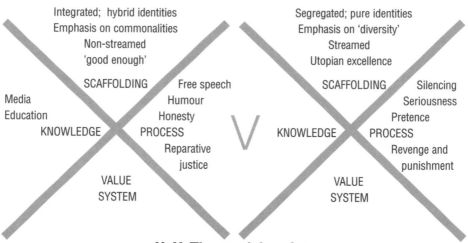

**XvX: The model so far**

are the ways of working, closely linked to values, arguing for an emphasis on free speech, honesty, humour and restorative justice. In the knowledge base, an argument has been made for media education.. In this final chapter I want to add in the rest of the model, starting with the knowledge base, then values and finally back to ways of working.

## The knowledge base

What do students need to know about extremism and the basis for challenging it? Three aspects are discussed here: teaching about conflict, counter-terror education and political education.

### Teaching about conflict

Our study of *Global Citizenship: the needs of teachers and learners* (Davies, Harber and Yamashita, 2004) asked young people what they wanted from global citizenship education. We found that one key thing they wanted was to know more about was war – in the current and not just the historical context. Both primary and secondary pupils wanted to know about the reasons for war, the reasons for hate and why we were selling weapons. A strong faction characterised Bush and Blair as 'terrorists'. All this related to the war in Iraq, about which many students felt they were short-changed by schools on the information and understandings they wanted. Teachers were reluctant to tackle the issues, sometimes because they feared intensifying feelings in their multicultural classrooms, and sometimes because of their own lack of knowledge or commitment. Some schools did join in the two million strong march in London against the war, but in other schools, students were punished for truanting if they joined the march. One headteacher actually declared that they would be better off praying than marching.

So at least two needs derive from this study: a need for political knowledge and information, and the desire to be active in some way. Both are problematic for schools that are risk averse. Just how active students can be allowed to be in this quest for active global citizenship, and what causes they can be encouraged to support? For some schools 'active' is code for 'politicised' and there is understandable concern about indoctrination or indeed radicalisation.

Nonetheless we found good examples of approaches for examining the war in Iraq and other contemporary conflicts. In 2003, one teacher was using 'The News in Numbers' for discussion each week, with a chart giving numbers on one side and the 'fact' on the other, for example

| 871,000 | the number of Iraqi refugees that it is estimated will be created if there is a war |
| 15m | the amount in £s that Gordon Brown has set aside to cover the cost of military action against Iraq |

It would make for interesting discussion today to consider how these figures were a gross underestimation. This multicultural school also created a war bulletin board for students to write down their opinions on cards to stick on the board and share with friends and staff. Another school followed the QCA Scheme of Work Unit 11: *Why is it so difficult to keep the peace in the world today?* with some classes pursuing also issues of asylum seekers. Students researched issues related to war and produced timelines on 'The Road to Conflict'. They used the internet and newspapers to research the views of British people in order to complete a two-way chart on 'Should Britain go to war?'. A Coventry school became involved in Coventry Peace Month, and teachers were also trying to find ways to respond to and explore the traumatic experiences endured by their refugee children. Schools were making good use of materials on the Holocaust, and at junior level, books such as *Zlata's Diary*, the account of a girl caught up in the Balkan conflict. All these initiatives show that war and conflict can be tackled across different areas of the curriculum, and that young people do respond positively to them. Any work in citizenship education on media and language analysis also gives pupils skills to look both at government rhetoric and at the way different communities and nations portray each other.

Yet, as said, teaching about 'the winds of war' creates extreme caution. Is 9/11 a 'teachable moment' (Nelles, 2003:17)? Ben-Porath (2006) reports that in the US, Maine's top educational office warned teachers to be careful of what they said in class about a possible invasion of Iraq, even before the war began, after receiving complaints that the children of soldiers were upset by anti-war comments at school. Similarly, Edith King recounts that US polls and surveys reported that large numbers of children felt that they were not being told about what was really happening in regards to the terrorism, or whether something bad would happen to them and their family. 'At times, teachers remained silent and did not encourage questions or discussions about the conflicts, the deaths and destruction resulting from warfare, suicide bombers and military action' (2006:17). King makes the point that not talking abut these aggressions and daily crises, not listening to children's concerns, does not protect them. It may communicate that the subject is taboo and that adults are insensitive. It is also important to see if children have any mis-understandings or unfounded fears. And as racist incidents have increased in the US and the UK following 9/11, teachers need to be vigilant and bring them into the open, taking active steps to stop the demonising of Islam.

We found in our study (Davies, Harber and Yamashita, 2004) that children want to know who is responsible for war. There can be a tendency to fudge the issue of responsibility – for example, King says 'UNICEF and UNESCO reports over the last decades have reiterated that wars are most important abusers of children; millions of children are victims of war' (p61). I know what she means; but this glosses over the fact that it is *people* that make wars, and who are the abusers, directly and indirectly. War should not be presented as some phenomenon that occurs almost spontaneously and inevitably. People make a decision to go to war or to support it or to condone it, as they do to commit extremist acts. However, King rightly – and sadly – points out how 147 coun-tries of the world have signed the Ottawa treaty to ban landmines, but US has not, and has been one of the largest producers and users of landmines in the world. 'Our nation-wide distraction with terrorism has not encouraged Con-gress to work to ratify the Ottawa treaty of other humanistic legislation to protect the world's children' (p63).

So critical civic education becomes even more important in times of conflict and terror. This is not just because of the threat to democratic stability but also the associated limits of freedom imposed by the *response* to it – internment, ID cards, and length of time allowed for imprisonment without trial. Public interest in politics does increase, as may participation – but the question is whether this participation is just unthinking patriotism or actions critical of inhumane practices. I would endorse Ben-Porath's promotion of 'expansive education', a political education for diversity, a 'conscious expansion of the scope of topics discussed and standpoints tolerated' (2006:122). Patriotism must be a subject for discussion, but so, too, must terrorism. It is important to test ideas in a safe environment, once the rules of engagement have been established. One useful exercise I have used with students is to 'design the sexist (or racist) school'. Asking them to design the ideal terrorist school or training camp would lead to interesting discussions of authoritarianism, militarism and ideology, and a critical view of their own education.

*Counter-terror education*

Does the current educational response to terror meet this need for critical, expansive education? In a review of contemporary initiatives, Sieckelinck (2007) describes different sorts of counter-terror educational strategy. One is the *Bosatlas*, the primary geography course in the Netherlands, also used by schools in Belgium, France and Scandinavia. It includes a map of international terrorism threat, with data based on research conducted by the American Assurance Company AON. There is not much information on how the map is to be used in geography classes: the publisher merely remarks that children will learn to look at the world through different glasses.

A second programme is clearer. A series of sessions about the dangerous attraction of radical ideals was developed for secondary students (age 15-18) by the Dutch National Counter-terror Coordinator. The aim is twofold: to obtain more information about how pupils deal with extremist convictions and to instruct children on the dangers of radicalisation. The pupils tackled questions such as 'Everything I am', 'In the name of', 'What is important to me', 'To attain your ideals, you have to stand for them and suit the action to the word' and 'My ideals stand above law' (Sieckelinck, 2007:2). This programme does seem more deliberative and would enable discussion of the link between ideals and action, coherence and morality. In one session the moderator asked an audience of 50 3rd grade pupils about who thought ideals could stand above the law. Only one hand rose, and that was their teacher's. She explained that some of her ideals were a critique of the law. Apparently, the pupils were 'taken by surprise', as 'standing for something' was not part of their normal repertoire. Sieckelinck explains: 'Although counter-terror education programs aim at neutralising dangerous – often ideal inspired actions, they run the risk of hitting youth ideal(ism) in its entireness.' (p4). Our task, it would seem, is how to preserve idealism-based agency and yet tackle extremist agency.

Another problem of specific counter-terror programmes is their specificity and inherent racism. There has been alarm about extremism on university campuses in UK and whether university authorities should try to monitor it and identify extremists. The original government guidelines rang even more alarm bells for many academics, with its suggestion that they should monitor 'Asian-looking' and Muslim students and report any concerns to Special Branch (UCU, 2007). Such programmes may in fact maintain the whole cycle. King reports that while 70 per cent of Al Qaeda's core leadership has been caught or killed, the organisation has carried out more attacks since 9/11 than it did in the three years before.

> History shows us that over the long stretch attacking terrorists only results in increases of terrorism, and this is what we are currently experiencing around the world. As long as there us a 'war on terrorism' it seems to bring attention and some significance to the various causes that use this means to engage in the conflicts worldwide. However, again as history conveys, when these militant groups are no longer being attacked, their membership declines. Social science research indicates that at least three priorities are of paramount importance in fighting terrorism: reducing inter-group conflict, creating incentives for the reduction of terrorism and socialising young people to reject violence as a means of problem solving (2006:154)

So the whole language of 'counter-terror' may well be unproductive in education. It is only one step away from the discredited 'war on terror'. In Whittaker's collection *The Terrorism Reader*, there is a chapter on counter terrorism strategies, but this contains nothing on education. At times army manual, at times criminology, the chapter ranges round increased security, reintroducing capital punishment, Identity Cards, internment without trial, computer searches and 'punishing' countries because of their involvement in terrorism. Admittedly, some of these are in response to 'state-sponsored terrorism' rather than individual or group activities. But in education we need to go further back, to the more preventative aspects, for example, tackling the 'moral disengagement' which Whittaker mentions in his chapter on 'ethical issues' and which we looked at in Chapter 2.

Finally there are dangers concerning how learners make use of the counter-terror training. Amnesty International (AI) has a *Twelve Point Guide for Good Practice in the Training of Government Officials*, but as Holland points out in the context of post conflict Angola,

> AI provides very specific instructions with regard to teaching students about torture. This is a subject that AI encourages the teaching of in the hope that thereby torture can gradually be eliminated as an interrogation practice. The point here is that AI

staff members have learned from experience that students don't always get the message AI is seeking to instil. Rather, some students have been found to be in danger of becoming more skilled torturers as a result of their having participated in these learning sessions. (2003:128)

I have developed a typology of teaching about conflict. First presented at a conference on 'Conflicted Societies' (which was conducted both in Jerusalem then Haifa as a good attempt at intergroup encounter), I then tried it out in other contexts (Davies, 2005 and 2006). I have slightly modified it so it relates specifically to the questions raised in this book. The model has two axes: negative⇔positive and active⇔passive, on which ten types are plotted. In the extreme corner of active/negative is the hate curriculum which exhorts students to kill or oppress enemies. Underneath is the 'defence curriculum', which teaches how to use weapons and landmines. But teaching that war is normal, as do many history books, while less 'active' is nonetheless negative. Ignoring conflict altogether is a very passive but also negative approach, as the discussion above has shown. I put 'tolerance' somewhere near the bottom, as seemingly positive but with possibly stereotypical overtones as discussed earlier. Going up on the positive side is the somewhat passive teaching 'about' conflict and causes, leading up to encounters with 'others' and then to active skills in conflict resolution. At the extreme corner of the active/positive quadrant, students are learning interruptive democracy, challenging inequality and actively campaigning for rights and peace.

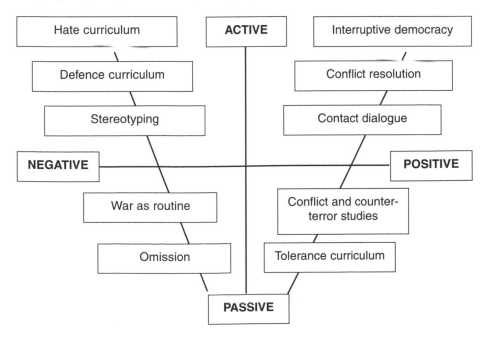

These are somewhat artificial divides, but the purpose is to show that conflict is 'taught' in schools in a number of ways, not all of which are positive or would lead to peace. In dealing with, or teaching about extremism, we would be looking for those strategies on the right hand side of the model, in particular those with the Active slant.

### A political citizenship education

Political education must be the base for all peace education. Peace education cannot, as Ben-Porath points out, be reduced to a utopian era of fluttering butterflies and economic profits or, alternatively, to the direct continuation of placid personal relations, as this fails to become a suggestive alternative to the reality of violence and hatred. She cites how only half a century ago Maria Montessori claimed that when educators fail to politicise education in order to tailor a proper response to the circumstances of war, they in effect act in the service of the war culture. It is not just about personal relations in the classroom. Ben-Porath has a critique of Betty Reardon's work on peace education which glowingly talks of the educational effort to form 'humane persons' in the Norwegian UNESCO Associated Schools, where boys 'have been weaned from competitive, aggressive behaviour by learning that 'It's Fun to be Nice'. Reardon apparently claims that 'were nations to learn this same lesson there would be a culture of peace (Reardon p187)'. As Ben-Porath drily comments, 'Aside from the principled deficiencies in a lesson plan that aims to teach that 'it's Fun to be Nice', the more pressing problem is that the method of transition from the personal to the political and international realm is not clarified' (p69). The programme neglects to consider nationalism and patriotism; and the fact that the successful experiment took place in a peaceful, democratic country like Norway also points to the necessity of having a differentiated and politically contextual account of peace education.

Our own Global Review of UNESCO Associated Schools (Davies, Harber and Schweisfurth, 2002) found some important work indeed happening around the UNESCO themes of peace, democracy and sustainable development, but also that some schools, particularly in conflict areas, were reluctant to tackle the issues of peace and conflict, preferring to focus on the UNESCO themes of environment or heritage. Recently, I talked to a head in a Sarajevo school for whom the major concern during the war had been the children's safety and somehow continuing their education in homes and garages when the school was destroyed. While he was currently forging a multicultural ethos in his new building, I cannot imagine an 'It's Fun to be Nice' programme when shells are dropping on the school.

A 'politicised education' or political citizenship education is not just learning the constitution or the history of political thinkers. It is about preparation and orientation for action and involvement. The task is to strike the balance between radicalisation and a more continuously doubtful stance. But one thing is at least to challenge indifference or denial. The Armenian genocide is still being denied by the Turks, who are able to pressure the US, France and the UK to do likewise, so as to secure arms contracts (Fisk, 2005). Writing about the Holocaust, Gallagher quotes Ian Kershaw's analysis:

> Popular opinion, largely indifferent and infused with a latent anti-Jewish feeling further bolstered by propaganda, provided the climate within which spiralling Nazi aggression towards the Jews could take place unchallenged. But it did not provoke the radicalisation in the first place. The road to Auschwitz was built by hate, but paved by indifference. (1984:277)

The question always asked after a genocide is: could it happen again? And could it happen here? Aguilar and Richmond's (1998) question on Rwanda is: how was it possible that education 'did not render genocide unthinkable'? The Balkans and the mass killings at Srebrenica took many by surprise; but we are currently watching the horrors of Darfur. As Gallagher soberly points out, 'If the Holocaust could be explained in terms of a particular national group or cultural history then it would be easy to avoid in the future. If it is explained by indifference, or something akin to indifference, it could all too easily happen again' (p6). A good political education therefore links to the values and skills of trying to take action against perceived harm and injustice.

## A value base: rights and the need for a secular morality

One argument for faith schools is that they provide a sound moral base. I am in full agreement that a strong value base is needed in school, but have already raised the dilemmas around choice, divisiveness and equity if this is religious. What is needed is a properly 'ecumenical' and universal value system, and I argue that the 'best fit' is to be found in human rights. All countries of the world have ratified the Convention on the Rights of the Child except the United States and Somalia (which currently does not have a functioning government that enables this state to ratify the international agreement). Groups in USA have been campaigning for participation and ratification as soon as possible (King, 2006).

Yet there is much work to do in persuading that a secular or humanist value system such as human rights actually exists as an ethical system. There is, sadly, a view that education is meaningless without an awareness of God or a spiritual Being. Mabud (1992) maintains that without the religious dimension 'it is not education at all but indoctrination into a particular worldview' (p90). That faith-based learning is equally much indoctrination seems to have escaped him. But his is not the sole voice. The Archbishop of Canterbury, Rowan Williams, rejects the suggestion that religion poses problems in education. 'Every religion has a concept of human dignity and worth which exceeds any account that secular people can give, and I think that's something very necessary in education', he asserts grandly (reported in Kingston, 2007). Leaving aside his ignoring of the many indignities done to others in the name of religion, this is breathtaking in its intolerance and superior attitude. Williams seems not to have heard of human rights conventions, specifically Articles 22 and 23, which since 1945 have pinpointed the protection of dignity as a basic right, and rights as indispensable for dignity.

Similarly, Husain recounts how during his time with Hizb, he was taught that there was no such thing as morality in Islam: it was simply what God taught. If Allah allowed it, it was moral. If he forbade it, it was immoral. There was no such category as 'feeling immoral'; one's own feelings – and presumably those of others – had nothing to do with it. Based on that premise, our responses would deem us either intellectual (good) or emotional (bad). (p102). This rather unemotional Captain Spock view of Islam cannot be mainstream, but it serves to enlighten the justification for violence, symbolic or real.

While I would propose a humanist and earthed alternative to a morality based on religion and the supernatural, I recognise that humanism's very nature, scope and contextuality makes it not instantly recognisable as a universal set of values. In what starts out as an interesting article on the nonsense of Intelligent Design, Christine Odone for example finally betrays her own prejudices against secularism. In arguing that 'most Christians' in Britain do accept evolution, she complains of Richard Dawkins being given television airtime to 'parade his ignorance of religious belief' when no theologian gets airtime to 'denounce the secularist moral vacuum' (Odone, 2005). There are many issues here: firstly, Dawkins is hardly 'ignorant' about religious belief ... but he can defend himself. Secondly, *Thought for the Day* is an entirely religious slot, and no humanist to my knowledge has ever managed to get airtime, in the face of this daily dose of supernatural homily sent up by the comic parodies such as 'What can we as Christians learn from the pop-up toaster?'. The real issue at stake here is the notion that secularism cannot have a morality, is simply a 'vacuum'. If this is indeed a widespread perception, and not just Odone's or the BBC's, then schools have a challenging job to do not just in accommodating secularism and humanism – and these are not 'identities' – but in seeing them as one solution to divisiveness.

Contemporary curriculum can also be seen as amoral. Fida Sanjakdar (2004) for example talks of how Muslim parents look for an education that builds Islamic morals, deeds, character and behaviour. This is understandable. But her critique of 'contemporary sexual health education' is less so. This curriculum apparently presents as normal or acceptable certain behaviours which Muslims believe as sinful:

> 'Free sex, 'safe sex', 'boyfriend/girlfriend relationships', for instance, are terms and concepts devoid of any responsibility and accountability and hence in direct violation of Islamic behaviour and Islamic law (*Sharia*). (p149)

Yet such a polemic misses the point that 'safe sex' is actually about responsibility and accountability. It is one thing to say that Islam prefers a certain definition of morality and another to accuse a curriculum of being 'devoid of any responsibility'. Doing so betrays a strong reluctance to engage with any other moral code, let alone the reality of adolescent relationships. Apparently in Islam, 'students are not supposed to know about the sexual act before they reach adolescence' (p160). Later, Sanjakdar talks of 'From an Islamic viewpoint, the area of most concern is 'the total absence of a guiding religious moral and values framework'. Total? 'Underpinned by Western liberal values, the curriculum is devoid of any others' (p154). It is the totalism which is the most worrying in this critique. One thing schools have always tried to do is promote moral education, even if only in order to keep discipline. The idea that it is completely impossible to have a morality without a religion is a myth which demands serious challenge. Sanjakdar complains of curriculum hegemony, using ideas from Apple and Giroux around cultural reproduction, apparently not mindful or caring about religious reproduction – and, from a 'Western liberal' view, keeping young people in ignorance. I digress into sex education here not as an expert but for two reasons: one is the need for recognition of the value of a secular morality in rights or humanism, and the second is the concern about the 'extremism' of views which seek equally to 'totalise' others.

So there has to be a set of values which is inclusive and yet open to scrutiny and change. Watson summed up the dilemma neatly with regard to citizenship education:

> Citizenship education is both the promotion of (assumed) common values (freedom, responsibility, honesty), irrespective of class, sex, gender ethnicity, culture and religion and, at the same time, is about encouraging young people to acquire the skills to question and evaluate values. (2004:266)

This presents Watson with a problem: 'how do you do the latter based on an assumption of the former'? (2004:266). As discussed in Chapter 3, national identity work does not solve this problem. But I argue that human rights does, for two reasons. First, it is made by people, and therefore can be scrutinised as man-made and the best bet for that historical era; and second, it is based not on ideals but on *entitlements* – it does not have a connotation of superiority or perfection.

The various covenants on rights can be debated, but they are indivisible and have a coherence. In contrast to religious value systems based on sacred texts, there is far less problem over which to select. Kahn (2006:363) quotes a widely circulated letter on the internet on the topic of scripture selection and the abomination of homosexuality, which makes a serious point:

- Lev 25:44 states that I may indeed possess slaves, both male and female, provided they are purchased from neighboring nations. A friend of mine claims that this applies to Mexicans, but not Canadians. Why cannot I own Canadians?

- I would like to sell my daughter into slavery, as sanctioned by Exodus 21:7. In this day and age, what do you think would be a fair price for her?

Rights also occupies ground that neither religion or science can. Scientific explanations do not have a particular morality in themselves, although social science might offer views on the contribution to social cohesion of values such as altruism or solidarity. Dawkins admits that science does not have an entitlement to advise us on moral values, but as he points out, this does not mean one cedes to *religion* the right to tell us what is good and what is bad. 'The fact that it has nothing else to contribute to human wisdom is no reason to hand religion a free licence to tell us what to do. Which religion, anyway? The one in which we happen to have been brought up?' (p57). As he points out, the Bible prescribes the death penalty for adultery, for gathering sticks on the Sabbath and for cheeking your parents. If we reject all this – as all enlightened moderns do – then which bits *do* we accept? 'And if we have independent criteria for choosing among our religious moralities, why not cut out the middle man and go straight for the moral choice without the religion?' For me, the moral choice, the independent criteria, are best situated in human rights.

As well as cutting out the middle man, the brilliant thing about a rights base is that it also circumvents the problem of 'tolerance'. I can accept your right to believe in a culture or religion without having to accept the religion itself. As argued earlier, belief systems by definition cannot be equal or equally valid; but our right to believe in what we want, as long as this does not cause harm to others, is – and must be – equally distributed. Rights and responsibilities together deny the possibility of indoctrination or imposition of beliefs. If I have the right to believe what I want, then so have you, and I do not have the right to impose my beliefs on you. Of course I might openly or sneakily try to persuade you; but I have no *mandate* to do this, whether from a supernatural power or any other source. Rights is not a belief system, it is an ethical system, and that is the crucial difference.

## Rights Respecting Schools

The above discussion can be concretised by giving a working example. UNICEF's Rights Respecting Schools is arguably the most promising initiative that we have nationally and internationally at the moment. It is an initiative which has developed from work in Nova Scotia and in the UK which is pre-mised on using the UN Convention on the Rights of the Child as a basis for all school life and ethos. In a Rights Respecting School (RRS) all children, teachers, ancillary staff and parents learn about the Convention and what this means for relationships and for learning. Key to this is obviously the twinning of rights and responsibilities: that if I have the right to something, I have the responsibility to accord you that right, and you have the same right and the same responsibility towards me. It is the ultimate reciprocity. If I have the right to education, then you have the responsibility to help ensure I get this right, or at least not hinder it. So, in behavioural terms, if I have the right to education and learning, you should not hinder this right by playing up and preventing me from listening – and vice versa. It is ridiculously simple in some ways, and that is the beauty of it all.

There are at the time of writing 245 accredited RRSs in the UK, primary and secondary. Schools apply for awards at two Levels, and are visited by UNICEF officers or partners who talk to children, teachers, parents and governors, observe lessons if invited and generally soak up the atmosphere. The visitors start by asking everyone to 'show me how you are a RRR', but this is matched against benchmarks for teachers/adults/community and for pupils. The benchmarks fall into four areas:

- knowledge and understanding of the UNCRC and its relevance to school ethos and curriculum

- teaching and learning styles and methods commensurate with knowledge and understanding of children's rights

- pupils actively participating in decision-making throughout the school

- committed leadership building a rights-based school ethos through strategic direction and appropriate professional development.

Significantly, the final benchmark, under the fourth category, is that '*pupils are empowered to work for change in the full awareness of how the UNCRC is a major instrument for improvements in children's lives worldwide*' – that is, indication of an active citizenship role as well as that within the school.

The use of the UNCRC permeates not just behaviour policy but also curriculum, in terms of thinking about the rights of the child when, for example, examining global issues such as water, health, HIV/AIDs, or child labour. I recently visited a small rural Rights Respecting primary school in Shropshire, where the children were learning about child labour in their area and in various parts of the world, linking this to the slave trade and to current trafficking. The infants and juniors had also followed the case of Alan Johnston (the journalist who was captured in Gaza), doing a mindmap on the rights he had lost (they said, including play!). The children's code of conduct which they had devised was based on their rights and responsibilities, but even more significantly, they talked of the responsibility of the teacher to educate them. This thus involved a dual responsibility – to help teachers learn about their teaching. Every assembly, for example, children took it in turns to complete a feedback sheet with smiley faces, on what the assembly was about, whether they enjoyed it, whether it made them think. (I mentioned this to some primary deputy heads in multi-ethnic Wolverhampton who blanched at the thought of pupil feedback on assemblies; it is a notoriously difficult area because of its basis of compulsory 'Christian worship'.) I then asked some Year 5s (9-10 year olds) whether they would give feedback to a teacher that the lesson was boring. They reflected on this for a while and then thought they probably wouldn't. They said:

- It wouldn't be respectful
- It might hurt their feelings
- They have the right not to be humiliated.

What can be seen from this is that children are not just parroting the conventions but are trying to make sense of them in their everyday lives and relationships. Operating on rights forms a basis for the unknown – when asylum seekers move in, the children can cope. This is better than artificial exchanges and visits, and provides reality and depth to intercultural work.

The head of this Church of England school talked about the original ingrained parochial, homophobic, racist culture surrounding the school. Parishioners made hate calls saying they were not proper Christians, the parents on the church council had stopped the pupils from visiting the Gurdwara, the National Front put up four candidates out of fourteen in the local elections; residents of nearby Manchester were referred to as 'niggers'. But with the advent of the Rights Respecting Schools programme, this changed. Children would stand up for other children who were 'different', for example those with special needs. They participated in the Junior G8 summit, engaging with children from other countries. The school was breaking down parochialism and hate with its insistence on respect and its more global vision.

One aspect is the distinguishing of identity and action – which has been a theme of this book. Singular, ascribed identities can be replaced by hybrid, fluid and conditional ones. In Rights Respecting schools, each day is a fresh day, in that behaviour is dealt with as it relates to rights, on that day, ideally without reference to previous infringements, avoiding 'you always ... you never...'. Children are not ascribed permanent behavioural identities – difficult of course, with persistent 'offenders', but at least they try. Instead behaviours would be examined in terms of how they affect others on that day – preventing them from learning, infringing their rights to play, infringing their right to protection from harm. Punishments are replaced by 'uncomfortable interviews' exploring the consequences of the behaviour and how to take responsibility for it. I asked, why 'uncomfortable'? The headteacher said that it was similar to how some criminals prefer prison to probation, because they do not want to take responsibility. Children may in fact prefer a detention, as this is mindless and inappropriate – it has nothing to do with them.

Part of the Rights Respecting ethos is democracy in practice – school councils, much dialogue, and obviously the emphasis on equality in rights. An action research project just completed on school councils in London secondary schools documented some radical work around both feedback to teachers and behaviour (Davies and Yamashita, 2007). Students were systematically trained to observe lessons and give teachers feedback on specific issues that the teacher wanted them to explore, for example, the balance between closed and open questions, or how much attention is given to girls and boys, to disruptive or passive students. Not only did the teachers learn, but the students said they became aware of how difficult teaching was – all that planning, and introductions, and keeping order. The behaviour panels also researched classrooms, identifying students whom the others thought caused the most mayhem, and talking with them. The stance was awareness raising more than straight admonition – 'do you realise how you stop the others learning anything'? This has clear resonances with Rights Respecting Schools, and UNICEF and School Councils UK are going to be working together more on this. As with peer mediation and peer mentoring, also often part of School Council work, other students can be more influential than teachers in changing behaviour or helping solve conflicts.

Part of RRS and School Council work entails changing the behaviour of teachers. This links back to the revenge questions tackled in Chapter 4. Teachers have to think about the right of the child to dignity, freedom from humiliation, and to be listened to. This is actually quite hard for teachers, who are not generally trained in listening skills. Listening to what children actually want and feel instead of what they ought to want and feel is alien to teachers steeped in a tradition of moral rectitude. What RRS underscores is the obvious point that teachers are not the sole or key repository of morals, and that students and teachers are equal interpreters and enacters of the rights. Teachers have to model respect, and again this is difficult for the teachers who do not, deep down, think that children have the same rights to respect as do adults, and who do not believe that children are entitled to the same rules of politeness, saving face, courtesy, and conversational turn-taking as would be expected in an adult-adult interaction. As one boy in a RRS told me, in his previous school, teachers knew about rights and responsibilities, but they hadn't *thought* about it. There, 'if you were bullied and went to a teacher, they'd say 'get on with it', they never had time for you. If they *thought* about it, it would be a nice school'.

There is then a persuasive combination of rationales for using the UNCRC as a basis for learning. Ian Massey, the Hampshire LEA inspector for intercultural learning, summarised these in a paper on the UNICEF website, and I summarise them even more briefly as:

- the Convention provides a framework that describes the global consensus on societal values for *all* children. Children learn that all children have rights, and this allows for development of a sense of connectedness with other children

- children learn they have rights *now* – solely because they are children. These rights are not earned or awarded at a particular age. This is of much greater interest to them than being prepared for what they may acquire in later life. Teaching can focus on pupils' self interest and current realities

■ children learn about their responsibilities, because other children's rights have to be respected (Covell and Howe, 2001). This is a positive tone, and better than much behaviour policy which centres round what children should *not* do. It also develops a positive and socially responsible identity which is more likely when children believe in and feel good about themselves

■ children come to realise that they have a responsibility to themselves to ensure that they take the opportunities offered by their rights.

■ the UNCRC avoids any tendency to moral or cultural relativism in discussion of social and moral dilemmas

■ the realisation that there are many situations where rights appear to conflict promotes the development of higher order thinking and reasoning skills.

■ difficulties faced by children can be seen as rights violations rather than individual weaknesses or failures

■ use of the UNCRC avoids the teachers' or schools' values being seen as isolated examples of political correctness. It demonstrates, for example, that codes of conduct are not unique to each school, but come from principles that are world-wide and expressed in the Conventions.

Many of these points are relevant to educating against extremism. The global reach of UNCRC is one, and is a good antidote to claims for global ascendancy or domination or universalism by particular political systems or religions. John Hanson Community school in Hampshire wrote on the UNICEF website how 'the school's values are now universal and transferable, rather than plucked from the 'liberal fog', and having relevance only for 5 school years'. Yet these universal – and lasting – values are not a blueprint. The point about apparently conflicting rights is a benefit, not a problem. It avoids absolutist thinking, the one correct answer. But it also avoids relativism, that any old answer will do, or that any culturally-based answer must be respected. When children and teachers know all the various rights but also know they occur in a context, this provides a basis for resolution or a 'least worst' compromise. This may be a utilitarian response, but it allows a 'greater good' to be specified rather than remaining at a philosophical discussion of whose 'good'. A key dimension is what actually constitutes a right. For example, parents do not have a right to beat their children.

In behavioural terms, a rights-based approach is superior to behaviourist techniques which reward students for the adoption of certain values but contain scant cognitive components and no critical thinking. It is also superior to the 'moral stories' approach favoured by some primary schools, where certain values such as honesty, perseverance, kindness, courage etc. are narrated as winning the day. Not only is this patently untrue in many circumstances, but apparently children do not actually accept these messages. Narvaez (2002) reminds us of how children actively construct their own meanings through their prior knowledge and may interpret the story differently, even negatively. Even democracy needs a context: while there is, rightly, a move towards students creating their own class codes and school rules, these can be separated from parental or wider community values and sometimes appear to be in conflict. As Massey points out, there is rarely any connection to wider national or international codes of social and moral responsibility.

This is not to claim that this approach can all be introduced overnight. Portway Junior School in Hampshire told how their Year 6 class was debating what aspects of the UN Convention they wanted as part of their charter, and whether it should have a section on immigrants.

> The children in the class were aware of the possibility of refugees joining the school. A member of the class had suggested that ALL Arabs were terrorists. A point that drew protests from the rest of the class and a number of rebuttals, including '*that would mean there were 9 million of them*'. To get to a stage where children were able to debate and understand the issues that will confront them for the rest of their lives has taken four years'. (UNICEF website)

The research continues on Rights Respecting schools. The findings so far indicate that adolescents show higher self-esteem and also feel valued, as well as more optimistic; those who received the rights curriculum perceived their classmates to be more accepting of ethnic minority children and perceived greater levels of peer and teacher support. There was a contagion effect, as learning about one's own rights results in support for the rights of others, including adults, and teachers' right to teach. There was a shift from adversarial and confrontational approaches to conflict resolution to the use of rights-based explanations. Teachers reported children using a rights-based discourse to settle problems, and they reported that children were readier to accept responsibility for their errors and behave appropriately when a rights-based explanation was offered for what is unacceptable (Covell and Howe,

2005). It makes sense when you think about it. So much bullying and play-ground fighting is about children hurling insults at each other, in an escalat-ing series of expletives and comments about their clothes, sexuality, mothers, in order to try to belittle and humiliate – just as warring groups do. Amazingly, replacing 'you big fat poof' with 'stop that, I've got the right to play' seems to work, at primary level anyway.

An important issue relates to the responsibility angle. Simply introducing human rights into schools may be counterproductive unless everyone accepts responsibility. Carter and Osler's study of the introduction of human rights into a boys' secondary school found at least one boy who saw rights as synonymous with weakness. 'If I had to say to someone I have a right to that, I would feel like I was asking their permission, they'd get the chance to say 'no' and then I would look stupid' (2000:345). Real men don't do rights. The prob-lem however seems to lie with this confusion of rights with permission: one primary school boy in John Lloyd's study of children's perceptions of citizen-ship, when asked if he had rights, said 'I am allowed to have chocolate after tea. I can have fish and chips on Wednesday' (Lloyd, 2006:120). Rights Res-pecting schools are precise about rights and try to make everyone responsible for them, not just the claimants.

## The link to democracy

A rights base also provides grounds for why democratic classrooms and schools are important. These are: systematic opportunities for children to participate in decisions that affect them (Article 12); children thinking and freely expressing their views (Article 14); and a climate where opinions can be expressed without loss of dignity (Article 39). There is compelling and in-creasing international evidence, which there is no room to describe here, that children with democratic teachers have more positive attitudes towards school, more respect for others and higher aspirations. They develop im-proved communication, participation and decision-making skills and greater social and interpersonal respect and responsibility (Alderson, 2000; Apple and Beane, 1999; Carnie, 2003; Chapman, Froumin and Aspin, 1995; Harber, 1997; Davies and Kirkpatrick, 2000; Harber and Davies, 2000; Schweisfurth, Davies and Harber, 2002; Trafford, 2003).

Yet it should not be assumed that the existence of democratic processes auto-matically solves conflict. In the Donnelly and Hughes study comparing Northern Ireland and Israel, all four primary schools used circle time as a key mechanism for encouraging cultural tolerance. However, the ways in which teachers dealt with issues relating to conflict varied. In Northern Ireland teachers mostly stated that they were either nervous of such discussion or that they did not see it as important in the integrated school context. Teachers in Israel tended to describe these discussions as cathartic and a natural part of the process of breaking down political and cultural boundaries. In the Israeli schools there was a sharing of experiences and stories of violence, and a desire to find a 'solution'. This resonates with the dialogue examples given in Chapter 2. In the Northern Ireland schools, teachers might deflect all this into a discussion of football, and avoid emotional or empathetic conversations. Discussions were deliberately and carefully managed to ensure that they did not stray into controversial or politically contentious areas, to avoid 'ill feeling' or 'breakdown in relations'. Ironically, newer teachers in the integrated schools scarcely felt like pioneers trying to engage in mediation, and simply saw it as a job.

Consequently, we have to be careful about what sort of democracy is being talked about, who defines it, and at what level. As Elworthy and Rifkind (2006) point out, in the minds of western élites assumptions are made that secular society denotes democracy, power-sharing and women's rights. 'In contrast, the experience of secular rule in the Arab world is linked with authoritarianism, whereas Islamic laws of governance include notions of inclusiveness and welfare which were not experienced under secular, authoritarian regimes' (p55).

Other unexamined assumptions can be the link between democracy and nationalism. A widely quoted view of education for democracy in time of conflict and terrorism is Kathryn Kersten's:

> Our children are living in perilous times. To prepare them to preserve their heritage of freedom in this dangerous world, we must place education aimed at cultivating democratic citizenship at the heart of the school curriculum, (quoted in Ben-Porath, 2006:116)

This starts to look dubious. The 'heritage of freedom' ideology is reminiscent of Bush's justification for attacking Iraq. But as Ben-Porath points out, it gets worse. The mark of 'true citizens' is to show the qualities of 'courage, loyalty, responsibility, gratitude to forbears, and a self-sacrificing devotion to the common good ... they must have ... a love for – and desire to perpetuate – the republic'. Ben-Porath calls this 'belligerent citizenship' – communal identity and nationalism as a project of loyalty and sacrifice. I see it as not far removed from political or religious martyrdom in its ideology. There seems to be no critique of government, only gratitude – for the slave trade? For Hiroshima? For Vietnam? Kersten apparently advocates the teaching of the 'character ideal' through heroic stories of patriotism, inspiring students to follow suit. This form of civic virtue is not only narrow but dangerous and pays little attention to pluralism and a pluralist history. It is even more disturbing when coming out of the 'education for democracy' school.

Hence in educating against extremism it is problematic to have unexamined concepts of democracy as equating with patriotism. Far more deliberative notions of democracy are required. I have previously argued for 'interruptive democracy' which is the active challenge to injustice, the habitual reflex of saying 'excuse me' when recognising the need for dissent (explored in Davies, 2004).

## Operational Base: Ways of working

Democracy is both a value and a process, and this leads into discussion of the third quadrant, the operational one, the ways of working. One important orientation is the resistance to polarised views, to the binary thinking which we have seen to characterise much extremist justification.

> George Bush gave an example of either/or logic when after 9/11 he said 'There is no middle ground. You are either with us or against us'. His statement is patently false: several other options were available – to be neutral or to try to mediate from the middle ground, for instance. Bush's *attitude* or *mind-set* – his logic or way of using words and thinking – led him to polarise the issue into only two choices, only one of which was 'correct'. He, and we, went to war with that mindset. (Colbeck, 2007)

As Colbeck then observes, it is far from easy – strictly speaking impossible – to think *thoroughly* critically. I cannot make a criticism and *at the same time* criticise the criteria I am using for that judgement. But we can be made aware of the basis of our criteria, their permanence, their origin, their universality or their particularism.

I have used chaos and complexity theory before to explore conflict and the role of institutions in this. One insight of complexity theory which is particularly valuable is the notion that for emergence into better forms, a system or organism needs to approach 'the edge of chaos' – that is, a messier form, experimentation, risk. What extremism does is actually revert to primitivism because of the lack of acknowledgement of complexity and a preference for absolutes, dualism, for good and evil. The role of education instead is to challenge that dualism, acknowledge multiple realities and approach the edge of chaos, as Robin Brooke-Smith (2003) argued in his book on leadership. Brooke-Smith was arguing for the edge of chaos to be used for school improvement; I propose it for anti-extremism. In concrete terms, that means comparative religion, comparative value systems – even exploring creationism if wanted or necessary, but as a religion, not a science. The opposite to absolutism and reductionism is comfort with ambiguity. It is also the fostering of 'critical (dis)respect' – working out which ideas and actions in a culture to respect and which to disrespect.

Openness and the presentation of alternatives can of course be hijacked, but that is a risk that has to be taken. Gary Younge (2004) reported an interesting dispute about a suburban American school which found itself in court after it tried to placate Christian fundamentalist parents by placing a sticker on its science textbooks saying evolution was 'a theory, not a fact'. A 2,300 strong petition of parents had attacked the presentation of 'Darwinism un-challenged'. Some wanted creationism – the theory that God created humans according to the Bible version – to be taught alongside evolution. The arguments were for a 'fair share', 'other explanations' and an 'open mind'. One parent said 'God created earth and man in his image. Leave this garbage out of the textbooks. I don't want anybody taking care of me in a nursing home some day to think I came from a monkey'. In 1987 the Supreme Court had ruled that creationism was a religious belief that could not be taught in public schools along with evolution. Since then creationism has been repackaged as the theory of 'intelligent design', attempting to bypass the question of the separation of church and state.

My argument in terms of learning about alternatives does not however extend to total relativism. Just as human rights can be a basis for examining the merits of the impact of different belief systems, a respect for evidence and probabilities has to be the basis for examining claims to 'truth'. In the end, the 'intelligent design' people fall back on the argument that we can't explain it, therefore it has to be some superior intelligence. Yet we have enough overwhelming scientific evidence now, from Darwin onwards, to support a factual explanation as opposed to a mystical one. Evolution is no longer a 'theory' any more than the law of gravity is. I accept that our notions of 'facts' do change – the earth is flat, lard is healthy, Elvis lives – but the function of schooling is to acknowledge this development while presenting the best evidence available at the time, and enabling learners to access and evaluate this evidence. This does not stop us wondering at the marvels and beauties of nature which are a result of evolution.

*Critical thinking*

Just as positive conflict is necessary, we also need 'positive extremism', as would be mooted by Socrates. His 'extreme principle' was that one should be committed 1) to act according to the views which currently are the ones that have the best reasons and arguments put forward for them, and 2) to search for even better reasons and arguments (quoted in Salmenkivi, 2007). This may seem to contradict the concerns about perfectionism raised in Chapter 1, but the main point is perhaps not the arrival at the 'best' solution but the continual process of searching and questioning.

I offer two examples of critical thinking with regard to fundamentalist attitudes, and the search for 'better reasons'. The first would relate to feminist pedagogy, which usually tried to challenge a multiplicity of widely accepted dichotomies, including that of cognition/emotion (Ben-Porath, 2006). It is not just about respecting the individual and building a positive self-conception. It is also that fear, hate and misconceptions must all be present in the classroom and dealt with, not flatly rejected. In reference to attitudes to lesbian, gay and bisexual (LGB) people (see Chapter 1) Kahn argues that teachers who are very religious should examine how their beliefs might influence the children they teach. (The studies showed that the stronger the religious conviction, the less tolerant individuals were towards LGB individuals). Kahn asks how educators approach students whose beliefs are anchored in authoritative biblical rhetoric. One tactic she uses is to provide contradictory information in the hope of inducing 'irritating doubt'. 'Students need to know that what they consider 'normal' and 'right' are socially constructed categories and therefore unstable, unfixed and mutable' (p365). You cannot just 'tell' students they need to protect LGB individuals from harassment.

> The common sense approach to changing beliefs is in a sense unsophisticated, not unlike simplistic approaches to multicultural education, where some individuals believe that a 'true' multicultural school is one where all of the ethnic history months each have their bulletin boards displayed in the hallways with their famous token African-Americans, Hispanics and Others. There is an assumption that given certain 'believable' information or outcomes, individuals will conform to desired behaviours or beliefs (i.e. if we show you famous African-Americans, then you will not be racist. If I am showing you famous African-Americans, then I am not racist)'. (p365)

Kahn sees a major obstacle to guiding students to deconstruct and actually 'see' the power of socialising agents such as the media, churches and schools as being that they are not in the habit of questioning the *status quo*. There is also the problem of agency: she found most of her own teacher trainees agreed that LGB people deserved the same rights and privileges as everybody else, but that only thirteen out of 43 thought it important to stand up to those who demonstrate homophobic attitudes. Is this contradictory? Or just an abdication of responsibility, the acceptance of a disjuncture between beliefs/ identity and actions? Kahn lists a number of strategies to break down inertia in prospective teachers – requiring students to identify their beliefs, examining inconsistencies, examining culture and histories of beliefs, debunking myths – for example that gay men are paedophiles, LGB are bad parents etc – providing resources, inviting speakers, and asking students to promise that they will not let derogatory language go by, and will affirm the identities of LGB youth.

The same strategies could of course apply to attitudes and actions towards any group, such as ethnic or religious minorities, and could apply to teachers whose own beliefs were founded not only in fundamentalist Christianity but in any extremist position.

### Ijtihad and 'truth'

Secondly, we have much to learn from the most crucial of jihads, which is *ijtihad*. This is the Islamic tradition of independent reasoning. Carrie Antal (2006) provides a useful and well researched discussion of ijtihad, claiming that the 'intellectual tool' of ijtihad is increasingly entering the discourse on development and reform in the Muslim world. Ijtihad, which literally translates as intellectual 'striving' or 'exertion' has historically been the fundamental process by which Islamic law and scholarship have developed. Progressive Muslims are arguing that the ijtihad is in fact every Muslim's duty and right to reasoned, critical analysis of questions whose answers are not found in the Qu'ran or *sunna* (established Islamic practices). Antal cites a number of scholars, NGOs, multinational agencies and Muslim religious authorities who are championing ijtihad as a tool that will enable Arab societies to reshape themselves for the 21st century. In judicial terms, it is in contrast to the practice of *taqlid* (following precedent). But many voices for reform in the region argue that shifting from taqlid to *juridical* ijtihad, while highly useful and necessary, is insufficient to achieve the sweeping changes that they believe are required to stimulate development in the region, and urge the encouraging of ijtihad at the *individual* level so that the Arab world might derive creative development solutions from any of its citizens.

> The promotion of critical thinking in schools, supported by a progressive curriculum and student-centered pedagogy, is seen as the first step in the propagation of individual ijtihad. (p2)

Manji inevitably puts it more strongly, pointing to the difference between Jews and Muslims in terms of critiques. Jews will actually publicise disagreements by surrounding their scriptures with commentaries and incorporating debates into the Talmud itself. 'By contrast, most Muslims treat the Qu'ran as a document to imitate rather than interpret, suffocating our capacity to think for ourselves' (2004:42). It is the 'perfect' scripture – not to be questioned, analysed or even interpreted, but simply believed. The *hadiths* (authoritative reports of what Prophet Muhamad said and did throughout his life) have a similar function, with all that is required being to submit to them.

> Do you see where this express train of goodness is actually taking us? To a destination called Brain-Dead. When abuse occurs under the aegis of Islam, the majority of Muslims don't know how to argue, reassess or reform. Which is just as well, we're told, since abuse can't occur as long as we stay true to the perfect text. Aaargh! What asylum logic! Such circular conditioning of the mind is enough to turn the brightest bulb into dimwits, and dangerous ones at that. (Manji, 2004:43)

Manji talks of how instead of acknowledging a serious problem with the practice of Islam today, Muslims have 'reflexively romanticised' Islam. 'The peer pressure to stay on message – the message being that *we're not all terrorists* – seduced us into avoiding the most crucial of jihads: self criticism' (p62). So she too turns to the different Islamic tradition of ijtihad.

Ijtihad is supported by the UNDP in their Arab Development report (2006), as well as by ISESCO (Islamic Educational, Scientific and Cultural Organisation), a multinational development agency based in Rabat whose researchers are drawn from across the Muslim world. The Arab Bureau for Education in the Gulf States (ABEGS), also strongly favours student-centred learning and the development of critical thinking skills for the promotion of academic excellence in scientific and technical fields. We can see that these organisations' arguments for ijtihad are more concerned with economic and scientific development than with using it as a barrier to extremism, but it is good that the interests coincide. A forum for National Dialogue in Saudi Arabia found local specialists proposing teaching ijtihad in local schools as part of a curriculum reform package aimed at reducing religious extremism and propensity towards terrorism. They urged the teaching of ijtihad in public schools to prevent the development of a terrorist mentality in the classroom and also to prevent the use of the highly authoritarian educational system as a tool for religious indoctrination (Dankowitz, 2004). Gesink (2006), writing about Egypt, regards the teaching of critical thinking skills as constituting one of many historically precedented applications of ijtihad.

However, high ranking religious authorities resist this spread of ijtihad as being 'destructive' of society, colluding with Zionists or serving American interests, and even call for protagonists to be brought to trial. The continuing debate about whether ijtihad can be legitimately engaged in only by religious authorities leads to more 'heretical' writing by Manji:

> Learning about ijtihad spurred me to ask: who are these religious authorities? I mean, does the Qu'ran recognise a formal clergy? Nope. Do the Qu'ran's wild mood swings make any interpretation of its text selective and subjective? Yep. So, it could be that the right of independent thinking, the tradition of ijtihad, is fact open to all of us? That by arrogating this right to themselves, the follow-my-fatwa ayatollahs are the actual heretics? (p64)

Significantly, the US government has also directed finance and research towards exploring the role of ijtihad in building peace, democracy and development in the Muslim world (Smock, 2004). Proposals include reforming religious curriculum to include the teaching and contrasting of all four Sunni legal schools, plus incorporating philosophy, logic, psychology, political theory and economics into the curriculum. The Washington think tank Centre for the Study of Islam and Democracy (CSID) has been active in promoting a vision of Muslim democracy in which ijtihad plays a fundamental role. Its director, Radwan Masmoudi, believes the majority of Muslims are moderates who desire a representative government but distrust the concept of democracy as they have experienced it so far, having been buffeted between the political objectives of religious extremists on one side and secular extremists on the other. CSID have developed an instructor's manual for the teaching of democratic governance that takes this distrust into account by framing democracy in terms of Islamic traditions conducive to free and representative governance, including *shura* (consultation) and ijtihad. 'The manual is replete with student-centered activities which develop students' critical thinking skills and call upon them to logically analyse information drawn from the Qu'ran and Hadiths to arrive at novel conclusions, in effect leading them to practice ijtihad as part of the lesson' (Antal, 2006:10).

Ijtihad would also encourage critical thinking elsewhere. In 2005, Tariq Ramadan said it was time to speak out – 'both against those who are doing these things in the name of our religion and against those who say that being a British citizen means blindly accepting all the decisions of the British government. Ours must be a constructive and critically participative loyalty' (p8). He also believes it is time for greater inter-religious dialogue, 'It is high time for Muslims to say that antisemitism is not acceptable. We have to ask questions of our own tradition and be self-critical about what is sectarian and racist'.

That means educating young Muslims in more than religious formalism. They must be taught that 'the capacity to promote social justice and the protection of the integrity of every individual, woman or man, rich or poor' is what determines authentic Islam' (Ramadan, 2005:8).

## Critical action and non-violence

The answer to extremism is not merely to be 'moderate'. Genocide cannot be done 'in moderation'. Having established critical thinking and a critical value base for this in universalist human and children's rights, we can turn to practical action. This is both about the big and abstract idea of 'building civil society' and also about individual acts of resistance to violence and extremism. One example is the international treaty to ban landmines. When Jody Williams, who won the Nobel Peace Prize for her work in bringing that about, was asked how she did it, she replied 'e-mail' (Garton Ash, 2004:251). We must 'refuse the illusion of impotence'.

It is interesting that extremist reform in Pakistan has not completely wiped out the human rights movement – why? Sen's take on this is that the resistance comes from

- using civil laws
- courage and commitment of civil dissidents
- fair-mindedness of many upright members of the judiciary
- the presence of a large body of social progressive public opinion
- effectiveness of the media in drawing attention to inhumanity and violation of civil decency, issues for the attention of a 'reflective public'. (2006:73)

It is not difficult to see the potential role of education in fostering all of the above – legal education, media education and an informed citizenship education. There is a problem that the US-led war on terror has been preoccupied with military solutions, and the importance of civil society has been neglected. The emphasis on always meeting 'Muslim leaders' to find solutions has bolstered and strengthened the voice of religious authorities while downgrading the importance of nonreligious institutions and movements. The problem is that we do not have 'secular leaders' or 'humanist leaders' – nor would I necessarily want to have people speak for me, unless I directly mandate them. But the whole message of this book is that we should locate the challenges to extremism in all civil society, not just specific sections of it. As Sen observes:

Efforts to recruit the mullahs and the clergy to play a role outside the immediate province of religion could, of course, make some difference in what is preached in mosques or temples. But it also downgrades the civic initiatives people who happen to be Muslim by religion can and do undertake (along with others) to deal with what are essentially political and social problems ... What religious extremism has done to demote and downgrade the responsible political action of citizens (irrespective of religious ethnicity) has been, to some extent, reinforced, rather than eradicated, by the attempt to fight terrorism by trying to recruit the religious establishment on 'the right side'. (2006:78/83)

I am therefore cheered by the growth of active non-sectarian citizenship education in many schools and countries, which encourages action in the community as well as in school. Our recent review for the Carnegie Foundation (Davies, Williams and Yamashita, 2006) on the impact of pupil decision-making in school and community looked at over 80 studies worldwide. We found evidence of young people taking action not just to improve the community, but also to hold local and national government to account – which was my third question for this book. Young people's J8 summits, Youth Parliaments and Local Government consultation groups may not have a lot of teeth, but they are at least teaching skills of advocacy, lobbying, negotiation – that is, creating change not through violent means but through legal and micro-political processes.

One large scale study found that in schools with a commitment to student voice, students were much more confident in expressing their views about a range of topics, including government policy, than students in schools where there were little opportunities for student voice (Hannam, 2004). Similarly, a project we have been involved in on developing School Councils finds – unsurprisingly – that students given powers and responsibility develop a sense of agency and improve their confidence to change things (Davies and Yamashita, 2007). This is not rocket science – but it is interesting how resistant some teachers still are to student involvement. One part of the project which involves pupils observing teachers to provide systematic feedback on teaching and learning evoked the response from one teacher: 'I'm not having kids watch me teach'...

So I do not underplay the individual and institutional barriers to an education which might tackle extremism. Nor would I or should I speak for those in far more difficult circumstances than I am or than children are in UK schools. For the Global Review for UNESCO on their Associated Schools (Davies, Harber and Schweisfurth, 2003), we asked schools what activities they were doing in the community for peace, tolerance and human rights. We were given some inspirational examples – kids on marches, peace vigils, advocacy work for non-violence in the community. But we also received bitter responses from children in occupied Palestine and Gaza strip who said a) that they were not allowed free movement, that the checkpoints, walls and brutality from Israeli soldiers prevented their doing anything and b) we should therefore be asking the Israelis about peace, not them. It would be facile to suggest some universal panacea or citizenship curriculum for education against extremism.

On the issue of faith schools, the judgement would be of on what actions they take, and for whom. Al Noori Muslim Primary school in Australia attempted to be part of the local community, repairing roofs after a storm and inviting them for tea. But what finally gained them acceptance was when the children wrote directly to Saddam Hussein to plead the case of Australian hostages in Kuwait, including the grandson of the school's neighbour. Muslims were being portrayed, for the first time, as both patriotically Australian and genuinely Muslim at the same time (Donahoue Clyne, 2004). This was a welcome change from the Australian press's usual images of hijab wearing girls sitting at the back of the class, as evidence of gender based discrimination, or worse, the association with terrorism. Using their weight for political influence might, admittedly, be one argument for denominational schools.

Omaar (2007) provides another practical example of this weight. He describes how young Somalis have opened a club in Ealing in London, a combination of café, meeting place and centre for community activities. Called *Talow*, which means advice and opinion, it provides a valuable service. 'Young men who have done time at young offenders' institutions such as Feltham and have become very devout Muslims, could easily, without a place like Talow, turn their sense of marginalisation into violence, as Yassin Hassan Omar did' (p208). Some are trying to build up a network of small businesses and others are trying to make their voices heard not through demonstrations but by voting – a key part of integration and a sense of active participation, however small.

## Critical idealism

We return finally to the purpose of promoting agency and political participation of young people. There are a number of paradoxes in arguing for a form of education which will challenge extremism. It is like the irony of a sign spotted at the World Trade Conference that read: 'Join The World Wide Movement against Globalisation'. The paradox can be summarised as wanting young people to have ideals; acknowledging that these ideals should not be or cannot be imposed or indoctrinated in a democratic society; and yet realising that to pursue ideals may lead into avenues which are seen as harmful. Sieckelinck and De Ruyter (2006) acknowledge some of these dilemmas.

> What we try to preserve through counter-terror education can only flourish by exchange of different ideals, while at the same time the educational entrance against extremism is apparently the warning against ideals. (p13)

The introduction to this book discussed how extremists and terrorists are often social or political idealists, acting primarily in a social space. Sieckelink and De Ruyter point out that 'it is expected that other people will become victims of the plans or the actions of the idealist', but then ask 'couldn't we offer children examples of worthwhile ideal inspired agency next to the counter-terror discourse, so that they can learn that it is good to live by ideals, as long as they reflect on how they express the passion for it?' (p15-16).

Immediately we see the problem of who decides what is 'worthwhile' and what is a 'public good'. For Sieckelinck and De Ruyter, 'reasonable passion' incorporates a sense of rationality (reflexivity), morality (not detrimental to others) and prudence (not at one's own expense). So counter-terror education should focus its efforts on encouraging children to have ideals but to pursue them in a 'reasonable' manner. It is not just a 'safety discourse'. The implication is that education should surface and discuss a range of ideals, so there is the reflexivity and the deliberation, but not promote one over the other, thereby downgrading the holder of that ideal. This was the problem of the BNP supporters in school, mentioned in Chapter 3. Where schooling or monitoring would need to become more strongly interventionist is over how those ideals might be pursued.

Useful distinctions and strategies could be drawn from proponents of advocacy for social justice (Cohen *et al*, 2001). In their manual on global action for the Oxfam Advocacy Institute, they distinguish *ideological advocacy* (groups pushing to make their beliefs and values dominant, battling others in the streets, in the halls of decision-makers and in electoral campaigns); *mass advocacy* (petitions, protests, non-violent civil disobedience); *interest-group advocacy* (organising round a specific set of issues, and lobbying); and *bureaucratic advocacy* (researchers, economists and consultants influencing decision-makers in the system). They give critiques of each of these forms and argue that social justice advocacy tries to extract and combine the strengths of each – drawing on people's experiences and finding ways to amplify their knowledge; building relationships with officials and experts; using organised mass action to engage decision-making systems; and translating protest into policy demands for specific institutional change, or moving 'from protest to politics' (Cohen *et al*, 2001:10). The manual is not aimed at schools, but could very valuably be drawn upon, not least in their use of mental models of political space and a human rights framework.

## Conclusion

The model can now be filled in. This is unashamedly bipolar, to make the contrast starkly. The X on the left summarises all the components of an anti-extremism education, versus the right-hand X in school (and society) which cements extremist divides and attitudes.

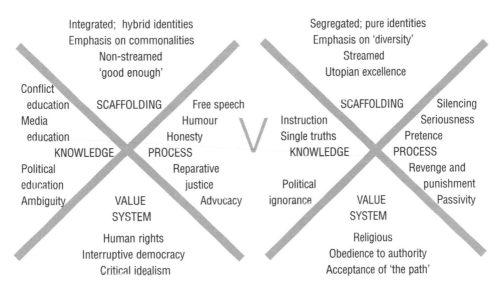

It must be stressed that *all* the components are necessary for anti-extremism education to be coherent. The rights base to values and school life gives young people a personal sense of worth, now. It provides immediate practice and the feeling of altruism in exercising responsibility, so that they will be less beguiled by extremist groups promising a special place in the world. The end-point of wanting to see rights for others as well as oneself is that schools should politicise – even radicalise – young people. Yet for idealism not to become extremist in the sense of causing harm, the book has shown that students and teachers need five types of criticality:

- a sound political education which includes conflict studies, comparative religion, non-nationalistic citizenship and political skills – *critical scholarship*

- sound understanding of universal rights and responsibilities – *critical (dis)respect*

- skills to weigh up alternative ideals and means to pursue them – *critical thinking*

- the acceptance that ideals should be provisional – *critical doubt*

- the acceptance that ideals and their holders can be mocked – *critical lightness*

The answer to extremism is not moderation, but a highly critical and informed idealism. Extremism's major enemy is also a lightness of touch.

---

### Math teacher arrested at airport

New York: a public school teacher was arrested today at JFK international airport as he attempted to board a flight while in possession of a ruler, a protractor, a set square and a calculator. At a morning press conference, Attorney Alberto Gonzales said he believes the man is a member of the notorious Al-gebra movement. He did not identify the man, who has been charged by the FBI with carrying weapons of math instruction.

'Al-gebra is a problem to us' Gonzales said. 'They desire solutions by means and extremes and sometimes go off at tangents in search of absolute values. They use secret code names like 'x' and 'y' and refer to themselves as 'unknowns', but we have determined that they belong to a common denominator of the axis of med-ieval, with coordinates in every country.'

When asked to comment on their arrest, President Bush said 'If God had wanted us to have better weapons of math instruction, he would have given us more fingers and toes'. White House aides told reporters they could not recall a more intelligent and profound statement by the President.

---

# References

Abrahams, N (2004) Sexual violence against women in South Africa. *Sexuality in Africa*, 1,3

Adie, K (2002) *The Kindness of Strangers* London: Headline

Aguilar, P and Richmond, M (1998) Emergency education response in the Rwandan crisis. In G.Retamol and R.Aedo-Richmond(eds) *Education as a Humanitarian Response* London: Cassell

Alderson, P (2000) School students' views on school councils and daily life at school. *Children and Society* 14, p121-134

Alexander, T (2001) *Citizenship Schools* London: Campaign for Learning/UNICEF

Ali, T (2005) *Rough Music* London: Verso books

Alibhai-Brown, Y (2007) 'Ignoring terror suspects' rights will achieve nothing more than to further brutalise them' *The Independent* Monday 16th July 2007.

Allport, G (1954) *The Nature of Prejudice*. Reading, MA: Addison-Wesley

Amnesty International (2003) *Annual Report* at http://web.amnesty.org/report2003/irn-summary-eng

Anderson, B (1983) *Imagined Communities: reflections on the origin and spread of nationalism* London: Verso

Antal, C (2006) Reviving Ijtihad: Islamic critical thinking for legitimate reform in the Arab States. Paper presented at the Comparative and International Education Society (CIES) conference, Baltimore, March 2007

Apple, M (2001) *Educating the 'Right' Way: Markets, Standards, God and Inequality* London: RoutledgeFalmer

Apple, M. and Beane, J. (1999) *Democratic Schools: Lessons from the Chalkface* Buckingham: Open University Press

Armstrong, K (2006) Interview with Steve Paulson, http://www.salon.com/books/int/2006/05/30/armstrong/index3/html

Ashrawi, H (2007) A life in the day. *Sunday Times Magazine* Sep. 9th 2007, p58

Babha, H (1994) *The Location of Culture* London: Routledge

Bakti, A (2003) Communication and Dakwah: religious learning groups and their role in the protection of Islamic human security and rights for Indonesian civil society, in W. Nelles (ed) *Comparative education, terrorism and human security: from critical pedagogy to peace building?* New York: Palgrave Macmillan

Barber, B (1995) *Jihad versus McWorld* New York: Times Books

Bardhan, P (1997) *The Role of Governance in Economic Development* Paris: OECD

Barnes, P (2006) The misrepresentation of religion in modern British (religious) education. *British Journal of Educational Studies* 54,4, pp395 – 411

Battle, J and Grace, G (2006) *Citizenship Education, A Catholic Perspective: Working for the Common Good.* London: Centre for Research and Development in Catholic Education

Baxi, U (1998) The development of the right to development. In J.Symonides (eds) *Human Rights: New Dimensions and Challenges* Aldershot: Ashgate/Dartmouth and UNESCO

BBC News (2007) *HK's Tsand apologises for gaffe.* http://bbc.co.uk/go/pr/fr/-/2/hi/asia-pacific/ 7042941.stm Published 2007/10/13

Ben-Porath, S (2006) *Citizenship Under Fire: Democratic Education in Times of Conflict* Princeton: Princeton University Press

Bertani, M (2004) Muslims in Italy: social changes and educational practices. In B. van Driel, (ed) (2004) *Confronting Islamophobia in Practice* Stoke-on-Trent: Trentham

Bird, L (2006) Teaching and Learning about war and peace: a qualitative investigation into the role of education processes in the Great Lakes Region of Africa. Unpublished PhD thesis, University of London

Blair, M (2000) 'Race', School Exclusions and Human Rights. In A.Osler, (ed) *Citizenship and Democracy in Schools* Stoke on Trent: Trentham

Blum, W (1999) A Brief history of US Interventions: 1945 to the present. *Z magazine,* www. thirdworldtraveler.co,/Blum/US-Interventions

Bohleber, W (2003) Collective phantams, destructiveness and terrorism. In S.Varvin and V.Volkan (eds) *Violence or Dialogue? Psychoanalytic Insights on Terror and Terrorism* London: International Psychological Association

Bond, D (1993) *Living Myth: Personal Meaning as a Way of Life* Boston: Shambhala Publications

Brohi, N and Ajaib, A (2006) Violence against girls in the education system of Pakistan. In F.Leach and C.Mitchell (eds) *Combating Gender Violence in and around Schools* Stoke on Trent: Trentham

Brooke-Smith, R (2003) *Leading Learners, Leading Schools* London: RoutledgeFalmer

Brown, A (2003) Church of England Schools: politics, power and identity. *British Journal of Religious Education* 25,2, pp 103-16

Buijs, F, Demant, F and Hamdy, A (2006) *Strijders van Eigen Bodem: Radicale en Democratische Moslims in Nederland.* (Home-grown warriors: radical and democratic Muslims in the Netherlands) Amsterdam: Amsterdam University Press

Burke, J (2007) Pope's move on Latin mass 'a blow to Jews'. *Observer* 8.7.2007, p31

Bush, K and Saltarelli, D (2000) *The Two Faces of Education in Ethnic Conflict. Towards a Peace-building Education for Children* Florence: Innocenti Research Centre, United Nations Children's Fund

Cairns, E (1996) *Children and Political Violence* Oxford: Blackwell

Callan, E (1997) *Creating Citizens* Oxford: Oxford University Press

Cannon, M (2003) Human Security and Education in a conflict society: Lessons from Northern Ireland, in W. Nelles (ed) *Comparative education, terrorism and human security: from critical pedagogy to peace building?* New York: Palgrave Macmillan

Carnie, F. (2003) *Alternative Approaches to Education* (London:RoutledgeFalmer)

Carter, C and Osler, A (2000) Human Rights, Identity and Conflict Management: a study of school culture as experienced through classroom relationships. *Cambridge Journal of Education* 30,3, pp335-356

Cassidy, S (2006) Novelist reveals what life is like for a teenage girl under the hijab. *The Independent* Monday 8th May 2006, p12

Catron, P (2008) Blinking in the Sunlight: A Fundamentalist Perspective, in M. Diamond (ed) *Encountering Faith in the Classroom* Sterling VA: Stylus Publishing

# REFERENCES

Centre for Religious Freedom (2005) Saudi Publications on Hate Ideology fill American mosques 2

Chapman, J, Froumin, I and Aspin, D (1995) *Creating and Managing the Democratic School* London: Falmer

Cheng, S and Jacob, J (2003) The Changing Role of Education in a post-September 11, 2001 world: perspectives from East Africa, Taiwan and the United States, in W. Nelles (ed) *Comparative education, terrorism and human security: from critical pedagogy to peace building?* New York: Palgrave Macmillan

Chomsky, N (1997) *Media Control in the Spectacular Achievements of Propaganda* New York, N.Y: Seven Stones Press

Cockburn, C (1998) *The Space Between Us: Negotiating Gender and National Identities in Conflict* London: Zed Books

Cockburn, T (2007) 'Performing' racism: engaging young supporters of the far right in England. *British Journal of Sociology of Education* 28 (5) pp547-560

Cohen, C, Phipps, J and Waters, B (2007) Diversity, Policing and alternative dispute resolution. Paper presented at the conference *Education and Extremism* Roehampton University, London, 5th-7th July 2007

Cohen, D, de la Vega, R and Watson, G (2001) *Advocacy for Social Justice: a global action and reflection guide* Oxfam America and Advocacy Institute. Bloomfield: Kumarian Press

Colbeck, J (2007) Either/or logic pushes us towards polarized 'black or white' thinking in extremes: towards 'Final Solutions' ('in the last analysis'), Holocausts and war. Paper presented for workshop at the conference *Education and Extremism* Roehampton University, London, 5th-7th July 2007

Colenso, P (2005) Education and social cohesion: developing a framework for education sector reform In Sri Lanka. *Compare* 35,4, 411-428

Coles, M (2004) Education and Islam: a new strategy. In B. van Driel, (ed) (2004) *Confronting Islamophobia in Practice* Stoke-on-Trent: Trentham

Connolly, P (2000) What now for the contact hypothesis? Towards a new research agenda. *Race, Ethnicity and Education* 3 (2) pp169-193

Cortes, C (2000) *The Children Are Watching: How the Media Teach About Diversity* New York: Teachers College Press

Covell, K and Howe, B (1999) 'The Impact of children's rights education: A Canadian study *International Journal of Children's Rights* 7, 181-183

Covell, K and Howe, B (2001) Moral Education through the 3Rs: rights, respect and responsibility. *Journal of Moral Education* 30, pp31-42

Covell, K and Howe, B (2005) *Rights, Respect and Responsibility* Report on the RRR Initiative to Hampshire Education Authority. Cape Breton: Children's Rights Centre.

Craig, D (2000) 'A' is for Allah, 'J' is for Jihad. *World Policy Journal* XIX (1) 90-94

CRE (2007) *A Lot Done, A Lot to Do* Final Report of the Commission for Racial Equality, London: CRE

Dalai Lama (2001) *Book of Love and Compassion* London: Thorsons

Dankowitz, A (2004) Saudi study offers critical analysis of the Kingdom's religious curricula. *MEMRI Inquiry and Analysis Series*, No 195

Davies, L (2004) *Education and Conflict: Complexity and Chaos* London: Routledge

Davies, L (2005) Teaching about conflict through citizenship education. *International Journal of Citizenship and Teacher Education* 1,2, pp17-34

Davies, L (2006) 'Understanding the education-war interface' *Forced Migration Review*, July, p13

Davies, L, Harber C and Schweisfurth, M (2003) *Global Review of UNESCO ASPnet schools* Birmingham: Centre for International Education and Research

Davies, L, Harber, C and Yamashita, H (2005) *Global Citizenship Education: The Needs of Teachers and Learners* Birmingham: Centre for International Education and Research

Davies, L. and Kirkpatrick ,G. (2000) *The EURIDEM Project: A Review of Pupil Democracy in Europe* London: Children's Rights Alliance

Davies,L, Williams, C and Yamashita, H. with Ko Man-Hing, A (2006) *Inspiring Schools : Impact and Outcomes* London: Carnegie UK

Davies, L and Yamashita, H (2007) *School Councils – School Improvement* Report for School Councils UK, Birmingham: Centre for International Education and Research

Davies, L (2007) *'Our Schools, Our Changes, Our Future': Baseline Primary Education Research in Angola.* Report to CfBT, Birmingham: Centre for International Education and Research

Dawkins, R (2005) 'Opiate of the Masses' *Prospect* October, pp 16-17

Dawkins, R (2006) *The God Delusion* London Bantam Press

DCSF (2007) *Guidance on the duty to promote community cohesion* London: Department for Children, Schools and Families

Decoene, J and De Cock, R (1996) 'The children's rights project in the primary school 'De Vrjldagmarkt' in Bruges, in E.Verhellen (ed) *Monitoring Children's Rights* The Hague: Kluwer

Dench, G, Gavon, K and Young, M (2006) *The New East End: Kinship, Race and Conflict* Profile

Dimitrijevic, J (1998) Human Rights and Peace. In J.Symonides (eds) *Human Rights: New Dimensions and Challenges* Aldershot: Ashgate/Dartmouth and UNESCO

Donnelly, C and Hughes, J (2006) Contact, culture and context: evidence from mixed faith schools in Northern Ireland and Israel. *Comparative Education* 42 (4) p493-516

Donohoue Clyne, I (2004) Educational Choices for Immigrant Muslim Communities: secular or religious? In B. van Driel, (ed) (2004) *Confronting Islamophobia in Practice* Stoke-on-Trent: Trentham

Elworthy, S and Rifkind, G (2006) *Making Terrorism History.* London: Rider

Epp, J (1996) 'Schools, Complicity and Sources of Violence' in J Epp and A Watkinson (1996) *Systemic Violence: How Schools Hurt Children* London: Falmer

Epp, J R and Watkinson, A (1996) *Systemic Violence: How Schools Hurt Children* London: Falmer

Extremismonthenet http://s170032534.websitehome.co.uk/extremismonthenet.html Accessed 29.11.2007

Evans, M (2007) 'Terror kids' inspired by net are West's big threat. *The Times* 7.11.2007,p8

Faas, D (2008) Constructing identities: the ethno-national and nationalistic identities of white and Turkish students in two English secondary schools. *British Journal of Sociology of Education* Vol 29 forthcoming

Feuerverger, G (2001) *Oasis of Dreams: Teaching and Learning Peace in a Jewish-Palestinian village in Israel* London: RoutledgeFalmer

Feinberg, W (2003) Religious Education in Liberal Democratic Societies. In K. McDonough and W. Feinberg (eds) *Citizenship and Education in Liberal-Democratic Societies* Oxford: Oxford University Press

Fisher, M (2007) *Culture of Fear and Education: An annotated bibliography* Technical paper no 28, In Search of Fearlessness Research Institute

Fisk, R (2005) *The Great War for Civilisation: The Conquest of the Middle East* London: Fourth Estate

Foggo, D and Aher, T (2007) Muslim medics get picky. *Sunday Times*, October 7th 2007, p1-2

Foggo, D and Thompson, C (2007) Muslim checkout staff get an alcohol opt-out clause. *Sunday Times* September 30th 2007, p3

Forest, J (ed) (2006) *Teaching Terror*. Maryland: Rowman and Littlefield

Free Muslims Coalition (2006) Reeducation of Extremists in Saudi Arabia. Press Corner: January 18th 2006, www.freemuslims.org/news/article.php?article=1241. Accessed 4.10.2007

Fuentes, A (2003) Discipline and Punish. Zero tolerance policies have created a 'lockdown environment' in schools. *The Nation Magazine* December 15 2003, pp17-20

Fukuyama, F (1992) *The End of History and the Last Man* New York: Free Press

Gallagher, T (2004) *Education in Divided Societies* Basingstoke: Palgrave Macmillan

Galloway, D (2006) Educational Reconstruction in the aftermath of war: some observations from the work of aid agencies in Bosnia and Herzegovina. In R. Griffin (ed) *Education in the Muslim World* Oxford: Symposium

Gaertner, S, Dovidio, J and Bachman, B (1996) Revisiting the Contact Hypothesis: the induction of a common ingroup identity. *International Journal of Intercultural Relations*, 20, Issues 3-4. pp 271-290

Gardner, E (2001) 'The Role of Media in Conflicts' in L.Reychler and T.Paffenholz (eds) *Peace-Building: A Field Guide* London: Lynne Reiner Publishers

Garton Ash, T (2004) *Free World* London: Allen Lane

Garton Ash, T (2006) The struggle to defend free expression is defining our age. *The Guardian* Thursday October 5th 2006, p23

Gereluk, D (2007) Bong Hits 4 Jesus: Defining the limits of free speech and expression in American schools. Paper presented at the conference *Education and Extremism* Roehampton University, London, 5th-7th July 2007

Gereluk, D and Race, R (2007) Multicultural tensions in England, France and Canada: contrasting approaches and consequences. *International Studies in Sociology of Education* 17,1/2, pp 113-129

Gesink, I (2006) Islamic Reformation: A history of Madrasa reform and legal change in Egypt. *Comparative Education Review* 50 ,3, 325 – 345

GfK NOP (2006) Attitudes to Living in Britain: A Survey of Muslim Opinion www.gfknop.co.uk

Ginsburg, M and Megahed, N (2003) Multiplo perspectives on terrorism and Islam: challenges for educators in Egypt and the United States before/after September 11, 2001 in W. Nelles (ed) *Comparative education, terrorism and human security: from critical pedagogy to peace building?* New York: Palgrave Macmillan

Gledhill, R (2005) 'Joke is on religion as Christians laugh at themselves. *The Times,* Monday, August 29th 2005, p20).

Goldenberg, S (2002) 'A mission to murder: inside the minds of the suicide bombers' *Guardian* 11th June 2002, p4-5

Gourlay, C (2007) It's weird up north as Scientology moves in. *Sunday Times* October 28 2007, p5

Gray, J (2003) *Al Qaeda and what it means to be modern* London: Faber and Faber

Gray, J, (2007) *Black Mass: Apocalyptic Religions and the Death of Utopia* London: Allan Lane

Grinberg, M (2006) Defamation of Religions v Freedom of Expression: finding the balance in a democratic society. *Sri Lanka Journal of International Law*, 18, July

Gupta, N (2002) *Mahatma Gandhi an educational thinker* New Delhi:Anmol publications

Hanman, N (2006) Unequal opportunities. *Education Guardian*, Tuesday May 9, page 5

Hannam, D (2004) *Involving young people in identifying ways of gathering their views on curriculum.* A study conducted for QCA in association with CSV. London: Qualifications and Curriculum Authority

Haque, A (2004) Islamophobia in North America. In B. van Driel, (ed) (2004) *Confronting Islamophobia in Practice* Stoke-on-Trent: Trentham

Harber, C. (1997) *Education, Democracy and Political Development in Africa* Brighton: Sussex Academic Press

Harber, C. (2004) *Schooling As Violence* London:RoutledgeFalmer

Harber, C. and Davies, L. (1997) *School Management and Effectiveness in Developing Countries* London: Cassell

Hayner, P (2002) *Unspeakable Truths: facing the challenge of truth commissions.* New York: Routledge

Hensher, P (2005) Responsible Free Speech? *Guardian Review* Saturday 19th September 2005, p6

Hobsbawm, E (2007) *Globalisation, Democracy and Terrorism* London: Little, Brown

Holland, T (2003) 'Teaching and Learning about Human Rights in Postconflict Angola' in Uwazie, E (ed) *Conflict Resolution and Peace Education in Africa* Maryland, USA: Lexington

Hood, R, Hill, P and Williamson, W (2005) *The Psychology of Religious Fundamentalism.* New York: Guilford Press

Howe, R and Covell, K (2005) *Empowering children: Children's Rights Education as a Pathway to Citizenship* Toronto: University of Toronto Press

Hoyle, B (2007) Football and the old Marxist who says that it explains the new world. *The Times*, Saturday October 6th 2007, p5.

Human Rights Watch (2007) Nigeria anti-gay bill threatens democratic reform. *Human Rights News* hrw.org/English/docs/2007/02/28/nigeria15431.htrr

Huntingdon, S (1996) *The Clash of Civilisations and the Remaking of World Order* New York: Simon and Schuster

Husain, E (2007) *The Islamist* London: Penguin

Iannaconne, L (1994) Why strict churches are strong. *American Journal of Sociology* 99, 1180-1211

Ignatieff, M (1997) *The Warrior's Honour: Ethnic War and the Modern Conscience* New York: Penguin

IHEU (2007) 'Combating Defamation of Religion' is unnecessary, flawed and morally wrong. International Humanist and Ethical Union, 23.7.2007 www.iheu.org/node/2751. Accessed 3.10.2007

International Crisis Group (2002) *Pakistan: Madrasas, Extremism and the Military* Islamabad/ Brussels: International Crisis Group (ICG), Asia

International Crisis Group (2005) *Understanding Islamism* ICG Middle East/North Africa Report No, 37, Mar 2005

Kahn, M M (2006) Conservative Christian teachers: possible consequences for lesbian, gay and bisexual youth *Intercultural Education* Vol 17,No 4 October 2006 pp 359-371

Kapferer, B (1997) Remythologising discourses: state and insurrectionary violence in Sri Lanka. In David Apter (ed) *The Legitimisation of Violence* New York: New York University Press

Kaplan, J and Ngorgo, T (eds) *Nation and Race: the developing Euro-American racist subculture.* Boston: Northeastern University Press

Kepel, G (2003) *Bad Moon Rising: a chronicle of the Middle East today* London: Saqi

Kershaw, I (1984) *Popular Opinion and political dissent in the Third Reich: Bavaria 1933-1945* Oxford: Oxford University Press

# REFERENCES

Kersten, K, (2003) What is 'Education for Democracy'? in *Terrorists, Despots and Democracy: What our children need to know.* Washington DC: Thomas B Fordham Foundation.

King, E (2006) *Teaching in an Era of Terrorism* Thomson

Kingston, P (2007) Making space for faith. *Education Guardian*, Tuesday January 30th 2007, p9

Klein, N (2001) *No Logo* London: Flamingo

Krech, R and Maclure, R (2003) Education and Human Security in Sierra Leone: discourses of failure and reconstruction. In W. Nelles (ed) *Comparative education, terrorism and human security: from critical pedagogy to peace building?* New York: Palgrave Macmillan

Lamb, C (2003) 'Mugabe bends minds in hatred camps' *Sunday Times* 9.2.2003, p27

Leoni, J (2005) Gender, Deviance and Exclusion Unpublished PhD thesis, University of Birmingham

*Let's Talk* 80:20 (2001) *Let's Talk: A Review* Bray, Ireland: 80:20 Educating and Acting for a Better World

Liese, J (2004) The subtleties of prejudice: how schools unwittingly facilitate Islamophobia and how to remedy this. In B. van Driel, (ed) (2004) *Confronting Islamophobia* in Practice Stoke-on-Trent: Trentham

Lister, D (2007) 'Airport hit by suicide bombers? You've got to laugh...' *The Times* Saturday July 7th 2007, p7

Lloyd, J (2006) Social Empowerment or Social Control: An exploration of pupils' prior knowledge of citizenship, and its application to appropriate teaching and learning in a junior school. Unpublished PhD thesis, University of Birmingham

London Development Education Centre (2002) *Undermining Education: New Labour and Single Faith Schools* London: LONDEC

London School of Islamics (2007a) Community Cohesion. *E-mail newsletter*, 18th August 2007, info@londonschoolofislamics.org.uk

London School of Islamics (2007b) Crusade for Fairness. *E-mail newsletter,* 1st March 2007, info@londonschoolofislamics.org.uk

Macintyre, B (2005) 'Saddam has only got one ball' *Times* 26.8.2005

Mabud, S (1992) A Muslim response to the Education Reform Act 1988. *British Journal of Religious Education* 14, pp88-98

Maher, S (2007) How I escaped Islamism. *Sunday Times* August 12th 2007, p19

Malik, S (2007) Schools are run by Islamic group Blair pledged to ban. *The Sunday Times* August 6th 2007, p10

Manji, I (2004) *The Trouble with Islam Today: A Wake-up call for honesty and change* Edinburgh: Mainstream Publishing

Mansfield, P (2003) *A History of the Middle East* 2nd edn, London: Penguin

Marciano, J (2003) 9/11 and civic illiteracy. In W. Nelles (ed) *Comparative education, terrorism and human security: from critical pedagogy to peace building?* New York: Palgrave Macmillan

Margolis, J (2007) 'Lessons in Tolerance' *The Independent* 1.2.2007, p6-7

Massey, I (2003) The case for Rights Respecting Schools http://www.unicef.org.uk/tz/teacher_support/assets/pdf/case_for_rrs_%2009_05.pdf Accessed 29.11.2007

Maylor, U and Read, B, with Mendick, H, Ross, A and Rollock, N (2007) *Diversity and Citizenship in the Curriculum Research* Report No 819 London: London Metropolitan University

McKinnon, C (2004) *International Criminal Tribunal for Rwanda* 98 Am.J.Int'l L , pp325-30

Merry, M (2007) *Culture, Identity and Islamic Schooling: A Philosophical Approach* Basingstoke: Palgrave Macmillan

Merry, M and Driessen, G (2007) Islamic Schools: Inhibiting or Enhancing Democratic Dispositions? Paper presented at the conference Education and Extremism Roehampton University, London, 5th-7th July 2007

Minority Rights Group (1994) *Education Rights and Minorities* London: Minority Rights Group

Minow, M (1998) *Between Vengeance and Forgiveness: facing history after genocide and mass violence.* Boston: Beacon Press

Narvaez, D (2002) Does reading moral stories build character. *Educational Psychology Review* 14, 2 pp155-171

Nawaz, M (2007) Why I joined the British jihad – and why I rejected it. *Sunday Times* September 16th 2007, p8

Nazeer, K (2005) Rushdie the warrior-poet. *Prospect* October 2005, pp76-77

Nazir, M (2005) Exploring the potential for educational change through participatory and democratic approaches in Pakistan. Unpublished EdD thesis, University of Birmingham

Nef, J (2003) Terrorism and the Pedagogy of Violence: A Critical Analysis, in W. Nelles (ed) *Comparative education, terrorism and human security: from critical pedagogy to peace building?* New York: Palgrave Macmillan

Nelles, W (ed) (2003) *Comparative education, terrorism and human security: from critical pedagogy to peace building?* New York: Palgrave Macmillan

Neumark, V (2005) Don't step on my religious sensibilities. *Times Educational Supplement* January 14th 2005, pp 28-29.

Nicolai, S (2007) *Fragmented Foundations: Education and Chronic Crisis in the Occupied Palestinian Territory* Paris: UNESCO International Institution of Educational Planning/Save The Children UK

NIPEU (2007) *Education for Social Cohesion and Peace (ESCP): A Comprehensive Framework for a National Policy.* Colombo: Ministry of Education, National Integration and Peace Unit

Novelli, M and Lopes Cardozo, M (2007) Conflict, Education and the Global South – towards a critical research agenda. Conference Position Paper, Dutch Ministry of Foreign Affairs/University of Amsterdam

Odone, C (2005) Chimps with everything: a ridiculous war. *The Times* 26th December 2005, p19

O'Connor, A (2007) Boy 'killed by teacher for doodling in book *The Times*, Thursday Nov 8th, p39

O'Farrell, J (2006) How many fascist dictators does it take to change a light bulb? *Amnesty Magazine* November/December 2006, pp 26-28

Omaar, R (2006) *Only Half of Me. British and Muslim: The Conflict Within* London: Penguin

O'Neill, S (2007) Lessons in hate found at leading mosques. *The Times*, 30.11.2007, 1-2

Orlenius, K (2007) The tolerance towards intolerance: values and virtues at stake in education. Paper presented at the conference Education and Extremism Roehampton University, London, 5th-7th July 2007

Ouseley Report (2001) *Community Pride and Prejudice: Making Diversity Work in Bradford* Bradford: Bradford City Council

Palmer, D (1995) The revolutionary terrorism of Peru's Shining Path. In Martha Crenshaw (ed) *Terrorism in Context* University Park, PA: Pennsylvania State University Press

Pape, R (2005) *Dying to Win: The Strategic Logic of Suicide Terrorism* New York

Parker-Jenkins, M, Hartas, D and Irving, B (2005) *In Good Faith: Schools, Religion and Public Funding* Aldershot: Ashgate

Parris, M (2001) The bigger they come the harder they fall *The Times* Saturday September 15th

Paulson, J (2006) The Educational Recommendations of Truth and Reconciliation Commissions: potential and practice in Sierra Leone. *Research in Comparative and International Education* Vol 1 no 4, pp335-350

Perry, W (1999) *Forms of Ethical and Intellectual Development in the College Years.* San Francisco, CA: Wiley and Sons

Phillips, T (2005) *After 7/7: sleepwalking to segregation.* Speech given at the Commission for Racial Equality, 22 September 2005. London: CRE

Pinson, H (2004) Rethinking Israelness: citizenship education and the construction of political identities by Jewish and Palestinian youth Unpublished PhD thesis, University of Cambridge

Policy Exchange (2007) *Living Apart Together: British Muslims and the Paradox of Multiculturalism,* by Munira Mirza, Abi Senthilkumaran and Zein Ja'far. London: Policy Exchange

Pullman, P (2005) Identity crisis. *Guardian Review,* Saturday 19th November 2005, pp 4-6

Ramadan, T (2006) We Muslims need to get out of our intellectual and social ghettos. Interview with Paul Vallely, *The Independent* Monday July 25th 2005, p8

Ramakrishna, K (2006) 'The Making of the Jemaah Islamiyah Terrorist' in J. Forest (ed) *Teaching Terror.* Maryland, Rowman and Littlefield

Reardon, B (2001) *Education for a Culture of Peace in a Gender Perspective* Paris: UNESCO

Richards, G (2001) *Gandhi's Philosophy of Education* New Delhi: Oxford University Press

Richardson, R (2004) Curriculum, ethos and leadership: confronting Islamophobia in UK education. In B. van Driel, (ed) (2004) *Confronting Islamophobia in Practice* Stoke-on-Trent: Trentham

Rizvi, F (2004) Debating Globalisation and education after September 11. *Comparative Education* 40, 2 pp157-171

Romain, J (2005) Faith Schools are a recipe for social disaster. *The Times* Saturday October 1st p9

Roy, O (2004) *Globalised Islam: the Search for a new Ummah* London: Hurst

Ruthven, M (2004) *Fundamentalism: The Search for Meaning.* Oxford: Oxford University Press

Sacks, J (2003 revised edition) *The Dignity of Difference.* London: Continuum

Salmenkivi, E (2007) Socratic extremism as an educational ideal. Paper presented at the conference Education and Extremism Roehampton University, London, 5th-7th July 2007

Salmi, J (1999) Violence, Democracy and Education. Paper presented at the Oxford Conference, September 1999

Sanjakdar, F (2004) Developing an Appropriate Sexual Health Education Curriculum Framework for Muslim Students. In B. van Driel, (ed) (2004) *Confronting Islamophobia in Practice* Stoke-on-Trent: Trentham

Schweisfurth, M., Davies, L. and Harber, C. (2002) (Eds.) *Learning Democracy and Citizenship: International Experiences* Oxford: Symposium Books

Sen, A (2006) *Identity and Violence: the Illusion of Destiny* London: Allen Lane

Sieckelinck, S (2007) The collateral damage of counter-terror education to adolescent ideal(ism) based agency. Paper presented at the conference *Education and Extremism*, Roehampton University, London, 5th-7th July 2007

Sieckelinck, S and De Ruyter, D (2006) Mad about Ideals. Educating for reasonable passion. Paper presented at the PESGB conference, Oxford

Silber, M and Bhatt, A (2007) *Radicalisation in the West: The Homegrown Threat* New York: New York City Police Department

Silva, N (ed) (2002) *The Hybrid Island: Culture Crossings and the invention of identity in Sri Lanka* London: Zed Books

Silver, E (2007) Israel's nightmare: Home grown neo-Nazis in the Holy Land *The Independent Extra* Tuesday 9 October 2007 pp2-5

Skolverket (2000) *A Good Enough School: A study of life at school and school's role in life.* Stockholm: National Agency for Education

Smith, A and Vaux, T (2003) *Education, Conflict and International Development* London: Department for International Development

Smock, D (2004) Ijtihad: Reinterpreting Islamic Principles for the Twenty-first century. *United States Institute of Peace*, Special Report 125, August

Smythies, J (2006) *Bitter Fruit* Charleston, SC: Booksurge

Steel, M (2004) Under this law, even God will end up in prison. *The Independent* Thursday 9th December 2004, p39

Steiner-Khamsi, G and Spreen, C (1996) Oppositional and relational identity: a comparative perspective. In A.Aluffi-Pentini and W.Lorenz (eds) *Anti-Racist Work with Young People* Lyme Regis: Russell House

Stone, R (2004) *Islamophobia: issues, challenges and action* Report by the Commission on British Muslims and Islamophobia, chaired by Dr Richard Stone Stoke on Trent: Trentham

Strike, K (2003) Pluralism, Personal Identity, and Freedom of Conscience. In K. McDonough and W. Feinberg (eds) *Citizenship and Education in Liberal-Democratic Societies* Oxford: Oxford University Press

Swinburne, R (2004) *The Existence of God* Clarendon Press

Symonides, J (1998) Introductory Remarks. In J. Symonides (eds) *Human Rights: New Dimensions and Challenges* UNESCO/Aldershot: Ashgate

Taheri, A (2006) Bonfire of the Pieties. Opinion Journal Wednesday February 8th 2006 From the *Wall Street Journal* Editorial Page http://www.opinionjournal.com/forms/printThis.html?id=110007934

Tamatea, L (2006) 'Gandhian Education in Bali: globalisations and cultural diversity in a time of fundamentalisms' *Compare* 36, 2 pp 213-228

Tawil, S and Hartley, A (eds) (2004) *Education, Conflict and Social Cohesion* Geneva: UNESCO, International Bureau of Education

Taylor, C (1989) *Sources of the Self: The Making of Modern Identity* Cambridge: Cambridge University Press

Teece, G (2005) Traversing the gap: Andrew Wright, John Hick and critical religious education. *British Journal of Religious Education*, 27,1, pp29-40

Teleman, D (2004) Are children 'intuitive theists'? *Psychological Science* 15,5, pp295-301

Thomas, N and Bahr, A (2008 forthcoming) Faith and Reason: Higher Education's Opportunities and Challenges, in M.Diamond (ed) *Encountering Faith in the Classroom* Sterling VA: Stylus Publishing

Toynbee, P (2001) Behind the Burka. T*he Guardian* Friday Sep 28th, p21

Toynbee, P (2006) Only a fully secular state can protect women's rights. *Guardian*, 17, 10, 2006, p7

Trafford,B. (2003) *School Councils, School Democracy and School Improvement: Why, What, How?* Leicester: SHA Publications

Tutu, D (2006) Tackling Extremism. Special Doha Debate, February 28th 2006, www.thedohadebates.com

UCU (2007) *University and College Union journal*, January 2007, pp41-41

# REFERENCES

UNICEF (2007) Rights Respecting Schools Award website http://rrsa.unicef.org.uk/ Accessed 29.11.2007

Ungar, R (2007) *The Self Awakened* Cambridge: Harvard University Press

UNIVERSAL ISLAMIC DECLARATION OF HUMAN RIGHTS (1981) www.alhewar.com/islamdecl/html/ Accessed 8.7.2005

Vallely, P (2007) A deadly scripture? Saudi fundamentalism in Britain. *The Independent Extra* Thursday 1st November 2007, pp 1-5

Van Driel, B (ed) (2004) *Confronting Islamophobia in Educational Practice* Stoke on Trent: Trentham Books

Wainaina, B (2006) 'How to write about Africa in five easy steps *Granta: The View from Africa*, Jan 15

Watson, J (2004) Educating for Citizenship – the emerging relationship between religious education and citizenship education. *British Journal of Religious Education* 26,3 259-271

Whittaker, D (ed) (2007 third edition) *The Terrorism Reader* London: Routledge

World Education Forum (2000) *Dakar Framework for Action: Education for All: Meeting the Challenge*. Paris: UNESCO

Yablon, Y (2007) Best versus possible practices: a critical perspective on current developments in contact hypothesis. Paper presented at the conference Education and Extremism Roehampton University, London, 5th-7th July 2007

Younge, G (2004) Evolution textbooks row goes to court. *The Guardian* Tuesday November 9th 2004, p12

Younge, G (2006) Let's have an open and honest discussion about white people. *The Guardian,* Monday October 2, p29

# Index

195